ᴀ Dishonoured Society

A Dishonoured Society

JOHN FOLLAIN

WARNER BOOKS

To R.

A *Warner* Book

First published in Great Britain in 1995
by Little, Brown and Company

This edition published by Warner Books in 1996

*This is a work of non-fiction and the
author acknowledges that any error is
his own responsibility.*

A CIP catalogue record for this book
is available from the British Library.

ISBN 0 7515 1445 4

Typeset by Hewer Text Composition Services, Edinburgh
Printed and bound in Great Britain by
Clays Ltd, St. Ives plc

Warner Books
A Division of
Little, Brown and Company (UK)
Brettenham House
Lancaster Place
London WC2E 7EN

CONTENTS

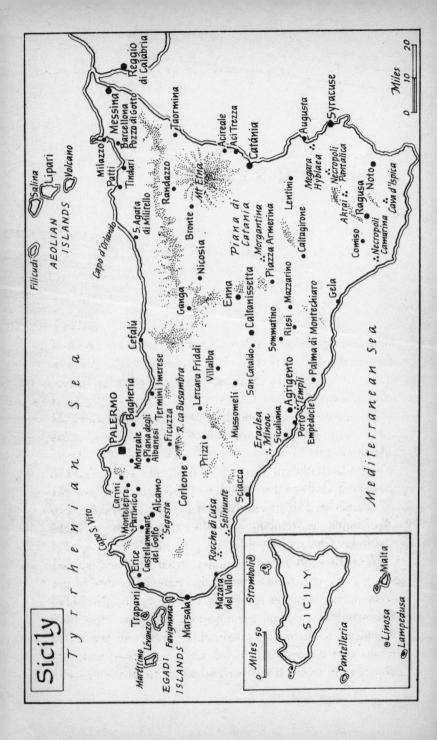

PREFACE

John Follain's book highlights in a very well-documented fashion the two essential characteristics of the Sicilian Mafia: its conservative nature and its growing inter-nationalisation.

The swing of the pendulum governs the relationship between the Mafia and the Italian State. Times of great repression are followed by great calm, and vice versa. When the Mafia hit the State, the State responded. If the Mafia did not hit the State, the State did not hit the Mafia. For instance, the main anti-Mafia laws are approved by parliament only after the murders of State representatives.

In practice, as Follain explains, what has been lacking in Italy is a permanent anti-Mafia strategy because of the cohabitation between the Mafia and the State. The Mafia is not only a criminal organisation, it is also a political organisation. It considers maintaining the *status quo* useful for its own interests and it has always operated with this objective in mind. It has woven links with politicians who could guard its interests, and it has killed politicians like Piersanti Mattarella (a Christian Democrat) and Pio La Torre (a Communist), who fought for social and political reforms.

Equally, decisions taken by politicians are always at the root of the modern transformations of the Mafia. The urban expansion of Palermo in the 1950s and 60s turned the criminal association, which until then had been a mainly rural organisation, into an urban organisation capable of establishing alliances with the administrators of a big city like Palermo as well as with building contractors.

The cohabitation is also apparent in the way sections of the political class periodically and violently attack the magistrates who have committed themselves the most to the defence of legality, accusing them of seeking only personal success, or of being pro-Communist. These charges were levelled at Judge Paolo Borsellino, accused of being a "professional of the anti-Mafia", and at Judge Giovanni Falcone, accused of being a friend of the Communists.

All this is a great source of strength for the Mafia and other similar organisations. That is why the anti-Mafia commission presented to parliament in 1993 a report on the relations between organised crime and politics, in which it explained the need to break these relations immediately.

The second characteristic of the Sicilian Mafia is its internationalisation.

This is due to various factors, chiefly the nature of the goods which are traded: drugs, arms and money. Trade in this merchandise involves establishing relationships with illegal groups from several countries, crossing many borders and in addition using many legal institutions (banks, financial companies, customs).

The need to recycle and invest the colossal profits

derived from criminal activities – Italian organised crime
has an annual turnover of some 69 trillion lire (£35 billion),
about 4.4 per cent of Italy's GDP – automatically requires
an internationalisation of the Mafia, which seeks out the
countries and banks that are the most welcoming and that
offer the greatest guarantees of discretion. The Mafia uses
its networks to invest in real estate in the south of France,
to send fugitives to Germany, to deposit money in Austria
or the Republic of San Marino or in certain English banks,
to set up large companies to recycle money in Russia, and
so on. Obviously, this is not new.

Mafia networks have much room for manoeuvre in
Europe because Europe is made up of contrasting legal
systems; the differences between laws on banking secrecy,
on the origins of invested money and on police powers
offer organised crime great opportunities for settling and
growth. It has been proven that the Mafia has already used
the opportunities which each country offered and continues
to offer. The Mafia acts according to expediency and it will
continue to expand according to this logic as long as it finds
no obstacles in its path. For instance, all the investigations
carried out in Italy, in parallel with many foreign countries,
reveal that there can be no major recycling without the
international trafficking of dirty money. Moreover, this flow
is possible because there is still too much international
indifference about where this money comes from.

It is impossible for a mafioso organisation to settle and
expand in foreign territory if in that territory there is anti-
Mafia vigilance. To be inattentive today, in Europe, means
to favour the growth of the Mafia. Thus to be effective, the
fight against the Mafia must be international.

Collaboration between the police forces of various countries in the struggle against organised crime has by
now reached a satisfactory level; relations between Italy

and Britain, Italy and the United States, and Italy and Germany in particular are excellent. All the same there is a difference between the internationalism of police investigations and the permanently national character of judicial procedures.

What is to be done?

One should aim at a realistic objective, to strengthen cooperation until the conditions are right for an international anti-Mafia zone. Clearly the Mafia operates in a supra-national field, and national borders, which still constitute a tiresome obstacle for legal authorities, are crossed with great ease by criminal organisations.

A first step towards an anti-Mafia zone would be to single out one type of offence in the legislations of the different countries concerned – for now one could start with the nations of western Europe – on which cooperation between police, judicial and banking watchdog authorities would be reinforced. The offence could be Mafioso criminal association, but collaboration could also extend, naturally, to the most common crimes involved like murder and drug-trafficking. Documents relating to such offences and valid as evidence in one country, if acquired with specific guarantees, could also constitute evidence in other countries.

With publication of John Follain's book, it will be harder for those in the Anglo-Saxon world who are responsible for the fight against organised crime to say: 'We did not know'.

Luciano Violante
President of the anti-Mafia commission (1992–1994)
Deputy-speaker of the Chamber of Deputies

1

THE FIRST MAFIOSI

The Myth

Judge Giovanni Falcone sped along the sea-front motorway
on his way into the Sicilian capital Palermo. Italy's leading
anti-Mafia crusader had been met by his bodyguards at the
city's airport, where his secret service jet landed after a
flight from Rome. A convoy of three armour-plated cars,
their engines running, awaited Falcone as he stepped off
the plane with his wife for a weekend break in his native
Sicily. Sirens blaring, the convoy joined the highway and
accelerated to a speed of 100 mph.

Only minutes later, a huge explosion scalped the motorway and punched a deep crater across three lanes, turning
all three cars into red-hot piles of tangled metal. The blast
catapulted the escort car travelling ahead of Falcone's
off the tarmac and into an olive grove more than a
hundred yards away. The three bodyguards in the car
were killed. Falcone and his wife died shortly after the

explosion. Four policemen in the last car were injured but survived.

The Mafia, which had never forgiven Falcone for his success in wringing confessions from supergrasses and sending many of its men to jail, had buried hundreds of pounds of TNT in a storm drain under the motorway. Lookouts on a hillside overlooking the site set off the bomb by remote control as Falcone's convoy drew close.

The murder of Falcone on the afternoon of 23 May 1992 was the worst Mafia outrage in a decade. The symbol of Italy's struggle against the Mafia, Falcone had long been top of its hit-list because of his triumphs against the secret society – including the 1986 trial of 338 Mafiosi who were sentenced to a total of 2,665 years behind bars, with 19 jailed for life. In killing Falcone, and his friend and colleague judge Paolo Borsellino two months later, Sicily's 'Cosa Nostra' ('Our Affair') showed its true face. The murders dealt yet another devastating blow to the Mafia myth – the attempt by its members, from lowly soldiers to powerful godfathers, to portray one of the world's most mighty criminal fraternities as a benign guarantor of order and ancient local traditions in Sicily, and themselves as champions of the poor and the weak.

Theirs, the mobsters say, is an élitist secret society, based on entrenched Sicilian values such as honour, family ties and friendship. They rarely refer to it as the 'Mafia', or to themselves as 'Mafiosi', because these words have unpleasant connotations. The labels they prefer include 'The Honoured Society', 'The Society of the Friends' or 'The Brotherhood' – but, most often, 'Cosa Nostra'.

Few have been more eloquent in their defence of the Mafia than the peasant-born Paolo Campo, a patriarch who built a criminal fiefdom near the hilltop town of Agrigento, on the south coast of Sicily, where incongruous ancient

Greek temples still lie open to the skies. In the summer
of 1985, Campo was a sick and frail old man. He and
the clans of Cosa Nostra, which had plagued the region
with impunity, were finally being brought to account. At
eighty-five, Campo faced a myriad of accusations which
included theft, racketeering and even murder, all of which
he denied despite damning evidence.

> I protest I am innocent of the crime of Mafia conspiracy
> in the sense that I have never committed a crime, nor
> have I associated with others for that purpose. I must
> say however that I was born and will die Mafioso, if by
> Mafia one means, as I mean, be good to your neighbour,
> give something to people in need, find jobs for the
> unemployed and give help to people in difficulty. In
> this sense I was born, I am considered and I consider
> myself Mafioso.[1]

Despite his plea of innocence, Campo was sentenced
to seven years in jail (cut to three years on appeal). But
fantasies like his have bewitched generations of Mafiosi,
and even many outsiders. Tommaso Buscetta, the first
Palermo boss to turn informer, described what led him
to join 'the great ideal' at the age of seventeen in the
aftermath of the Second World War: 'In my day a young
man was attracted by the respect he could receive from
others because he was considered a man of honour . . .
who had to act within the norms of a man of honour,
because all the things that I have known inside Cosa Nostra
are beautiful – with the exception of murder, which is a
necessity.'[2]

A generation later, another Mafioso who betrayed the
organisation's secrets to the authorities, Gaspare Mutolo,
showed it had lost little of its hypnotic power. Several of

his uncles were members, and he too joined as a teenager, recruited personally by the Godfather Salvatore Riina: 'I was fascinated by people who in my imagination were wise figures, to whom others turned to ask for advice . . . Of course, if you look at the Mafia today, after what it has done, you see it differently, but the Mafia until the 1970s, as I remember it and as I imagined it, was completely different. The Mafiosi were the people in command, they were the wise ones. You never thought of the violence.'[3]

How did the Mafia become such a powerful object of fascination for generations of young Sicilian criminals? Part of the answer is to be found in the ancient and noble ancestry which the 'men of honour' have created for their organisation, twisting the popular Sicilian legend of the Beati Paoli from which they claim to descend.

The Beati Paoli was a secret association said to date back to the twelfth century, whose members according to folklore were Robin Hood-like figures defending the poor against the abuses of Sicily's foreign rulers. In the words of one chronicler, this was 'an occult and mysterious force . . . Common people, artisans, sailors, bourgeois, lawyers formed this terrible body, which took it upon itself to judge the actions of men, to re-examine judicial sentences and to repair the ills caused by those in power.'[4]

Their motto was 'Voice of the people, voice of God'. Meeting at midnight in caves and tunnels dug under the palaces and streets of the Sicilian capital, the sect would mete out cruel punishments in occult rituals. 'They hid both their good and their bad deeds under a mantle of hypocrisy. By day they would genuflect at the altars and pray . . . at night they would lie in wait, wrapped in their greatcoats, and roam the streets with a rosary in their hands and a dagger hidden close to their hearts.'[5]

In the slums that litter Palermo, in the labyrinths of dark alleyways that lie behind the dilapidated façades of its baroque palaces, youngsters were brought up on the sect's romanticised activities. The most detailed account was given by the Palermo-born Luigi Natoli, who published the 800-page historical novel *I Beati Paoli* in a local newspaper between March 1909 and January 1910. Natoli, writing under the pen-name 'William Galt', set his swashbuckling tales of duels, kidnappings and assaults on nunneries in seventeenth-century Palermo.

Today's Palermo still pays tribute to this legend. In the heart of the old city above a vaulted cellar in the Mercato del Capo, where a stallholder stores his crates of fruit and vegetables, a stone plaque proclaims: 'Sede degli antichi Beati Paoli' ('Seat of the ancient Beati Paoli'). In the late 1970s, the novel was turned into a hugely popular television serial.

Countless Mafiosi have been influenced by the tales of the Beati Paoli. For Buscetta, the Mafia has the same values, the same duties, as the sect. A low-ranking 'soldier' of the Mafia, Leonardo Vitale, told how he was made to 'repeat the sacred ritual of the Beati Paoli' at his initiation ceremony.[6] Another debonair man of honour, Salvatore Contorno, was nicknamed 'Coriolano della Foresta' after the novel's hero.

But in fact there is no historical justification for Cosa Nostra's claim that its origins can be traced back to a sect such as the Beati Paoli, or even to the time when it is said to have been active. What the two do share however is a deep-seated antipathy towards authority, which in Sicily has taken the form of a long line of foreign powers that have ruled the island over the centuries. It is in this history of foreign rule that the true origins of the Mafia can be found.

The Mafia was born as a surrogate for foreign authorities in a role they failed to play, that of protecting the property of Sicily's landed gentry. What started as a way of life in rural society, a tool of absentee landowners, grew into a hierarchical association with its own rituals and rules very loosely based on traditional popular values. A conservative force, the Mafia was to help quash attempts to overthrow Sicily's feudal legacy and infiltrate the new-born Italian State, becoming thoroughly entrenched on its home ground before extending its empire to the Italian mainland and much further afield.

The Birth of Cosa Nostra

Sicily has always been a land of conquest. A castaway in the heart of the Mediterranean, and that sea's largest island, it is a natural stepping-stone between Europe and Africa, and between the Levant and the West. It was once part of a land-bridge joining Africa and Europe. Only a couple of miles separate Sicily from the Italian mainland at the narrowest point of the Strait of Messina. The distance between the Scylla and Charybdis of Greek mythology is so short that there have long been plans to throw a bridge across the Strait. But the sea effectively divides the two lands like a vast desert or a formidable chain of mountains. The writer Leonardo Sciascia said of his native island, a region of exceptional fertility for most of its history, that it had been invaded a thousand times but 'cut off from the history of great peoples and great cultures'.

Phoenicians, Greeks, Carthaginians and Romans invaded

Sicily. The Roman writer Cato branded Sicily 'the granary of the republic, the nurse at whose breast the Roman people feeds'. Many more followed, including Vandals, Arabs, Normans, Spaniards, Bourbons and Germans. The Second World War brought American and British troops. The last to conquer the island were the (northern) Italians at the time of unification.

Most of these invading nations governed from abroad. The Arabs and the Normans (Sicily's Golden Age), who occupied the island in turn, made it the centre of their empires. But it was ruled from afar from the period of French Angevin rule (1268–82) until 1947, when it was granted regional government – a belated official recognition of its identity.

Today's Sicily, the biggest region in Italy, is pockmarked with the scars left by the long series of invaders. Its interior of mountains and plateaux is as empty and torpid as Palermo is crowded and bustling. Although green in spring, the cornfields which cover most of the interior and south coast are parched and desert-like by midsummer. Drugged by the hot scirocco winds from Africa, it is a world far removed from the rich green belt of vines, lemon and orange trees and olive groves which stretches along the north and east coast to girdle the foot of Mount Etna. Driven from the interior by the barrenness of the countryside, the majority of today's five million Sicilians live in the provinces of Palermo and the second biggest city, Catania, in the east.

The teeming capital Palermo, the hub of the island since the ninth century, lies sprawled across a fertile valley, at the bottom of a wide bay on the island's northern coast. The valley, rich in lemon and orange groves, is the beautifully-named 'Conca d'Oro' ('Golden Shell'), enclosed by a chain of mountains over which towers the limestone hulk of Mount Pellegrino. One of Sicily's few plains and spread over some forty square miles, it owes its name to the 'Aurata Conca' of fifteenth-century writers who related the popular legend that the river Oreto once had a bed of auriferous sands. In more recent times, the name came to refer to the gold of the citrus fruit groves. Today, there is little gold or green left on the plain – the centre of the shell in particular has been smothered in concrete and tarmac.

A treasure-trove of bygone splendour and romantic decay, Palermo is a bedraggled patchwork of contrasting architectural fashions – its palaces, churches and monasteries sum up Sicily's turbulent history of invasion. The imposition of foreign art and culture has spawned a typically Sicilian fusion of styles.

The flamboyant cathedral boasts Norman, Gothic and neo-classical features. Nearby is the Norman royal palace which was started by the earlier Arab occupiers, under whom Palermo became one of the most important cities in the world. Strung out along the noisy avenues that cut through the city are Spanish baroque palaces, blackened by pollution from the city's incessant traffic. Many of these crumbling buildings are cloaked in ugly scaffolding, which seems at first sight to be the only prop preventing their collapse.

Behind the faded operatic scenery of the nobility's palaces, the hovels of the poor in the Saracen city centre have changed little over the centuries. Many of the houses threaten to cave in, but few have been abandoned. An Arab legacy fires the narrow flagstone streets into life in the mornings with the shouts of some of the most picturesque markets in Italy. They look and feel more like the souks of north Africa and the Middle East than their counterparts on the Italian mainland.

As well as making their mark on the capital, the string of foreign occupants left a deeper scar running through Sicily – they made it a fertile breeding-ground for those who took the law into their own hands, like the Beati Paoli and the Mafia. The island's inhabitants learnt to be distrustful of authorities which so often ruled them from afar and failed to impose law and order, and so rarely put the Sicilians' interests first.

The Roman Catholic Church, the one institution entrenched enough to fill the vacuum left by the absence of a respected, rather than feared, authority, failed to step into the breach. Instead, it helped foster popular mistrust of those who supposedly enforced law and order in the name of officialdom. The precepts laid down by the archbishop of Palermo in his *Taxae Cancelleriae et Poenitentiariae Romanae*, which was published between 1477 and 1533, allow for witnesses who have given false testimony to judges in court to be pardoned. Another clause allows a suspected thief or criminal to keep as 'his property rightly gained and acquired' any illegal gains, providing he obtains an edict from the Church and gives alms of an adequate value. [7]

Far from preaching respect for the established authorities, the Church in Sicily went as far as instituting its own form of private justice. The advent of the Holy Inquisition, launched by an envoy of the Spanish King Ferdinand the Catholic in 1487, soon blanketed the island with a web of several thousand watchdogs appointed to wage war on heresy. They became so powerful that they were allowed to carry arms despite a general ban and were exempted from having to answer for their actions – including murder, fraud and extortion – to the judiciary.

As a secretive society defying authority, the Inquisition was to prove a precursor of the Mafia. But it is more than three hundred years later in the first half of the

nineteenth century in western Sicily, under the rule of
the Neapolitan Bourbons, that the Mafia is believed to have its
roots. The island was then part of the Kingdom of the Two
Sicilies, which comprised not only Sicily, but the whole of
mainland Italy south of Rome. Sicily's feudal system had
seen little change in centuries – even at the end of the
eighteenth century, two-thirds of the population was under
the jurisdiction of feudal barons. When revolutionary ideals
conquered France in 1789, Palermo was still refining the
privileges of the aristocracy. While the rural economy in
the north of the Italian peninsula was being modernised,
in Sicily time stood still.

The countryside was bare and unyielding, a far cry
from the fertility that had enriched the island's earlier conquerors. The Bourbons' short-sighted agricultural
policies bled the rich volcanic soil and helped reduce
much of the Sicilian interior to a parched wasteland.
An eighteen-volume parliamentary investigation into the
conditions of life in the countryside, launched in the late
nineteenth century, found that malnutrition was common in
many parts of Sicily and in southern Italy, and that malaria
claimed thousands of victims every year.

Giuseppe Tomasi di Lampedusa, author of the classic
novel *Il Gattopardo* (The Leopard) set in nineteenth-century
Sicily, remembered 'the immense scenario of feudal Sicily,
desolate, suffocating, oppressed by the midday sun'. On the
annual journey from Palermo to their inland wheat-growing
estates, his family could not find a single tree to give
shade at lunchtime.[8] In the novel, Lampedusa described
a landscape of extremes:

. . . Sicily, the atmosphere, the climate, the landscape of Sicily. Those are the forces which have
formed our minds together with and perhaps more than

alien pressure and varied invasions: this landscape which knows no mean between sensuous sag and hellish drought; which is never petty, never ordinary, never relaxed, as should be a country made for rational beings to live in . . . this climate which inflicts us with six feverish months at a temperature of 104°.[9]

Bandits proliferated. The Bourbon rulers, ensconced in the royal palaces and fortresses of Naples on the mainland and in Palermo, were too remote and too weak to maintain law and order in the mountainous regions of western Sicily. Their regiments garrisoned the big cities, but there were no police to deploy in the countryside. The nineteenth-century ethnologist from Palermo, Giuseppe Pitrè, wrote that in the eighteenth century no traveller, even if provided with an escort, set out on a journey into the hinterland without first making a will, going to confession and receiving communion.[10] Banditry in Sicily endured until the nineteenth century, and was still common in some areas into the twentieth.

The Bourbons' failure to meet the demand for law and order spawned a system of private protection which was heavily reliant on the use of violence. This demand for security and protection was intensified by the abolition of feudalism. In the southern regions of the Italian mainland, a law repealing feudalism passed in 1806 came into force immediately. But, in Sicily, an 1812 law was much slower to take effect, and feudalism survived for another eight years.

In 1813, Sicilian landowners forced the Bourbon King Ferdinand to sign a decree setting up 'compagnie d'armi' – small groups of armed men on horseback whose task was to drive bandits from the countryside. They were given powers to maintain public order and protect the landowners' property. However, recruited locally, they collaborated with thieving bandits or cattle-rustlers from neighbouring provinces in committing crimes outside their mandated territory.

Several decades after their creation, the Tuscan sociologist Leopoldo Franchetti was to write of such groups: 'They arrive at a village in the evening, go to the inn, leave their arms in a corner, and start drinking with the muleteers, the cart-drivers, with all kinds of people. They talk to everybody, greet everyone, they know everybody . . . They are accomplices of the wrongdoers, either because they are scared of reprisals, or because they have a share in the booty [of crimes].'[11]

In 1838 Pietro Calà Ulloa, the Bourbon king's public prosecutor for the town of Trapani on Sicily's north-west coast, sent a report to the Justice Ministry in Naples. Underlining the lawlessness which then prevailed, Ulloa described the 'strange and dangerous remedies' used by the Sicilians. Although his study makes no mention of the term 'Mafia', the similarities are striking:

There is no employee who has not prostrated himself at the nod and whim of a bully, and who has not at the same time thought of drawing profit from his office. This general corruption has made the people turn to exceedingly strange and dangerous remedies. There are in many villages unions or brotherhoods, kinds of sects, which they call parties, of no political colour or aim, who never hold meetings, with no link other than dependence on a leader, who can be a landowner, or a priest. A common fund covers the need to exonerate an official, or to defend him, or to protect a defendant, or to charge someone who is innocent. They are like so many kinds of governments inside a government. The

absence of guardians of law and order has caused the
number of crimes to multiply. The people have reached
a tacit understanding on crime. When thefts occur,
mediators come forward to offer transactions for the
recovery of the stolen property. The number of such
deals is infinite. [12]

Ulloa's report exposed the Bourbons' inability to impose
some measure of authority. It also gave a graphic foretaste
of how the Mafia was to take over the duties of the
authorities and become a state within the State.

The first Mafiosi emerged as instruments of the ruling
class, of the absentee landowners who were anxious to
defend their *latifondi* (great landed estates) at a time when
feudal reform was threatening their way of life. Unlike their
northern counterparts, the landowners of the Mezzogiorno
(the Italian South) lacked a tradition of entrepreneurial
mercantilism to fall back on. They had long been used
to living in the capital and at court. They valued their
estates, which produced chiefly wheat, only in terms of
the income they generated, and took no interest in their
daily management or in the plight of the peasants who
worked for them. Instead, they became heavily reliant on
rural entrepreneurs who were quick to take advantage of
their masters' indifference.

This new breed of entrepreneur, the *'gabellotti'*, were
usually of peasant origin. They leased the *latifondi* from the
landowners, owned some land and cattle and were feared
by their peers. Their objective was always to make slaves
of the day-labourers, and pay the landowners an ever-
decreasing rent, eventually granting them loans at extor-
tionate rates of interest.

The *gabellotti* in turn recruited guards, the *'campieri'*, to
protect the estates from bandits and marauders. Two status

symbols highlighted the superiority of the guards over the peasants. They were authorised to carry arms, which peasants were not; and the *campieri* rode on horseback, while peasants travelled on foot or on donkeys or mules.[13]

A report by Carlo Alberto dalla Chiesa, a paramilitary carabiniere captain who was to rise to the rank of general before he was murdered by the Mafia, details the roots of the organisation in the town of Corleone south of Palermo. Corleone was to become notorious as the home of one of Cosa Nostra's most ferocious clans. In this poor, provincial hinterland as in much of Sicily, the land in the early nineteenth century was divided into vast *latifondi*. Dalla Chiesa wrote that the noble landowners, most of whom lived in Palermo, were for the most part satisfied with their comfortable lives, and cared little about the peasantry.

This, he explained, made for 'a society which was undoubtedly decadent and prey to those profiteers, the *gabellotti* and the *campieri* . . . [The latter] were taken on for their lack of scruples and for their dubious reputations, safeguarding with the use of force the properties which had been entrusted to the *gabellotti*.'[14] Thus the *campieri* ensured that the landowners and estate managers did not need to rely on the law of the State.

Sicily's new, parasitical rural middle class – the managers and their guardians – soon came to be known as Mafiosi. Dalla Chiesa called them the 'first matrix of a vast Mafioso web'.[15] Among their earliest crimes was the protection they granted to outlaws. Following a raid on an estate, these entrepreneurs were well placed to negotiate a deal among interested parties because they knew or could trace those involved. Generations later, the Mafia had lost little of its rural origins. This century's Godfathers were almost invariably of humble origin – Vito Cascio Ferro who reigned in the inter-war years was the son of an

illiterate peasant; Calogero Vizzini who died in 1954 was
the son of a day-labourer; his sucessor Genco Russo had
worked as a shepherd as a young man before becoming
a *gabellotto*; and more recently Salvatore Riina was also a
day-labourer's son.[16]

Born as an instrument for the defence of agrarian interests, the Mafioso came to replace the absentee landowner
to the extent that he supplanted him in the exercise of
his rights. He blackmailed his former master, imposing
as the price for his services an absolute freedom of action
in his dealings with the peasants. In return the Mafioso,
through his network of guardians, shielded the landowner
from his peasants' grievances, assured him the services of
badly-paid day-labourers and the peaceful enjoyment of
his estate's income.

The Mafia on Stage

There is little agreement on the origin of the word 'Mafia'.
It surfaced for the first time in an official document in
Palermo in 1658, in a list of heretics who had been
converted by the Act of Faith. One witch on this list was
referred to as 'Catarina la Licatis a nomata ancor Maffia',
meaning she had a reputation as a spirited character.[17]

Giuseppe Pitrè heard the word being used in a popular
neighbourhood in the capital, meaning above all 'beauty,
self-confidence, pride, graciousness, perfection, excel-
lence'.[18] A beautiful girl had '*della mafia*', and might
be dubbed '*mafiusa*'. Even a woman selling brooms in the
market used the term to describe her wares. It was used
with different meanings in different parts of the country.

In Tuscany for example the word '*maffia*' meant poverty, in Piedmont a '*mafium*' was a mean individual.

It seems likely that the word derives from one or more Arabic words in common usage during the Arab domination of Sicily from 827 to 1061: '*mahias*' (meaning daring, impudent); '*Ma àfir*' (a Saracen tribe which held sway over Palermo); '*maha*' (grottoes of tufo stone near Marsala on the north-west coast where persecuted Saracens and other fugitives sought refuge). Another possible origin is '*mu' afâh*' (an association which administered its own private justice), a combination of '*mu*"' (health, vigour, strength) and '*afâh*' (to persevere, to protect).[19] Most of these origins underline one or several aspects of the Mafia ideal – a secret society of fearless men acting for the good of the local community.

In 1862 the Mafiosi were portrayed on stage for the first time. A new comedy, *I Mafiusi di la Vicaria* (*The Mafiosi of La Vicaria*), performed at Palermo's Sant'Anna Theatre, took the capital by storm. Set in the city's Ucciardone jail, the play by Giuseppe Rizzotto and Gaspare Mosca shows how the mobsters were in almost complete control of life inside the prison. The Mafiosi are respected by other inmates, who are impressed by the association's strict hierarchy and its well-defined customs including an initiation ceremony.

Rules enforced by the mobsters demanded for example that new prisoners pay them an 'entry tax'. Mosca, a schoolteacher, said the idea for the play had come from the owner of a taverna, who had been his chief source of information. The play toured Italy – calling at Rome, Turin and Milan – and even travelled as far as South America. It did so well that it was expanded into a trilogy, with *I Mafiusi in progresso* (*The Mafiosi in Progress*) and *I Mafiusi all'osteria* (*The Mafiosi at the Inn*) as its sequels.

The success of these plays did much to popularise the word 'Mafia'. Its first official use was in a report sent by Count Filippo Gualtieri, prefect (government representative) in Palermo, to the Minister of the Interior in 1865. He wrote: 'What is . . . certain is that not only are there criminals, but they are also organised. The mafia exists. The very word suggests association. This association of criminals is a large and long-standing sore, and when it rears its head it shows that someone is manipulating it.'[20] Gualtieri reported that many landowners, although remaining honest, had allied themselves 'at least in silence' to the Mafia, fearing their property would otherwise be damaged. Gualtieri called for the military to intervene.

A decade later two Tuscan sociologists, Leopoldo Franchetti and Sidney Sonnino, travelled through Sicily to study the plight of the peasantry, making the first-ever investigation into the phenomenon of the Mafia. Franchetti was struck by the beauty of the Sicilian landscape and immediately convinced he had discovered an El Dorado. But after hearing stories of horrific violence, he was soon writing that he 'felt everything change around him little by little. The colours change, the appearance of things is transformed . . . After a number of such stories, all that scent of orange and lemon blossom begins to smell of corpses.'[21]

Equally overpowering is the anarchic society in which the Mafia evolves:

There is an extremely unequal distribution of wealth; a total absence of the concept of equal rights for all; a predominance of individual power; an exclusively personal character to all social relationships. All of this is coupled with hatreds of a very harsh nature, as was inevitable; with the passion for vendetta; with the concept that he who does not seek justice himself and does not take his own revenge is not honourable. In such a state of affairs, nothing prevented the maximum violence of customs and a sublime contempt for human life.[22]

Franchetti and Sonnino defined the Mafia as an 'industry of crime and violence' in cahoots with the landowning classes. Franchetti wrote that there was no Mafia in eastern Sicily because the landowners there had a monopoly of force, and were more united and less absenteeist than their counterparts in the west of the island, which includes Palermo. His advice to the government was that 'to save Sicily, the State should govern without the co-operation of the Sicilians'.

Into the Political Fray

Franchetti and Sonnino were among the first to study the new Sicily that came into being after the demise of the Kingdom of the Two Sicilies. The old Bourbon regime had been swept away in the name of Italian unity by the popular hero Giuseppe Garibaldi. Within three weeks of landing at the port of Marsala in western Sicily in May 1860 with a thousand volunteers, or 'Redshirts', Garibaldi had occupied Palermo. The 'Dictator', acclaimed as a saviour, advanced on Naples and defeated the Bourbons. By an overwhelming majority in a plebiscite, Sicilian voters chose to join the new Italian united kingdom.

The birth of the Italian State did little to slow the Mafia's rise. Undeterred by the fledgling State which was too weak to assert itself, Sicilian landowners continued as before to rely on the Mafiosi to run their estates. Northern Italy, the heart of the new State's administration, saw these criminals as a strictly Sicilian phenomenon (as they then were) and showed no desire to mobilise against them.

In fact, the triumph of the movement for Italian unity marked a qualitative leap in the Mafia's involvement in political affairs. From then on, the secret society was to grow from strength to strength as it infiltrated local, regional and national government. In sealing pacts with those who exercised power at local level, the feeble central government in effect recognised the right of Sicilian property-owners to organise themselves. For the first time in an Italian region, the central authority acknowledged a power other than itself.

Already in 1865, the Palermo prefect Gualtieri had stressed that the main characteristic of the Mafia organisation was that its members had links with political parties. One of its earliest ventures into the political fray was under the rule of Garibaldi. Sicilians were called to vote for an assembly which was to decide on the island's annexation to the new kingdom of Vittorio Emanuele. Mafiosi hawked election manifestos from house to house, threatening voters who were slow to do as they were told.

The links between the Mafia and politicians, forged through the exchange of mutual favours, were strengthened after the Left formed a national government in 1876. One parliamentarian, Colajanni, denounced the fact that 'the Mafioso mentality no longer springs exclusively from the police, the prince, the landowner, the *gabellotto*, the *campiere* and the armed companies. The influence of the deputy and often of the simple candidate has been added to these and often prevails over them.'[23] Extensions of the suffrage in Sicily from 1882 onwards played into the hands of the Mafia because the poorest classes, when they were given the right to vote, were often forced to yield to pressure from the Mafiosi to elect their candidates.

As the Mafia drew closer to government and politicians, it became confident enough to murder a respected public figure. On 1 February 1893 Marquis Emanuele Notarbartolo, a former director of the Bank of Sicily and a former mayor of Palermo, was stabbed to death on a train from the town of Termini Imerese to the Sicilian capital. He was knifed twenty-three times and his body thrown out of the train. He had been campaigning against corruption inside the bank.

The investigation that followed revealed that a member of parliament had ordered the Mafia to carry out the murder. This was a historic turning-point for the secret society. It was the Mafia's first so-called 'delitto eccellente' ('excellent crime', or murder of a leading personality). The next did not come until 1971, when the Mafiosi killed a public prosecutor – the first in a long line of magistrates to fall victim to the Mafia.

Shortly after the Marquis' murder, his son Leopoldo accused Raffaele Palizzolo, a parliamentarian and one of the bank's governors, of ordering the killing. He repeated the allegation to the Prime Minister, Marquis Di Rudinì, who had been a personal friend of the victim. The Premier expressed his sympathy and then asked: 'But if you know definitely that the guilty man is Raffaele Palizzolo, why don't you have him assassinated?'[24]

The deputy Palizzolo, investigators concluded, had ordered Notarbartolo's death because he was afraid the latter's campaign would reveal his own corrupt activities. He was tried three times and sentenced to thirty years in jail. But the verdict was overturned by the Supreme Court. The affair prompted a Sicilian member of parliament, Giuseppe de Felice Giuffrida, to protest in November 1899:

'This institution [the Mafia] isn't the shame of the island; it is the shame of the government which supports it.'

Defending the Status Quo

The Mafia was born as a conservative movement, and its first concern was to prevent the impending social revolution. It transformed itself gradually into an industry of crime whose immediate objective was to stamp out peasant attempts to rebel against a miserable existence. Its aim was also to prevent the industrial revolution, under way much earlier in Britain and mainland Europe, from eroding the Sicilian economy's agricultural base. To these ends the Mafia allied itself with other forces seeking to preserve the feudal regime, always ready to use violence where necessary.

In the aftermath of the First World War, landowners became increasingly dependent on a growing number of Mafiosi retainers to control a restive labour force and help sway the elections in which peasants had recently started taking part. The reforms of 1913 and 1919, which extended the suffrage to all adult males, as well as the hardships of the war and restrictions on overseas emigration by Sicilians, had exacerbated tensions between peasants and their overlords. Peasants staged mass occupations of farms and estates. The authorities and the Mafia joined ranks against the rebels. Many trade unionists were killed.

But it was after the Second World War that these tensions came to a head. Sicilian peasants waged a struggle that had been fought decades if not centuries earlier in mainland Italy, and in other European countries.

The peasant movement, in its efforts to evict the estate managers from the land, clashed with the Mafia. From 1944 onwards, Socialists, Communists and trade union leaders sought to undermine the power of the landowners. They also denounced the many pacts which were being struck between the Mafia bosses, the new Christian Democrat Party and a rising Separatist movement which campaigned for independence from mainland Italy.

The peasants tried to wrest land from their rulers by setting up co-operatives. Mafia leaders repeatedly defeated such attempts, forming co-operatives of their own and buying the land themselves. The Godfathers Calogero Vizzini and Giuseppe Genco Russo acquired properties in this way.

Estate managers reacted with extreme violence to the peasants' demands, often murdering the movement's leaders. As for the State, it protected both the murderers and those who commanded them. The killers were invariably acquitted if they were taken to court, or simply never found.

In September 1944 the regional Communist leader Girolamo li Causi visited Vizzini's realm, the town of Villalba in central Sicily. The Godfather, who took turns with his nephew to serve as mayor of the town and who also controlled the local branch of the Christian Democrat Party, had asked the visitor to avoid discussing local questions at his rally 'out of respect for the hospitality offered to him'.

But when the combative Li Causi addressed a crowd in the town square, he spoke of the local estate Vizzini had acquired. He denounced the Mafioso estate manager who exploited the peasants' labour with what he branded a culture of robbery. Vizzini, who had been listening to the speech, shouted: 'It's not true!' As if at a pre-arranged signal, Vizzini's men immediately started shooting at the crowd, throwing five small bombs into the panic-stricken throng. Fourteen people were injured. Vizzini later boasted that he could do even better – one nod from him would be enough to have all the trade union offices in the province burnt down.

Worse was to come three years later in the small town of Portella della Ginestra. The Mafia hired the flamboyant Salvatore Giuliano, the most famous Sicilian bandit of all, in an attempt to break the momentum of the peasant movement. On 1 May 1947 hundreds of peasants from the town celebrated labour day with their families by symbolically occupying a local estate, their red banners raised in the air. As the regional Socialist secretary addressed them, shots rang out. The peasants cheered at first, thinking the shots had been fired in celebration, not realising that they were the target of gunmen. Some 800 machine-gun rounds were fired at the rally, killing eleven people and injuring seventy-one.

According to a recent account by the supergrass Mutolo, the shooting was a mistake.[25] The plan, Mutolo said, had been merely to frighten the peasants by firing shots into the air. But the machine gun had slipped from the hands of one of the bandits, with the result that rounds were fired into the crowd. Mutolo said Giuliano was a fully-fledged member of the Mafia, unlike the bandits he commanded.

Under the Mafia's protection, Giuliano and his henchmen were able to wreak havoc in the area of Montelepre west of Palermo. They evaded capture by hundreds of policemen and troops who had been sent in as reinforcements. Altogether they murdered an estimated total of 430 people in the region.[26] Giuliano did not appear to have any clear strategy – he attacked carabinieri barracks, destroyed Communist Party offices, attacked army troops and even killed some Mafia bosses. The police did not catch up with him until after his death on 4 July 1950, when he was murdered by his cousin Gaspare Pisciotta. Deciding that Giuliano had become a liability, the Mafia itself had been largely instrumental in Pisciotta's betrayal.

At a trial in Viterbo on the Italian mainland, Pisciotta told a stunned court that the Interior Minister Mario Scelba, a Sicilian, had ordered him to kill his cousin. He shouted: 'We are one body alone: bandits, police and Mafia, like the Father, the Son and the Holy Ghost.'[27] It was one of the earliest admissions of the ties between the Mafia and politicians. But as the trial concerned only the killings at Portella della Ginestra, the court ruled that Pisciotta's statement could not be taken into account. Sentenced for his part in the killing of the peasants, Pisciotta was jailed in Palermo's Ucciardone prison. In February 1954, he died there after drinking coffee laced with strychnine.

Peasants and bandits were not the only victims of the Mafia's efforts to resist change. At least fifty trade union leaders and politicians of all parties, mostly Socialists and Communists, were slaughtered between 1945 and 1952. The spring of 1948 was a key time for the peasant movement. An alliance of Communists and Socialists had won a relative majority in regional elections in 1947, and the dominant conservative parties feared this success could be repeated in the general elections of 1948.

Among the most notorious victims was Placido Rizzotto, a young Socialist trade unionist in the Mafia dominion of Corleone south of Palermo. On the evening of 10 March 1948 he disappeared after he was seen being led away from the town by a local Mafioso. Soon afterwards, a thirteen-year-old shepherd boy, shouting and suffering from shock, told his father that in the hills around Corleone, he had seen bandits breaking the skull of a man.

The doctor at the local hospital, Michele Navarra, who was also the local Mafia boss, prescribed a tranquilliser to calm the boy. The teenager died soon after Navarra's injection. After the autopsy, the carabinieri reported that he had died of a huge intoxication, which had prompted 'acute delirium'.[28] Navarra said he deeply regretted giving the wrong injection. Rizzotto's remains were found nearly two years later. His body had been thrown down a ravine.

The Mafia's tactics in delaying agricultural reform effectively maintained the status quo for several years, until the autumn of 1949 and the following spring, when there was a wave of fresh attempts by peasants to wrest control of the land. Tens of thousands of hectares of land were occupied by peasants who in many cases got as far as sharing out and even sowing their new fields.

Thousands of them were arrested together with hundreds of the movement's leaders and many received long jail sentences. But despite the repression the movement grew, eventually prompting the Sicilian regional assembly to approve agrarian reform in 1950. Renewed pressure from the landowners prevented this from coming into force for another five years.

Apart from allying itself with the landowners against the challenge from left-wing parties, the Mafia also joined forces with the Movimento Indipendentista Siciliano (MIS), a Separatist movement which aimed to make Sicily part of the United States of America. This was not because the Mafia believed the Separatists would achieve their objective quickly, but because it saw this force as a means of preserving the status quo.

Of no small importance was the fact that the Separatists promised to wipe the slate clean where Mafia crimes were concerned. Part of the first Separatist manifesto, published clandestinely in Catania in 1942, read: 'The new history of the free and independent Sicily will have to start under the flag of concord and pardon. We shall forget all sins which will be redeemed with behaviour worthy of Sicilians . . . Woe to traitors! . . . The past will be forgotten, not the future.'[29]

In the last years of the Second World War, the Separatists were among the main supporters of the chiefly feudal equilibrium then prevailing in Sicily. The Godfather Calogero Vizzini himself was among those Mafiosi who joined the MIS. Vizzini put in an unexpected appearance at a Separatist congress in 1945. Asked whom he could speak for, he answered: 'I have only to whistle, and every man in the province of Caltanissetta will vote Separatist.' Only a couple of years later, Vizzini dropped the Separatists by the wayside and swung the Mafia behind the new Christian Democrat Party.

The Sicilian Mafia had long forged its own links with the United States. As far back as the late nineteenth century it had given birth to the American Mafia, extending the reach of the secret society beyond Sicily for the first time. The Sicilian brotherhood was much later to boast settlements and affiliates both across the Italian mainland and in several European countries.

It was not until 1963, in testimony by the American supergrass Joe Valachi to the McClellan commission of the United States Senate, that the expression 'Cosa Nostra' was used publicly for the first time, as the name of the American offshoot of the Sicilian Mafia.[30] In Sicily itself, the expression eventually became the men of honour's preferred name for their own organisation.

The Italian criminals first made American newspaper headlines in 1890, when a police captain in New Orleans was murdered. Two rival Sicilian clans were fighting for control of both the docks and the city's fruit trade. The police officer was murdered because he was allied to one of the families. When ten Sicilians were acquitted of the murder, they were lynched by a crowd.

Among the Sicilian Mafiosi's first victims in the United States were their fellow-countrymen. They extorted money from many of the vast numbers of Sicilians – more than 800,000 – who had emigrated to the United States between 1901 and 1914.[31] These extortion rackets were the first signs of life of the forerunner of the American Cosa Nostra, the Black Hand secret society, named after the sign which appeared on letters demanding extortion money.

One of the first Sicilian immigrants was also one of the first Godfathers of the Sicilian Mafia. Vito Cascio Ferro, who emigrated to the United States in 1900, swiftly became one of the leaders of the Black Hand. He was instrumental in turning the newborn extortion rackets into a lucrative industry.

Cascio Ferro is believed to have murdered a New York detective, the Italian-born Joe Petrosino. Petrosino had proved himself an arch-enemy of the secret society, and was responsible for the deportation from the United States of numerous clandestine Sicilian immigrants. Among those police had arrested was Cascio Ferro himself, seized along with a group of forgers in 1903.

The long arm of the Mafia took its revenge many years later, after the bosses of the Sicilian and United States Mafias decided upon Petrosino's death at the first of a string of meetings between the two societies. Petrosino was shot four times in Palermo's city centre in the Piazza Marina in March 1909, shortly after his ship had docked in the city. He had sailed to Palermo to uncover the secrets of the Black Hand's forefathers. Cascio Ferro was at first a prime suspect for the killing, but he was cleared by magistrates at an early stage of the investigations. A member of parliament swore that Cascio Ferro was dining at his house at the time of the murder.

The Godfather, whose criminal record until 1914 was a collection of acquittals on charges such as racketeering, kidnapping and arson, was to boast years afterwards: 'In my whole life I have only killed one person, and I did that disinterestedly . . . Petrosino was a brave adversary, and deserved better than a shameful death at the hands of some hired cut-throat.'[32]

The murder shocked both Italian and American public opinion. At that time, the Sicilian Mafia was still very much steeped in the rural economy, and the killing of such a leading investigator in Palermo's city centre was almost unheard of.

Prominent Palermitans claimed that the organisation was neglecting its traditional role as a guarantor of order in feudal communities. They argued it was turning into a more violent and ruthless organisation in which the accumulation of wealth had become the key objective. The myth spun by the secret society was again raising its ugly head. The truth was that the Mafia was simply showing its true nature.

Many inside and outside the Mafia believe a distinction can be made between the 'old' (rural) and the 'new' (gangster) face of the brotherhood. Drug trafficking is most often quoted as the cause of this supposed degeneration. Based in the cities, the new Mafiosi are seen as having more in common with the gangsters of Chicago in the 1930s than with the traditional Sicilian model of the 'man of respect'.

In his evidence to the anti-Mafia commission of the Rome parliament, the informer Buscetta caused hilarity among parliamentarians when he told them: 'It was drug trafficking that distorted Cosa Nostra, which made it lose

its values. Don't laugh, please. I was born this way and
it's difficult to change. I believed in it.'[33] The activities of
Cosa Nostra may well have evolved, but its violent tactics
have endured. There has always been a 'new' Mafia ready
to chase the 'old', and there is invariably little to choose
between the two.

The first time a conflict between the old and the new was
recorded was in 1873, when the brother of a police officer in
Monreale outside Palermo, in league with the authorities,
created a new local Mafia. The not-so-secret society was
set up under the cover of the local artisans' club, with
the purpose of limiting the power of the established
Mafiosi.

The statute of the new association included the rule:
'Abide by the oath and keep the secret; the punishment for
those who do not will be death within twenty-four hours.'
But the established society and its upstart rival gradually
persuaded themselves that they should work together, and
eventually merged.

More recently the Mafia myth has begun to suffer some
hard knocks from within its own ranks. A supergrass from
Catania, who followed in Buscetta's footsteps, scorned
the attempts by some Mafiosi to pass themselves off as
modern-day Robin Hoods:

It's true that in the old days the Mafia did not want poor
people to be treated unjustly. But that was because it
wasn't in its own interests. What do you think one could
steal from someone who didn't have anything? It would
have been stupid to steal from the poor. You would have
made very little out of it and you would have made
yourself unpopular.[34]

But this man of honour is an exception. Few of his

contemporaries would share his prosaic outlook. The myth to which Buscetta clings is firmly entrenched in the consciences of most of his former acolytes.

Anchored to such a fantasy, the Mafia extended its empire to all the activities on which Sicily's economy was founded – all forms of power, including the choice and election of candidates to the national parliament. Conceived to supplant the State in the protection and conservation of the big landed estates, the Mafia blossomed into a criminal 'state within the State', at the same time taking care to nurture the myth that moral values were its guiding principles.

2

THE MAFIA CANON:
SIN AND RETRIBUTION

Blood and the Virgin Mary

'Are you ready to enter Cosa Nostra? Do you realise there
will be no going back – you enter Cosa Nostra with your
own blood, and you can leave it only by shedding more of
your blood.' The criminals standing before the clan boss
nod in silence. They are about to take the biggest step
of their career in the underworld – an age-old ritual will
pluck them from the lowly ranks of common crime and
anoint them as the hallowed 'men of honour'.

'Hear the commandments of Cosa Nostra,' the patriarch
continues. 'You will not touch the women of other men of
honour. You will not steal, nor will you exploit prostitution.
You will not kill other men of honour save in cases of
absolute necessity. You will never speak of the affairs of
Cosa Nostra in front of strangers, nor will you introduce
yourself on your own to other men of honour.'

The candidates for initiation are now ready to swear their allegiance to the secret society. The first is asked in which hand he holds a gun. The boss pricks the index finger of that hand with a pin, to draw blood and stain a paper image of the Virgin Mary at the Annunciation, the patron saint of Cosa Nostra.

The boss then sets the image alight and drops it into the cupped hands of the candidate, who swears his allegiance to the society as he passes the burning image from his left hand to his right hand. 'As paper I burn you, as saint I adore you, as this paper burns must my flesh burn if I betray Cosa Nostra.'

That oath is a profession of loyalty with no possibility of return. The initiated is now a man of honour. Belonging to Cosa Nostra will from now on be a way of life for him, permeating his every act and impossible to escape from. His fellow-mobsters gather round to embrace and congratulate him, and slip him cash presents of several hundreds of pounds. The event is celebrated with a lavish banquet.

This is a scene which has been repeated thousands of times across Sicily – in remote hilltop villages, in lively coastal cities, even in jails. For the infant Mafioso, it is a ritual that sets him high above the humble ranks of common criminals to a prized status which automatically commands honour and respect. Antonino Calderone, the nephew and brother of powerful Mafiosi from Catania below Mount Etna, boasted of his exalted position despite turning informer:

You must forgive me for this distinction I make between the Mafia and common crime, but it's important to me. It's important to every Mafioso. We are Mafiosi, the others are just the rabble. We are men of honour. And not so much because we have sworn an oath, but because we are the elite of crime. We are very much superior to common criminals. We are the worst of all![1]

Influenced by the ceremonies of the legendary Beati Paoli sect of Palermo, the ritual is the outsider's first contact with the folkloric, even religious, trappings of Cosa Nostra mythology.

With its appeal to traditional Sicilian values such as honour, friendship, family ties and private justice, the initiation liturgy encapsulates the commandments Mafiosi describe as their 'code of honour'. They are ready to cling to this code of behaviour through thick and thin because it allows them to justify the existence of Cosa Nostra as a champion of worthy values. But in fact this code is trampled underfoot by bosses who manipulate it to help them crush a rival.

Mafiosi seek to portray their association as a brave, benign force which refuses to be suppressed. Buscetta, even after he had committed the worst sin in the eyes of the secret society and turned informer, defined the Mafia as 'a way of behaviour, a way of conceiving friendship and existence. It's an idea of certain values.'[2]

Cosa Nostra patriarchs are past masters at passing off the organisation, and themselves, as the embodiment of Sicilian wisdom. The Godfather Vizzini was asked at one trial in 1949 to explain the meanings of the phrases 'man of respect' (a euphemism for Mafioso) and 'Mafioso culture'. So successful was he in answering the judges' queries that he was described in their verdict as a man of 'much authority and prestige' who had 'asserted himself because of his personality'. There was no mention in the sentence of the word 'Mafia'.[3]

Such attempts to identify it as a diffuse and indistinct

mentality played into the hands of the criminal organisation for decades, hoodwinking researchers, judges and
members of parliament alike (although the ties of some
politicians to Mafiosi meant that they did not need too much
prompting). Giuseppe Pitrè, the ethnologist, wrote in the
late nineteenth century that the Mafia was 'a state of mind,
a philosophy of life, a conception of society, a moral code,
a particular susceptibility predominant among Sicilians'.[4]

Even the president of the anti-Mafia commission in the
1960s, Senator Pafundi, fell for the Cosa Nostra line in a
colourful diagnosis:

> the Mafia in Sicily is a 'mental state', it pervades
> everything and everybody, at all levels . . . The Mafia
> has ended up in the blood . . . It is above all in
> the ancestral mistrust of laws and therefore in their
> avoidance, which in Sicilians has the nature of an
> epidermic voluptuousness . . . a mental state which
> bewitches, fascinates, infects.[5]

Soldiers and Cardinals

The religious overtones of Cosa Nostra's initiation ritual are
no accident. For a young Sicilian Catholic, the ceremony
is like a second baptism. Before him is a boss imitating
the local Roman Catholic priest in threatening dire punishments if commandments are violated.

As he joins the secret society, the new Mafioso sees Cosa
Nostra as a Church, an institution he can identify with.

It is his first encounter with the association's professed respect for popular values, in this case the religion of most Sicilians. 'Even if they call themselves "soldiers", they are in fact generals. Or rather cardinals of a church which is much less indulgent than the Catholic Church,' judge Falcone said of the men of honour.[6]

Religious symbols are a statutory ingredient of the initiation ritual, which can vary slightly from clan to clan. The holy image is usually of the Virgin at the Annunciation (whose feast day is 25 March), but other saints can be used too. To draw blood, clan bosses traditionally use a thorn from an orange tree, or a hat-pin. The family holding sway over the small town of Riesi in central Sicily had, and may still have, a gold hat-pin kept exclusively for such rituals.

Even the earliest accounts of this ceremony, which has changed very little since the last century, show how much it owes to the Church. The first report dates from 1877. Candidates for membership of the Stuppaghiari brotherhood in Monreale outside Palermo had to smear the effigy of a saint with their blood and then burn the effigy as they swore allegiance. A decade later, the Fratuzzi sect of Bagheria ended its rite of initiation with the new member firing a pistol at a crucifix to show that 'after shooting at the Lord, he would have no difficulty in murdering his father or his brother.'[7]

Today's Mafiosi see no clash between the values of their code of honour, which is supposed to regulate the workings of Cosa Nostra, and the Ten Commandments of the Roman Catholic Church. Men of honour see themselves as Catholics, and have thought up odd ways of accommodating their two religions: 'There are many Catholics among us,' said one supergrass. 'For example, one of the rules of Cosa Nostra bans killing on Fridays because, for us, it's a day of mourning. It will seem strange, but all we men of honour have the Bible, we pretend to be saints, even if we know the consequences. We are Catholics: as a matter of fact, I am a Catholic and I belong to Cosa Nostra.'[8]

Religious paraphernalia is harnessed to the less charitable of the Mafia's activities. In 1958, the Godfather Don Genco Russo summoned the young Luciano Leggio, a notorious killer from Corleone, to murder the town's increasingly arrogant Mafioso Dr Michele Navarra. Genco Russo, entertaining Leggio at his home, pronounced the name of Navarra and then kissed Leggio on his forehead, chest and shoulders while reciting the ritual formula: 'I give you the life of the traitor, in the name of the Father, the Son and the Holy Spirit. Amen.'[9]

The particularly sanguinary Palermo boss Filippo Marchese had the habit of crossing himself every time he had a trouble-maker strangled and his body dissolved in a barrel of acid. The Cuntrera brothers, drug barons who had emigrated from the dirt-poor village of Siculiana, had the effigy of the black Christ flown over from their home-town to Canada and Venezuela so that their soldiers could carry it in processions.[10]

The Mafiosi's 'Church' can even claim its own Holy Father. Michele Greco, a Palermo chief with the bearing of a distinguished man of the cloth and given to reciting long extracts from the Bible at his trials, was known to mobsters as 'The Pope'. Reluctant to divest himself completely of his holy mantle, Greco said in a court appearance that he had found out about the nickname from newspapers, and added: 'They call me "The Pope" but I cannot compare myself to popes, not even to the present one. But as for my serene conscience, as for the depth of my faith, I can even feel equal, if not superior to them . . . I have read a great deal, especially the Bible.'[11] When the

Palermo maxi-trial of several hundred Mafiosi neared its end, Greco gave a sinister blessing to the judge: 'May the Lord be with you in your decision and give you eternal peace.'[12]

But unlike the all-embracing Catholic Church, Cosa Nostra seeks to feed its reputation as an élitist organisation by refusing to let all-comers taste its lures: 'enrichment, the realisation of a world which offers all a young man asks of life'.[13] Those banned from entry include women; homosexuals, who are deemed morally unworthy; policemen and magistrates or their relatives; and the sons of men of honour who have been killed by Cosa Nostra. The latter are excluded because, were they to join, fellow-mobsters would be forced according to the rules to reveal who had carried out the murders of their relatives.

The Mafia has recently added a new category of men who cannot be allowed to join, for pseudo-moral reasons – men whose mother or sister has had a lover are banned because their honour is tainted.[14] Save for these restrictions, it casts its net very wide. Not only can criminals join but also lawyers, doctors, princes, even priests – anyone who stands to make a contribution to the common cause by joining the brotherhood.

Young criminals are watched closely, in case any show promising signs of decisiveness or arrogance. Cosa Nostra will rear them like a surrogate mother, train them, teach them to shoot, to plant bombs, to kill. Once they have been picked out, most candidates are required to undergo some sort of test, which can include stealing motorcycles or cars, collecting protection money or even carrying out a murder. This not only allows clan bosses to judge their mettle, it can also serve to force a potential Mafioso to go so far that he cannot pull back.

Vitale, a boss who became the first man of honour to repent and reveal Cosa Nostra's workings to the police in the 1970s, was told by his Mafioso uncle to shoot a horse dead. Having passed that test, he was then ordered to shadow a criminal who had defied the supremacy of Cosa Nostra, ambush, and murder him. That task also completed, Vitale was enrolled – at the age of only seventeen.

For some young Sicilians, however, their ancestry can be enough to fulfil the secret society's entrance requirements. Asked why he had been recruited, the informer Messina put it down mostly to 'family tradition'; the Mafia, he said, had been his nursery. His grandfather had been the head of a clan, and he claimed he could trace his family's membership through no fewer than seven generations.

His grandmother's cousin had kept him under observation from boyhood and little by little revealed the secrets of the Mafia to the young Messina before he went through the initiation ritual, thus breaking the rule that mobsters should not talk about its business to outsiders. At the age of twenty-five, Messina swore his allegiance after serving four years in jail for theft and other crimes.

The supergrass Calderone, whose uncle founded the first clan in Catania, was asked to do very little. He was told to drive the car of a family friend, a doctor, who had been threatened by a rival gang seeking extortion money. Calderone's presence at the wheel served to warn all and sundry that the doctor was under his uncle's protection.

Calderone explained how the indoctrination of a potential Mafioso begins at an early age. When a boy realises his father, his older brothers and the friends of the family are men of honour, 'The Mafia becomes everything for the youngster. In such an environment there aren't many influences from outside, people don't read many newspapers or books. Even today few go to school and even fewer go to church.'[15]

But when Calderone sought to revoke his membership, he found to his cost that this is impossible for a man of honour. He had begun to fear for his survival after his brother was shot dead apparently by rival mobsters. Calderone asked the local boss to be allowed to leave his clan. But the boss told him that a Mafioso could not leave Cosa Nostra. He had to choose between staying in the clan or being murdered because he knew too much. Calderone chose to stay, but he was not kept informed as well as previously of the clan's affairs. 'I had to live with the fear that one day they would call me to a meeting and murder me,' he said years later.[16]

The Law of Silence

'As saint I adore you, as paper I burn you, as this paper burns must my flesh burn if I betray Cosa Nostra.' The oath of allegiance is the foundation stone of the men of honour's solidarity – an unyielding law of silence, or 'omertà'.

This commandment of the code of honour is the Mafia's first bond of association, as well as a protective shield. The brotherhood was defined as 'crime plus intelligence and omertà'[17] by Buscetta, who turned informer in 1984 after more than four decades in Cosa Nostra. Before any

physical sanction is enforced, the Mafioso who breaks the
oath of silence is a moral outcast because he has shown
himself to be a traitor and unworthy, a man who has lost
all claim to honour.

In this perverted canon, silence becomes a measure of
a man's moral worth. The word *omertà* itself is derived
from '*omu*' in Sicilian dialect, meaning not just 'man'
but someone who has the pride, courage and sense of
responsibility of a man who is respected in his community.
Without obeying this law of silence, the man of honour
cannot be an '*omu*', he cannot maintain his superiority
unchallenged.

Any betrayal of the law of silence brings shame on the
family of the man of honour. 'He has stripped us brothers of
our dignity, so much so that we are ashamed even to walk,'
said Stefano Calzetta after his brother Vincenzo, a lowly
mobster, violated his oath of allegiance. Rita Sinagra, the
sister of another informer, even denied the traitor was her
brother in order to show how he had been ostracised by his
own family, describing him to the police as 'a relative of
my father'.[18]

These families may be turning their backs on the traitors
out of fear of reprisals, but they are also underlining how
its law of silence is grounded in Sicilian popular culture.
The Mafia has adapted itself to a traditional value to justify
its existence and gloss over its more sinister doings with a
spurious legitimacy.

Only for a few rare periods of Sicilian history have its
official rulers succeeded in guaranteeing safety and public
order to its population. *Omertà*, the fear of falling victim
of those you denounce, has its roots in the conviction
that questions of honour are resolved by private violence.
Silence is a form of self-defence for a people whose
temperament has been shaped by a legacy of invaders

into 'a combination of apparent submission and loyalty to tradition combined with intense pride.'[19]

'The man who is really a man never reveals anything, even when he is being stabbed,' says one Sicilian proverb. A host of sayings encapsulate the popular wisdom that the safest bet is to avoid revealing too much, to a friend or to authority: 'Testimony is good as long as you don't harm your neighbour'; 'He who is deaf, blind and silent lives a hundred years in peace'; 'The priest covers the chalice and we must cover each other.'

Popular songs also reflect this traditional Sicilian reluctance to collaborate with authority. Islanders are diffident towards the strangers who for centuries invaded their land, and the Mafioso minority often supplanted these foreign rulers. The songs show the peasants' attitude towards the association and the bandits of the countryside:

> Don't pay attention if you are called,
> Pretend to be stupid and stunned.
> When the shoot-out is over
> The dead and the wounded will be counted.[20]

From its earliest days, the Mafia has manipulated this trait of Sicilian character. An anecdote from the early 1900s illustrates the Mafioso's respect for the rule of *omertà* when he is challenged by authority. A policeman patrolling country roads on horseback chanced on a Mafioso moments after he had ambushed and shot a man from behind a hedge. The body lay sprawled at the mobster's feet, and his double-barrelled gun was still warm. The policeman arrested him. The Mafioso's steadfast answer to all questioning was: 'I know nothing, I have seen nothing. But if even this nothing were prejudicial then I know less than nothing, I saw less than nothing.'[21]

The law of silence extends to the very identity of Cosa Nostra, as well as that of its members. Mobsters are forbidden to introduce themselves as men of honour to strangers, and can do so only if there is a third Mafioso present known to both parties. There is a set formula for such presentations. The man introducing the two to each other must say, 'He is Cosa Nostra [Our Affair]', 'This is the same thing' or 'He is like me and like you.'[22]

The only time a boss publicly violated the rule that the organisation's existence must never be acknowledged was during the so-called 'maxi-trial' of more than 300 mobsters in the mid-1980s. An eleven-year-old boy, Claudio Domino, had been shot dead by gunmen during the trial, and the press speculated that the Mafia was to blame.

Palermo's Giovanni Bontate stood up in court to speak out on behalf of those on trial. He read out a statement protesting 'against vile and baseless accusations. We are men, we have children, we understand the grief of the Domino family . . . We reject the hypothesis that such an act of barbarity could even touch us.'[23] Bontate even asked for a minute's silence to mourn the boy's death.

Many Mafiosi disapproved of Bontate's statement. By reading it out, he had tacitly acknowledged the existence of Cosa Nostra, as an organisation which dissociated itself from the boy's murderers.

Writing down its secrets is equivalent to blasphemy. One of the few men of honour who attempted to commit the organisation's workings to paper was the Palermo mobster Michele Cavataio, an ambitious maverick who in the early 1960s sought to rearrange the families of the capital according to his designs.

Cavataio drew a map of Palermo showing how the clans

should carve up the various neighbourhoods between them, and whom he would like to see heading each Mafia family. He made the mistake of showing this map to several bosses, and they sentenced him to death for breaking a golden rule.

The law of silence can be breached only by men of honour talking among themselves. They are, formally at least, under an obligation to tell the truth. Otherwise, said one supergrass, 'nobody understands anything any more, and this gives rise to great confusion . . . If nobody knows who killed somebody, or if people suspect the wrong person, then nobody is sure of anything any more, not even of their own lives.'[24]

When they discuss their dealings, today's Mafiosi speak a jargon derived from the slang of thieves, pickpockets and criminals who run prostitution rackets. This language boasts an abundance of terrifying neologisms reflecting the men of honour's activities. '*Capottu pisanti*' (literally, 'heavy overcoat'), for example, refers to a body encased inside a column of cement. There are a dozen different words for 'murder'.[25]

Sharp and to the point, the nature of the jargon has changed little as Cosa Nostra evolved. As early as the last century, one observer commented: 'It's strange that in these hot and imaginative countries, where the ordinary language is so mellifluous, hyperbolic and figurative, that of the Mafiosi is brief, sober, blunt.'[26]

The use of such jargon can help to isolate men of honour from the outside world. When the informer Contorno testified in court, he refused to speak Italian and insisted on using what he called the Mafiosi's slang. An interpreter had to be called in. Although he was testifying for the authorities, Contorno wanted to be sure his former acolytes understood his every word as he described an attempt on his life and the composition of the Palermo clans.

Men of Honour

When the young mobster Giuseppe Marchese fell in love with a thirteen-year-old girl called Rosaria, the elders of his Mafia clan sought to bring him to heel. It was not the girl's age they objected to, but her family. Rosaria, they told him, was no match for a promising man of honour like Marchese, who had been sworn in at the early age of seventeen and murdered his first victim – on the orders of the Godfather Riina himself – only two years later. Rosaria's parents were separated, and this violated the Mafia's respect for family ties.

Marchese's brother Antonio, also a soldier, told him that the only solution possible under the Mafia's code of honour was to murder Rosaria's father. There would be no objections to the marriage once Rosaria had been made an 'orphan', he said. Antonio Marchese even offered to do the job himself as a brotherly favour.

Giuseppe Marchese pretended to agree, but did nothing. Later, his brother insisted: 'You are going to ruin yourself and ruin your family with this marriage. If you won't kill him, we shall.' Marchese told magistrates years later: 'I broke off our relationship because if I had accepted I would no longer have been able to look Rosaria in the eye.'[27]

Cosa Nostra puts a high price on honour, or at least its distorted view of the concept. Mafiosi like to call themselves men of honour, or men of respect. Their commandments are known collectively as the 'code of honour'. Theirs is the Honoured Society. The name can be taken literally. Honour, or paying lip-service to it, is one of the pillars that supports the entire structure.

The ideal is a sham, as one informer was to learn after being dazzled by the worthy commandments expressed during his initiation ceremony:

What beautiful words! What beautiful principles! And how many times in the years that followed I came across the lack of respect for these rules, double-crossings, betrayals, murders carried out precisely by exploiting the good faith of those who instead believed in these rules. I had no choice but to realise that the real Cosa Nostra was very different from that which was presented to me on that occasion.[28]

As early as 1874, the prefect of Girgenti (today's Agrigento) had listed in a report to the Interior Ministry a series of rules which he said were supposed to guide the actions of Mafiosi. He concluded that 'the Mafia can however be defined as criminal silence, shameless courage, impudent falseness, treachery in intimate personal relations, resistance to all moral and civil rules'.[29]

Cosa Nostra's ideal of honour demands that a Mafioso show courage and demonstrate he has the ability to take revenge. It also demands sexual propriety in female relatives. The man of honour is respected, and feared, because he is willing to use violence to assert his dignity if need be. In 1889, Pitrè defined the Mafia as 'the consciousness of one's own being, the exaggerated concept of individual strength . . . from which springs an intolerance of superiority in others, and – what is even worse – of bullying by others.'[30]

In more recent times, some mobsters shook their heads

in disapproval when the Palermo boss Filippo Marchese commissioned five soldiers to murder his brother-in-law in jail. The execution was carried out by fellow-inmates, but one informer told investigators that, according to Mafia honour, Marchese should have righted the wrong himself. 'For my blood it must be my hand,' the supergrass explained.[31]

The Mafioso's honour is also measured by the chastity of the women in his family. For the Mafia, which has an exalted sensibility for traditional sexual roles, feminine purity is seen as directly related to the virility of its menfolk. Any doubt about the first inevitably stains the reputation of its disciples.

Cosa Nostra has taken on board the popular Sicilian saying: 'The gun and the wife are not made to be lent.' A man of honour's sisters must stay virgins until their wedding or they bring dishonour to his house. This echoes the ancient custom that a young Sicilian wife was required to prove her virginity on the first night of her wedding. The couple had to hang their bed-sheet out of the window the following morning so that relatives and the rest of the village could pay tribute to the stained linen as a symbol of the newlyweds' honour.

The law laid down by Cosa Nostra does tolerate Mafiosi, and especially bosses, betraying their wives. But if they do have extramarital affairs, men of honour must conduct them with discretion in order not to publicly humiliate their spouses. '. . . if I rebuke a young man, or try to kill or force him to marry a woman only because he has had a relationship with her, I must be the first in the neighbourhood – where the Mafioso is respected by men and women – to set an example,' said one soldier.[32]

If a mobster slept with the wife of another man of honour, the latter was automatically entitled to murder the lover, according to Palermo's Buscetta. Buscetta himself was isolated within Cosa Nostra and deemed untrustworthy partly because he had married three times and had an unstable private life. The Mafia does not tolerate divorce, let alone a second or third marriage. Marriage vows sworn before a priest are as sacrosanct as the oath of allegiance sworn before a clan boss. When Buscetta confronted Riina in court in November 1993, the first meeting between the two men in thirteen years, he accused the Godfather of masterminding a string of murders, including those of his relatives. Riina remained stonily silent, except for a single retort which underlined Cosa Nostra's attachment to its code of honour: 'I don't want to talk with this immoral man,' he said.[33]

The commandment that affairs should not lead to the break-up of a marriage can cause a Mafioso to commit the most serious offence against the secret society and turn informer. Baldassare di Maggio, a driver and general dogsbody for Riina, saw his career in the organisation come to a sudden halt when he left his wife and two children to flee with his mistress. Di Maggio had a son by his mistress. His superiors told him he could never rise to become a clan boss because he had broken the rules.

An embittered Di Maggio gave himself up to the police and revealed Riina's whereabouts, enabling them to arrest the Godfather. For Di Maggio, the breach of rules was used as a pretext to outmanoeuvre him. 'They say I had betrayed the rules of the Mafia by betraying my wife and getting myself a mistress. Balls! Everybody had mistresses. The truth was that [my rival] was jealous of the fact that his father had a preference for me.'[34]

The Palermo Mafioso Francesco Marino Mannoia traded his revelations for the chance to break free from the rigid code of honour. Marino Mannoia, who refined heroin for the clans, was married to the wife of a local boss. When he fell in love with a woman who had no contact with the Mafia, he felt he had no choice but to flee because his brother-in-law would never have allowed him to divorce. He made a pact with the investigators – he would reveal all he knew in exchange for the guarantees necessary to start a new life with his girlfriend far away from Sicily.

The Women of Cosa Nostra

Apart from her faithfulness, the ideal companion for a man of honour is a devoted wife who obeys the oath of allegiance to Cosa Nostra without ever having sworn it. '. . . a wife, even knowing her own husband is a criminal and a murderer and seeing the kind of people he talks to, is ready to accept any sacrifice for the love of a man who is faithful and who loves her. There are women, wives or mothers of Mafiosi who are worthy of admiration for the sacrifices they make.'[35]

Women play a significant role because they are a key link in the chain of relations which holds Cosa Nostra united. Family ties help to bind members of the Mafia, and constitute one of the fundamental characteristics of its structure.

Mafiosi refer to clans as families. And it is the clan which must come first and foremost for the mobster, as must the family in popular Sicilian culture. The family unit is important as a model for the structure of the organisation. Weddings cement alliances between clans, and serve to bury the hatchet after decades of feuding between rival families.

But the Mafiosi's women are traditionally held at arm's length by Cosa Nostra and appreciated only for their trustworthiness as keepers of their menfolk's secrets. For Calderone, women could resign themselves to the murder of a husband but not to the loss of a son. Revealing the workings of the secret society to one's nearest and dearest is a betrayal of the oath of allegiance:

When a woman is wounded in her dearest affections, she doesn't reason any more. *Omertà* no longer means anything to her. Cosa Nostra no longer exists, no arguments or rules can restrain her . . . The Sicilian man of honour knows this, and tries to keep wives, sisters and mothers far from Cosa Nostra affairs. He does this to protect them, to safeguard them, to save them, because if the woman knows something things go badly. Either he has to kill her or he has to have her killed by someone else.[36]

In recent years, however, these women have come to play an increasingly important part in the day-to-day business of Cosa Nostra. They have carved out roles for themselves as drug-couriers, kidnappers, business partners, and even become informers.

Unlike the Camorra, the Neapolitan cousin of the Mafia, there are few cases of women in command. Concetta Fausciana, wife of a jailed boss in Gela on Sicily's south coast, was an exception. She ran an army of a hundred or so teenage mobsters entrusted with collecting protection money from local shopkeepers. The soldiers would set bombs off or shoot if necessary to intimidate traders who were slow to pay up. Fausciana taught her recruits how to shoot and paid them £150 a month out of the funds of Cosa Nostra.

Antonietta Bagarella, married to the jailed Godfather Riina, managed twenty-seven plots of land in her husband's name, as well as two flats. Saveria Benedetta Palazzolo, wife of Riina's lieutenant Bernardo Provenzano, was a shirt-maker by profession but already in the 1960s had an estate worth £100,000 and owned shares in a wine-making co-operative. Both these women had healthy bank balances. 'Women do well for themselves in the Mafia. Being the wife of a Mafioso means the enjoyment of many privileges, big and small. Women are attracted by the Mafia,' said one supergrass.[37]

Such privileges can include an extreme form of protection from sexual harassment. In the mid-1970s, the wife of Nitto Santapaola, the Catania boss who was jailed for life for the 1982 murder of General Dalla Chiesa, passed her driving test. Her instructor, who had no idea who her husband was, flirted with her and asked: 'Don't I deserve a kiss now?' Shortly afterwards two mobsters were dispatched to the driving school to kneecap the instructor but they got the wrong man and wounded his brother by mistake.[38]

Women have played pioneering roles in betraying Cosa Nostra to the authorities, or in persuading their men to do so. After her husband and adopted son were murdered in clan warfare, Serafina Battaglia knocked on the door of her local police station to reveal the truth behind twenty-four murders that had rocked the town of Alcamo, and to denounce thirty Mafiosi.

The men she accused were brought to trial to face her, and she told the court: 'If the women of those who have been murdered took the step of speaking out as I am doing because I am thirsty for justice, the Mafia would have ceased to exist in Sicily a long time ago.'[39] The men of honour were sentenced in the first trial but were all acquitted fifteen years later.

Battaglia's decision to break ranks, and similar moves by Mafiosi rebelling against the strictures of the code of honour, show how the canon has come under increasing pressure in recent years. As a set of commandments based on traditional, almost medieval, values, it has proved too uncompromising. The greatest challenge to this code has come from the '*pentiti*' (literally, 'penitents' or 'repentants'), who have broken their oath of allegiance.

The Oath Betrayed

'Men of the Mafia, I know you are here . . . I forgive you but you must go down on your knees. If you have the courage to change . . . but they don't want to change, they don't change . . . If you have the courage to radically change your designs, be Christians once again.' The words of the young widow Rosaria Schifani rang out at a funeral mass in a packed Palermo cathedral. A few days previously she had lost her husband, one of three bodyguards blown up by a bomb which killed Falcone and his wife in May 1992.

Schifani's words, broadcast live on state television, played a key role in prompting two men of honour, Messina and Marchese, to become *pentiti* and collaborate with the magistrates.

Messina, grandson of a Mafioso and deputy head of the

clan of San Cataldo, told the investigators: 'I no longer recognise myself inside the organisation and when I saw on television the widow of the policeman Schifani speak and pray to the men of the Mafia, her words struck me like rocks.'[40] Messina had been angered by the murder of his best friend and feared he was earmarked for the same fate.

The collaboration of Marchese, who had been sentenced for murder and drug trafficking, highlighted the frailty of the law of silence. Marchese was the brother-in-law of Leoluca Bagarella, who was in turn the brother-in-law of the Godfather Riina. And yet here was Riina's own relative, although family ties had long been the most solid link in the organisation's chain, turning his back on such an illustrious kinsman.

The first to break the oath of allegiance was Leonardo Vitale, born and bred in Palermo. After his initiation at the age of seventeen, he turned his back on the Mafia in 1973 following a crisis of conscience for religious motives. 'One becomes a man of honour by [following the Lord's commandments] and by refraining from killing, stealing or striking fear into people,' Vitale told the investigators.[41]

He denounced the untouchables of the Palermo élite, including a Christian Democrat city councillor and a prince. Vitale also revealed the crimes he had himself committed, chiefly collecting extortion money, and the misdoings of other mobsters. He was the first to warn the police of the standing of Riina, who was soon to become Godfather.

But those he accused were almost all acquitted. Vitale himself was declared mentally disturbed, tried for his crimes and sentenced. He spent a decade in jails or mental homes. The Mafia took it upon itself to confirm the importance of Vitale's testimony after the State had failed to do so. Seven months after he was released from jail, Vitale was shot dead on his way home after Sunday mass in December 1984.

'My only fault was to have been born and brought up in a family steeped in Mafiosi traditions and in a society where all are Mafiosi and for this reason are respected, while those who are not are despised,' Vitale wrote in a document handed to the police before his death.[42] In 1985, magistrates wrote in their indictment for the Palermo maxi-trial that Vitale's ability to remember and relate events he knew about had not been impaired by his alleged madness, because he had suffered neither from hallucinations nor from delirium prompted by fear of persecution, nor any other serious psychic anomalies.

That trial, at which 338 mobsters were given long jail sentences, was made possible by the betrayal of Buscetta, the first Mafioso of rank to entrust his vendetta to the State. Unsurprisingly, it had taken a decade for a man of honour to follow Vitale's lead. But the testimony of Buscetta, or Don Masino as he was known, was to have a far more destructive effect than Vitale's.

'I remain a member of Cosa Nostra in the same spirit as when I joined,' Buscetta told the magistrates when he began his testimony in 1984.[43] He was rebelling against the bloody rise to power of the clan from Corleone, the 'Corleonesi'. His decision to break ranks was one of the hardest blows Cosa Nostra has suffered. It helped to show up the Mafia-imposed *omertà* as more the fruit of fear than the result of a Sicilian subculture. In time it pushed many other men of honour into following suit, shattering the myth that Cosa Nostra was a tight-knit, impenetrable force.

Born the last of seventeen children to a Palermo family,

Buscetta was initiated at an early age. He rose to become 'The Boss of Two Worlds', accused of being one of the co-ordinators of Cosa Nostra's drug empire, with contacts in Brazil, Peru, Bolivia, Colombia, the United States and Europe. The member of a Palermo clan, he was also accused of several murders.

Buscetta broke the law of silence because he wanted to use the State for his vendetta and because he believed the Corleonesi family had overturned the code of honour. He blamed that clan for his sons' disappearance. Neither son had been a man of honour. They had fallen victim to the *'lupara bianca'* ('white shotgun', after which the bodies of those murdered are never recovered) despite Buscetta's refusal to become involved in an attempt to counter the rise of the Corleonesi. That he had been asked to do so by a leading rival of the Corleonesi was enough.

Asked after his betrayal of the secret society whether he still considered himself a Mafioso, Buscetta answered: 'If you mean by Mafioso a man who keeps his word, who has dignity, even being as they say *pentito*, but I am not all *pentito* . . . I define myself as a man disappointed by the Mafia, a man who has contributed so much to the Mafia and who sees his own children murdered for no reason, disappear into thin air. I don't think any father could go on living in such an environment.'[44]

Before turning informer, Buscetta attempted to commit suicide by swallowing strychnine. 'I wanted to stop causing trouble for my family,' he said later.[45] He talked for forty-five consecutive days, and his testimony enabled the magistrates to issue 366 arrest warrants. Buscetta was offered money by Cosa Nostra to feign madness so that his testimony would be made invalid, but he refused. The day after his refusal, his brother-in-law was shot dead.

Buscetta's collaboration with the authorities was unprecedented in that he set an example for other Mafiosi to
follow. In one case, he was instrumental in prompting
another mobster to betray the oath of allegiance. Salvatore
Contorno was a bodyguard and hit-man in the service of
the Palermo boss Stefano Bontate. Contorno's family was
decimated by the Corleonesi after he testified.

The jailed Contorno, who had learnt of Buscetta's
collaboration with the authorities, asked to meet his
former accomplice. When the two met in a prison cell,
an overwhelmed Contorno dropped to his knees before
Buscetta and kissed his hand, as if paying homage to
a monarch. The Boss of Two Worlds put a hand on
Contorno's shoulder and told him: 'Cosa Nostra is finished
now. Totuccio, you can talk.'[46]

Cosa Nostra's Vendetta

The secret society's revenge was extreme, even by its
own savage standards. In November 1989, three women
were found shot dead in a residential area in the heart
of Palermo. The killings bore all the hallmarks of a
Mafia raid, but police were at first at a loss for a
motive. If the killers were men of honour, this would
be the first time that the organisation had targeted
women.

Investigators found the key to the murders, and had
to rewrite the criminal organisation's rule-book, when
they discovered that all three women came from the
same family. They were the mother, sister and aunt of
Marino Mannoia. Cosa Nostra had swiftly carried out its

unprecedented vendetta as soon as it heard that he had turned informer. His reaction was to refuse to collaborate any further with the authorities.

The killings were a desperate attempt to stem the stream of Mafiosi who had followed Buscetta's lead in renouncing the society. Faced with such a challenge, the Mafia did not hesitate to admit tacitly the hypocrisy of its code of honour, which had until then banned the taking of women's lives.

Marino Mannoia was a rare catch for the authorities. He was the first on the side of the Corleonesi clan to betray his oath of allegiance after it had won a bloody war for supremacy against rival families. Dubbed 'The Chemist' because of his skill as an expert refiner of heroin, he was the first to turn informer in four years. He was able to give the magistrates priceless information, since he had been a confidant of the Corleonesi and also because many families employed him, impressed by his professional reputation.

The murders of his female relatives raised eyebrows even in Cosa Nostra itself. One Mafioso, Gaspare Mutolo, asked Leoluca Bagarella, lieutenant of the Godfather Riina, why Mafia rules had been violated and the women murdered. Bagarella replied that Marino Mannoia's betrayal was the reason, but added that the three women had also offended the organisation by giving him moral support. Had they broken with him, they would not have fallen prey to the killers.

Mutolo testified: 'The most terrible thing for me was when they started killing women and also a few children . . . I remember that in years past, if for example there was the order to kill someone, if he happened to be in the company of his wife or daughter, they watched them, then went away and postponed the execution. But this rule no longer holds.'[47]

The mobsters coined a new expression for the murders of informers' relatives – 'vendetta trasversale'. This new form of retribution was the most macabre side of Cosa Nostra's attachment to the family as the base of its entire structure. The Corleonesi threw their net wide: victims included anybody – friend, relative or mere acquaintance – who could provide assistance to the supergrass or who refused to help the clan take its revenge.

Contorno lost twelve relatives. Buscetta, who had already lost his two sons before he turned informer, was to have eleven relatives – including a brother, a brother-in-law, a nephew and his son-in-law – shot dead.[48] Years afterwards, Buscetta vented his frustration against his jailed rival, Corleone's Luciano Leggio:

> I have something more than him. I know where his son is, but I did not go to kill him because he did nothing to me, and then, who knows, maybe he will become a good person. If I had the possibility, I would kill him, in any circumstance, even in court. If somebody brought me a gun, I would do him in in front of the judge. It's not fury, it's not anger. It's just that I am a father. I accept any kind of battle against me, but I am not against someone who has nothing to do with it.[49]

When a man of honour like Buscetta seeks to contact police authorities to turn informer, all Mafiosi are duty bound to track him down and murder him immediately, without seeking permission from their bosses. The Cosa Nostra 'Church' has no room for the Christian teaching of forgiveness. Instead it is guided by Sicilian sayings such as 'Blood washes blood', 'Vendetta is the best forgiveness' and 'If I live I will burn you, if I die I will forgive you.'

Punishment can also come from within the turncoat's family, for whom the fear of retaliation can prove too much to bear. In March 1994 Enrico Incognito, a boss in the

town of Bronte on the slopes of Mount Etna, was shot dead
by his brother because he had betrayed Cosa Nostra. The
thirty-year-old Mafioso was gunned down when he opened
the door of his home to his relative. A friend of Incognito's
had been filming his confession on a home videocamera at
the time, and filmed the murder too. Investigators said Cosa
Nostra might have given his relatives an ultimatum to carry
out the killing.

The unprecedented revenge taken on informers is only
one of the sanctions it imposes to enforce its code of
honour. It is merciless with those who transgress its
canon. To make sure the commandments are respected,
the Mafia has its own system of tribunals and sanctions,
which runs in parallel to, and rather faster than, that of
the Italian State.

Antonino Salomone is one of the few men of honour who
have managed to disobey the organisation and survive.
Salomone, in his sixties at the time, decided to give
himself up to the police rather than execute an order from
the Palermo clans to murder Buscetta. The wily Salomone
asked a police officer to say he had arrested him because
he feared reprisals by the Mafia.

Clan bosses can decide to put a mobster who has
offended the code of honour, for example by speaking
of the society's affairs to his wife, under observation for
six months or so, during which time he is not told of
the family's business. Or he can be '*posato*' (literally, 'set
down') when the members of his clan expel him and are
ordered to avoid him. The offender is forbidden to speak
of Cosa Nostra.

But sanctions are not always so lenient. All too often
Cosa Nostra's system of justice has only one sentence for
malefactors – death. This has become increasingly the
norm as the ruthless Corleonesi clan rose to supremacy.

All Mafiosi are by their very nature capable of carrying out such sentences. Asked according to which criteria killers were chosen inside the Mafia, one informer told the investigators: 'All those who are part of Cosa Nostra are killers. The word "killer" does not exist for us.'[50]

Mafiosi see themselves as executioners whose actions are justified by their legal system – Cosa Nostra's code of honour. The more murders they commit, the greater their prestige and charisma within the society. At the mid-1980s maxi-trial, Riina and his lieutenant Michele Greco were accused of being responsible for fifty-two and fifty-one murders respectively. The Palermo boss Filippo Marchese, feared by insiders and outsiders, boasted the record number of murder counts, fifty-eight.

'I felt as one who was doing his duty towards a community, a brotherhood. I was doing what was right. I wasn't the judge, of course, but I was doing what they had ordered be done. Later I too gave orders to do it,' said Buscetta. He added: 'It's so easy to press the trigger and see the other fall. And immediately you have a sense of liberation: I have done what I had to do, and in the best way.'[51]

Cosa Nostra knows how to be patient. Gaetano Badalamenti, on his appointment as boss of the Palermo families, ordered a mobster to murder a man because a decade or so earlier he had dared to slap the Italo-American gangster Lucky Luciano in the face. Badalamenti, notes a supergrass, 'was proud to let it be known in the United States that the offence had been washed with blood, albeit tardily'.[52]

Mafiosi usually like to carry out such sentences quietly. Shooting a victim with a kalashnikov or some other weapon is a last resort, in cases where he cannot be ambushed. Cosa Nostra prefers to strangle its victim and then burn the body, dissolve it in a barrel of acid, or bury it after covering it with chemicals so that it cannot be identified should police find it a few months later.

Often the victim is led away to his death by someone known to his relatives, so that several days go by before the family calls in the police to report a disappearance. An informer explained: 'When somebody is strangled, the family believes for a time that the son or husband has gone away. The police cannot draw up its report. If it does, it's more difficult for the judge to pass sentence, because there is no body for evidence.'[53]

Strangulation can be a tiresome business, but the outcome makes it all worthwhile, according to the heroin refiner Marino Mannoia, who confessed in court to having committed twenty-five murders. 'Do you realise how much strength is needed to strangle a man?' he asked judge Falcone. 'Do you realise that it can take up to ten minutes and that the victim writhes, bites, kicks? Some even manage to break free from the rope. But at least these are "clean" killings.'[54]

Bodies are spirited away in a variety of ways. Marino Mannoia helped police to uncover a Mafia cemetery for victims of gangland warfare in Palermo. They dug up human bones under a motorway flyover on the outskirts of the city. He also revealed that Cosa Nostra had built death chambers along the banks of a river which had become an open sewer. Bodies of rival Mafiosi were left to soak in baths of acid in the chambers and then dumped in the river, which flowed out to sea.

The Corleonesi clan is largely responsible for making the disappearance of victims a common practice in Cosa Nostra. Previously the Mafia relied more often on the traditional technique of using the bodies of its victims to publicise its code of honour, to warn future generations of Mafiosi of what fate awaited them if they violated its commandments.

Death itself became a ritual. If a hand was cut off and placed on the body's chest, the message was that the victim was a petty thief who stole when he knew he should not. If the eyes were scooped out and placed in the victim's clenched hand, this meant that he was a good shot who had killed someone linked to Cosa Nostra. Replacing a dead Mafioso's wallet with prickly pear cactus showed he had stolen money or property placed in his trust by the society.[55]

A singer, Pino Marchese, was found with his genitals in his mouth. Mobsters took this to mean that he had had an affair with the wife of a man of honour. Such symbolism can travel. Pietro Inzerillo, brother of the Palermo boss Salvatore, was found in the boot of a car in New York with a bunch of banknotes stuffed into his mouth and covering his genitals. He had shown himself to be too greedy.[56]

Such didactic techniques can also apply to the murders of outsiders. In January 1993 Giuseppe Alfano, a journalist on the Catania daily *La Sicilia*, was shot dead. He had long campaigned against the Mafia, writing about electoral fraud and corruption in the small town of Barcellona Pozzo di Gotto near Messina in north-east Sicily. Gunmen ambushed him on his way home one night. He was shot in the mouth. In the Mafia's language, this was a punishment for someone who talked too much.

The threat of sudden death can become an obsession for a man of honour. The informer Gaspare Mutolo, asked by a lawyer during a trial whether he had lived in fear of being killed during his time as a Mafioso, shot back: 'Why, who is there who is not scared of being killed every day? Excuse me! Why, do you feel at ease when you walk around Palermo?'[57]

The Catania supergrass Calderone warned his former brothers that they would never be able to shake off such obsessions if they remained in the organisation:

Go to another place, in another continent, in another world as far as possible from Sicily. Because here everything always ends the same way. You die. And you will die, and your children will die too . . . Death calls death as blood calls blood. It is a thing without end. [The Catania boss] Nitto Santapaola was terrified of this, but all he would do was to say: 'We must kill even the sons of those we have killed.' He would say this because he feared the sons of the dead would grow up and kill him, or would kill his sons. The great terror of you Mafiosi is born of this . . . They have murdered too much, they have killed too many enemies.[58]

3

A STATE WITHIN
A STATE

The Rule of the Clans

The neighbourhood of Ciaculli is one of the most Mafia-infested of Palermo, hugging the coast on the city's southern outskirts. The authorities like to give a wide berth to the area, where the clan bosses' grim, bunker-like houses are the only landmarks. Even the local council finds it difficult to penetrate much of the district, and many of Ciaculli's more desolate streets have no name.

For years the feared killer Pino 'Little Shoe' Greco, who boasted an almost legendary reputation, imposed a reign of terror on Ciaculli. In early 1983, at the height of the warfare between rival Palermo mobsters, many households there were sent anonymous and threatening letters ordering them to move out of the area.

The letters were effectively ultimatums. Some families abandoned Ciaculli immediately, but others tried to stay.

The stubborn ones had their cars set on fire and were mercilessly harassed until they fled. Greco had ordered these families out because he suspected they were acting as informers for his rivals.

'Pino Greco wanted to "reclaim" the territory of Ciaculli,' explained Buscetta. 'He forced all the families who could not guarantee absolute loyalty to abandon the territory, including those composed only of women because the men were under arrest or on the run.'[1]

Ciaculli is no oddity. It is by no means the only neighbourhood of Palermo, or of other Sicilian cities or towns, where organised crime carries such political weight. That the Mafia should have the final say on where Palermitans are allowed to live underlines how far it has come since its birth in the great landed estates of rural Sicily. Nothing has slowed its spread into the urban areas of Sicily, where it directs the activities of legitimate businesses by levying 'protection' money, and by fixing tenders for public contracts.

The men of honour have extended their reach even further afield. The Mafiosi's enthusiastic entry into international drug trafficking has allowed them to assert themselves on the Italian mainland and abroad, enslaving other criminal organisations in the south of the country.

Cosa Nostra can claim total dominion over vast swaths of Sicily. Far more than a banal criminal organisation, it is to all intents and purposes an illegal 'State'. The secret society has a Machiavellian relationship with the Italian State. As a criminal structure, it does not recognise and violates the latter's laws. But in its exploitation of political allies to fix tenders for public works, Cosa Nostra implicitly recognises the State's authority and penetrates its institutions. The brotherhood has its own territory, and a population of men of honour and their acolytes. The code of honour is its constitution. The Mafia also boasts its own institutions, a huge budget and an implacable judicial system to try those who fail to obey its laws.

Territories are carefully divided up among the various clans, which exercise almost absolute supremacy over them. Appealing to their code of honour as their guide, many bosses have successfully imposed themselves as leading figures in their community, with a recognised role to play as guarantors of law and order. Sicilians frequently turn to the local boss rather than the legal authorities when they have a problem to solve. The anti-Mafia commission was forced to admit that in many areas the institutions of the Italian State commanded less respect than the rules and men of Cosa Nostra:

> [The Mafia] also manages to obtain consensus by peaceful means . . . in many areas of the country the Mafia is no longer either an anti-state or an organisation seeking to overthrow the legal authorities. The Mafia in these areas constitutes a recognised, respected, efficient and feared 'government'. The Mafia wields institutional and political power. It decides with no possibility of appeal on the life and death of citizens, controls economic activities demanding tributes on the most obvious signs of wealth and has a monopoly on coercion.[2]

In practice, this means that Mafiosi wanted by the police can spend years 'on the run' living in their own neighbourhoods, where their authority is strongest, with no fear of being denounced. 'We would go out as usual, but we knew at what time the police patrols would be back,' explained one informer. 'When we had to move a body or something . . . we knew that, say from 1.30 pm to 3.30–4 pm, we could walk around freely and that evenings from 6.30 to 8.30–9 pm were usually quiet.'[3]

Holding sway over such neighbourhoods, or territories, is the basic unit of the Cosa Nostra state, the autonomous 'family' or clan. Loosely based on real family ties, the clan can govern a single district in a city like Palermo, or one or more of the small towns of central Sicily. Each Mafia family has its boss – the *'capofamiglia'* – flanked by a counsellor, who occupies a privileged position outside the hierarchy. The *capofamiglia* answers to a *'capomandamento'* – the 'colonel' – who is responsible for three or more neighbouring families.

Below the clan boss come what could be called the sergeants of Cosa Nostra. The *'capodecina'* ('head of ten') commands up to thirty *'soldati'* (or *'picciotti'* in Palermo), who make up the rank-and-file. These soldiers are tied inextricably to their Mafia family at the initiation ceremony, during which they swear their allegiance with their blood. The Mafiosi pledge to obey unfailingly their immediate superiors, who take precedence over their own true families: 'if the boss calls, you have to be available to the point of leaving even the wife when she is giving birth,' said one former hit-man.[4]

Soldiers claim they elect their bosses 'democratically', at meetings specially called for this purpose. 'The Mafia is a democratic organisation, said one informer, '. . . there are no secret ballots, voting is by show of hands, in front of everybody . . . It's always the whole family which decides. The boss is elected by the rank-and-file, by the men of honour, who have the same power as the *capodecina*.'[5] But almost invariably the result is a foregone conclusion because there is only one candidate. And in recent times, the Corleonesi clan has encouraged

Mafiosi to bypass such procedures. Increasingly, they do not trouble to vote a boss out of office, they simply murder him.

The clans are fond of staging ritualistic board meetings to hold elections and carry out other business:

> Usually we sit around a table on which somebody has placed the sacred image of the protector of the town, which in our case [San Cataldo] was the Virgin of the Annunciation. At the head of the table sits the boss with the deputy and the *capodecina* next to him. The boss or the deputy stands up, followed by all the participants, who observe a very strict silence and the following formula is pronounced: 'In the name of the family of San Cataldo I declare this meeting open. Here everything can be said and outside nothing can be said because all that must be said about Cosa Nostra must be said in this place.'[6]

There are about thirty soldiers in each clan. The biggest Mafia family, that of Santa Maria del Gesù in Palermo, has some 200 members. The 180 or so clans of Cosa Nostra (67 of them in Palermo and the surrounding province alone) can claim a fighting force of roughly five thousand soldiers, most of whom are in Sicily. On an island with a population of some five million people, this figure gives a ratio of about one man of honour for each thousand Sicilians.

But this is a conservative measure of Cosa Nostra's strength, according to investigators. They say it numbers nearer 10,000 henchmen than 5,000 in Sicily because many others apart from fully-fledged men of honour have to be included. The mobsters call these ousiders *'avvicinati'* (close to Cosa Nostra). They are not only accomplices; they can carry out all the activities of a Mafioso and have a real and proper role in the organisation.[7]

The Government of Cosa Nostra

The clans of Cosa Nostra have absolute control over the affairs of their territory. No Mafia murder can be committed within its borders without the go-ahead from the local boss. But when the victim is to be a magistrate, politician, police officer or journalist, the clan must bow to a higher authority.

This authority is the Mafia's ruling junta, the 'Cupola', whose members are representatives drawn from the Sicilian provinces. Only the Cupola can decide on the murder of a public figure, and it has the power to delegate such an execution to men of honour from various families without having to inform the boss of the territory where the killing is to take place. The clan's authority is waived because any crackdown by police after the murder would affect Cosa Nostra as a whole.

The Cupola, as its name implies, crowns Cosa Nostra's rigid, hierarchical edifice. It is the government of the Mafia state, and like the fragile coalitions of its Italian counterpart, is often rent by factional infighting. Each Mafia province is supposed to carry equal weight, but in practice it is traditionally that of Palermo which has most influence.

Mafiosi fear their own government, convinced that its justice is unstoppable. 'If it is decided that all informers have to be killed, from the first to the last, there is no turning back. Even if the men change, even if a long time goes by and those who join the commission do not know me or the other informers, we mustn't deceive ourselves. They won't forget. The Mafia does not forget,' said one supergrass.[8]

The Cupola grew out of attempts in the 1950s to set up some form of ruling council to resolve disputes inside clans, on the suggestion of Joe Bonnano, one of the bosses of New York's five families. A commission was swiftly set up for Palermo and the surrounding province, followed by similar bodies for other provinces.

But it was not until 1975 that the Sicilian clans were able to agree on setting up a body representing all the families on the island: the Cupola, as it came to be called. The brainchild of Pippo Calderone, a boss from Catania in eastern Sicily, it decided as its first edict to ban kidnappings in Sicily, because they prompted too much police activity. The death penalty was decreed for those who disobeyed this edict.

Calderone also drew up a statute, endorsed by the Cupola's members, to govern relations between clans. But as Calderone's brother Antonino was to tell the investigators after turning informer: 'These rules are beautiful, but they are a Utopia. They are a nice trinket which all pretend to admire while they deal in drugs, kill, steal and suit themselves. Mafiosi have heaps of rules which, in effect, they are always violating.'[9]

Mafiosi have repeatedly sought to circumvent the pyramid structure of Cosa Nostra in order to increase their own influence. In the 1960s several Palermo bosses, snubbing the hierarchy as enshrined in their new provincial commission, recruited men of honour who could answer only to them.

These lieutenants were placed outside the traditional clan structure, out of reach of the *capodecina*. More

recently, the Godfather Riina has appointed his own allies
to head clans, flouting the established practice of allowing
soldiers to elect their own bosses.

Don Calò Vizzini – the Mafioso as Mediator

When Calogero Vizzini, the Godfather who had nursed the
Mafia through Fascism and the Second World War, died
peacefully in July 1954 two weeks after celebrating his
seventy-seventh birthday, an extraordinary procession of
pilgrims came to pay their last respects.

Those who braved the beating sun and shuffled behind
Vizzini's horse-drawn hearse in his fief of Villalba in
central Sicily, a town of more than 4,000 inhabitants,
included five government ministers, fifty-two members
of parliament from the Christian Democrat Party, three
bishops and sixty clergymen, as well as the heads of all
the Cosa Nostra families.

The 'capo di tutti capi' ('boss of all bosses') had always
looked and acted like a distinguished country gentleman –
he never swore, and he was often seen devoutly reciting
the rosary with local priests. His friends hung a big pall
of black velvet over the door of the local church. Above
it, an enormous placard proclaimed:

With the skill of a genius
he raised the fortunes of a distinguished household.
Wise, dynamic, tireless,
he was the benefactor of the workers on the land
    and
in the sulphur mines.

Constantly doing good,
he won himself a wide reputation
in Italy and abroad.
Great in the face of persecution,
greater still in adversity,
he remained unfailingly cheerful.
And today,
with the peace of Christ
and in the majesty of death,
he receives from friends and foes alike
that most beautiful of all tributes:
He was a gentleman.[10]

Don Calò was a 'benefactor', 'constantly doing good' –
tributes to a typical Mafioso mediator. More often than
not, the people of his town would ask him to resolve their
disputes. A clan boss, through acting as a go-between,
acquires legitimacy in the eyes of the people, and thus
consolidates his power at the expense of the institutions
of the State. This role fits the Mafioso like a glove because
of his reputation as a 'man of respect', implying that he
exercises more power than most, and denoting his origins
as part of a new class which insinuated itself between
peasants and landowners. There could be no more solid
base for the Mafia pyramid.

Vizzini justified himself by appealing to the historical
failure of authority, whether foreign or not, to assert itself
in Sicily. 'The fact is that in every society there has to
be a category of people who put things right, when they
get complicated,' he said in one of the few interviews he
gave. 'Usually they are State officials. Where there is no
state, or it does not have enough strength, there are private
citizens.'[11] A card sent to friends and relatives in America
to mourn his death lavishly praised him as a man who had

shown 'that his Mafia was not delinquency but respect for the law, defence of every right,'[12]

To help them acquire the authority to mediate, mobsters invoke their code of honour and present themselves as role-models valid for the common people — faithful to their friends, ready to do or return a favour, but also ready to use violence so that such values are respected. Bosses are on a par with their lieutenants, or even with their enemies. Ideally, they do not show off their weapons or take advantage of other people's misfortunes, and always pay their debts. Above all, these men of honour show respect for all and never seek to intimidate others.

Vizzini himself, who usually shunned publicity, gave a humble picture of himself. 'It's curious! People think I speak little out of discretion. No. I speak little because I know little. I live in a village, I only rarely come to Palermo, I don't know many people. And I'm getting on now, I'm more than seventy years old.'[13]

The Mafioso's role as referee in social conflicts, or general fixer, has lost little of its importance since Vizzini's death. His immediate successor as Godfather, Genco Russo, described himself as having '"the soul of a whore", that is a heart which loves everyone, especially the poor, the people who need help . . . Many people owe their life to me: my power, as you call it, derives precisely from the feeling of friendship and gratitude of so many men, for the help, the succour I gave all those who needed it.'[14]

In the week before one trial, Genco Russo was able to draw up a petition to defend his good name. Seven thousand notables and peasants from three villages, including his home town of Mussomeli, a large agricultural centre, swore to his honesty and civic virtues. Genco Russo proved a slippery fish. Charged sixteen times for offences including murder, theft and extortion, he was always acquitted except once. He was found guilty of failing to vaccinate his cattle as the Fascist regime demanded.

Even today bosses can be asked to resolve a dispute between a young man and his fiancée, or find jobs for the unemployed. In Catania, meeting such demands became a full-time occupation for the boss Pippo Calderone. He ran an office where he could receive the dozens of people who called on him every day. When the stream of petitioners became a flood, Calderone was forced to rent a flat next door to his office to serve as a waiting-room.

'They came from all over Catania and also from the province, and Pippo never said no to anybody, he would take all the problems of the others on himself . . . They were common people, with everyday problems, who saw in Pippo a personality, a figure qualified to help,' his brother Antonino said years later.[15]

Some were looking for work or wanted the clan to deal with thieves in their neighbourhood, others needed help to get hospital treatment, or simply asked for money. Seeking power rather than wealth, Pippo Calderone would never accept payment for his services. His only reward, according to his brother, was that grateful supplicants would send him generous presents at Christmas.

Some communities manifest their gratitude more brazenly. The arrest of the Mafia boss Sebastiano Ferrara sparked an effusive public display of support from residents in the village of Cep outside Messina in eastern Sicily. When the police seized him from his refuge – he had been hiding behind a kitchen dresser stacked with pasta and bottles of tomato sauce, a crowd of locals assembled outside and cheered and applauded Ferrara as he was dragged into the open. A few days later, some 300 people demonstrated outside the courthouse in Messina in support of the boss. They said he kept the village's streets clear of crime and drugs. The thirty-two-year-old Ferrara was sent to trial on charges of murder, extortion and Mafia association.

Even judges have been known to seek the good offices of Cosa Nostra. One magistrate in Messina was arrested and charged with asking several soldiers to ambush and shoot a university professor. The professor had repeatedly given the judge's nephew poor marks in examinations. Informers told police the mobsters had granted the judge his favour and kneecapped the professor with five gunshots.[16]

Pax Mafiosa

Corleone, buried in the uplands south of Palermo, is the capital of the Mafia state. No busy metropolis, it is a small agricultural town whose one claim to fame is the ferocious breed of Mafiosi it has spawned. The bosses of the Corleonesi, Luciano Leggio and Salvatore Riina, have successfully defied the established clans of Palermo to rule supreme over Cosa Nostra.

The clan rules with such a tight hold over its home town that its citizens are among the safest in Sicily, if official statistics are any guide. The truth is that any crimes which are committed are either not reported or are resolved by Mafia justice. Common criminals are simply not allowed to operate. Thefts and kidnappings are banned. Even the authorities are forced to recognise that Corleone is in the iron grip of a *'pax Mafiosa'*.

At the local barracks of the carabinieri, cells stand empty and desktops are cleared save for routine paperwork. 'The *pax Mafiosa* has been in existence since the Corleonesi took over in the 1960s,' says the commander, Captain Francesco Iaccono, a dashing moustachioed figure whose black uniform is set off by immaculate white gloves. 'We keep statistics of crimes that are reported to us and for those we find out about. We have had no reports of crimes and are not carrying out any investigations. There's been nothing in the town in ages. I can't remember anything bigger than the theft of an oil barrel from a farm outside the town.'[17]

As well as acting as mediators, the 'men of respect' often take it upon themselves to guarantee some form of law and order for their community. This is the policing arm of the Mafia state. It has scant regard for the Italian authorities, and bans mobsters from denouncing crimes to the police. The only exception is if a man of honour has his car stolen, because it could be used in a crime committed by outsiders and cause him trouble.

The Mafia's laws are its code of honour, which can be enforced on outsiders, or used to clear an area of disruptive common criminals. In Palermo, the brother of the supergrass Marino Mannoia was ordered to kill a man (who was not a Mafioso) because he had made advances to a number of women in the clan's territory.

Marino Mannoia also told the magistrates that another hoodlum was murdered in the mid-1970s because he had disfigured a young foreign woman in an attempt to snatch her bag. The thief was killed 'to warn all common criminals that such behaviour was not allowed. At that time robbers and bag-snatchers who caused too much trouble in various neighbourhoods of the city were got rid of.'[18]

Shortly after the ruling Cupola banned kidnappings from Sicily in 1975, a gang outside the organisation seized a builder's wife in Monreale near Palermo. Men of honour intervened to free the captive, and all her kidnappers were killed save for the woman who guarded her. She was spared because of her sex. One informer quotes the boss who ordered the reprisals, Gaetano Badalamenti, as telling his subordinates: 'I'm not giving you the order to kill a woman, but if somebody feels like it he can: I won't do it.'[19] No one took him up on the offer.

The Mafia's policing arm protects traders too, not just the community as a whole. Businessmen or shopkeepers who regularly pay 'protection money' to the local clan are sometimes helped to rid themselves of any other extortion rackets. The Catania boss Nitto Santapaola was always keen to score points off common criminals in the city. If a trader complained he was receiving threatening telephone calls from gangs demanding money, Santapaola would go to the premises and stay there until the next call came:

He would answer the phone and say: 'I'm Nitto, do you know me?' The other would answer: 'Yes, I know who you are', and add that he needed money to help people in jail. Nitto would give them an appointment in a square and the other man would come to see him. I remember that two youngsters went to see him after asking him for 300,000 lire (£150). When they met they said to him: 'If it's your business, Nitto, we don't want any money.' Nitto however forced them to take the money and after three days he sent his brother to kill them.[20]

Santapaola had four children murdered in the mid-1970s simply because they were bag-snatchers operating in his territory. The boys, the youngest of whom was only twelve, were abandoned for two days as one mobster, Antonino Calderone, pleaded for their lives. All four were eventually strangled and thrown down a well. One executioner, tormented by his task, was unable to pull the noose tight round the neck of one of the boys. Unsure whether his victim was still alive, he threw him into the well all the same.[21]

The men of honour's writ runs even in places where the Italian State could be expected to have the upper hand – in jails. When a man of honour is sent to prison, he does not lose contact with the brotherhood. Quite the contrary. The organisation gives both him and his family financial assistance, including meeting lawyers' fees, and keeps him informed about what is happening outside the prison. 'This is because belonging to Cosa Nostra involves the way of being and thinking of the individual, and cannot be interrupted or suspended by any event, save in cases of expulsion,' an informer explained.[22]

Despite the fact that a jail contains inmates from different Mafia families, a new clan is set up inside the prison and its boss is entrusted with solving its members' day-to-day problems. Criminals can be initiated into the family with the traditional ritual held inside the jail. As soon as a mobster finishes serving his sentence, a meeting of his clan is called and he is introduced to any new family members.

In return for assistance, the soldier is expected to bear his sentence with dignity. Feigning madness to seek more lenient treatment is frowned upon because it shows he is incapable of facing up to the prospect of long years in prison. Mafiosi can also be banned from seeking to escape because those left behind would have to suffer a tighter regime. The code of honour holds good for inmates too. In one incident, mobsters complained to the prison authorities because they did not want their wives to visit when pimps were present.[23]

Those of rank are duty bound to set an example in bearing the weight of a jail sentence, starting with the way they dress for their trials. Suits and ties are mandatory. Asked why the men of honour invariably dress with care on such occasions, one boss explained to his lawyer: 'Every one of us, especially if he is sentenced for life, must be dressed as though at any time he could be freed and go for a stroll down via Ruggiero Settimo [in Palermo]. Never think even for a moment that a life sentence really means a life sentence.'[24]

The bosses often have much more authority in the running of a prison than the governor himself. Palermo's Ucciardone jail is no exception. Built as a fortress by the Bourbons in the heart of Palermo near the harbour, it has been dubbed the 'Grand Hotel' by the Mafiosi, who would order in lavish meals from the capital's best restaurants when they had something to celebrate.

'We had everything!' boasted one informer of his time at the Ucciardone. 'They found a store with everything you can think of: money, whisky, champagne . . . I had the keys, I even passed on some knives . . . Drugs were the only thing we didn't consume.'[25]

When inmates tried to riot in 1976, the police and carabinieri forces surrounded the jail, ready to break in and stamp out the protests. But it was a peaceful intervention by Buscetta that defused the conflict. Buscetta, whose standing during his six years in the Ucciardone was such that new arrivals would seek him out to pay their respects, was taken out of his cell and allowed to walk freely through the corridors. By the end of his tour, the demonstrators had been pacified. 'Signor director, it was only an unpleasant misunderstanding,' Buscetta told the governor with a modest smile.[26]

Cosa Nostra's Income Tax

In December 1989, police raiding a refuge used by the clan of Francesco Madonia, which controlled northern Palermo, made an unprecedented discovery. They found concrete proof that the Madonias levied what was effectively an income tax on the overwhelming majority of shops and businesses in their fiefdom.

The evidence was an accounting ledger filled with the names of various clan members. The name of each man of honour was followed by a list of shops or businesses he was designated to tax. The book also showed how much each trader was to pay. The eighty-four bars, restaurants, shops or other businesses listed each handed £100–250 to the clan every month.[27]

Many of the traders whose names appeared in the ledger denied paying any protection money to the Madonia clan. When a judge rebuked them for failing to co-operate with the investigators, they argued that they had lied because they feared possible reprisals. Months went by before any arrests were made, because the police were given little help in their struggle to identify the Mafiosi named in the book – more often than not, they had only a nickname to go on.[28]

The businessmen's silence showed how effective the Madonia clan's extortion racket was as a means of governing its district. The sums paid to the clan may seem small, but their symbolic importance is great. Mafia intimidation weighs so heavily on the traders that recourse to the clan's 'protection' becomes indispensable if they are to earn a decent living.

In fact it is often the traders themselves who turn to the local Mafiosi to seek protection. The very few who try to resist this custom become victims of reprisals, usually arson attacks. The result is a diffuse atmosphere of coercion which in turn helps to strengthen people's reluctance to co-operate with the authorities in fighting the Mafiosi.

Other Mafia activities such as drug trafficking may bring in more lucrative profits, but only extortion gives a clan political control over its territory. The Italian State has been elbowed aside by that of Cosa Nostra, which alone decides whether shops stay in business or are forced to close. More than anything else, extortion is a typical Mafia crime. Intimidation can be effective only if the victim does not run to the police. Only a Mafioso, and not a common criminal, can approach a target with the certainty that yet again the law of silence will not be broken.

The Mafioso must have established himself as a man of respect, as a pseudo-guarantor of law and order before he can levy his tax. 'When I introduce myself to you, you must feel my weight and you must sense it, but not distinctly,' said Buscetta as he described the ideal approach. 'I will never come to threaten you, I will always come to you with a smile and you know that behind that smile there is a threat hanging over your head. I will not come to you and say: "I shall do this to you." If you understand me, well and good; if not, you will suffer the consequences.'[29]

As ever with the ideal Mafioso, the rule is to be discreet and not too greedy. Showing a bizarre deference to the Christian calendar, clans have the habit of demanding extra payments only on important feast days such as at Christmas and Easter.

Discretion was a precept taught by the man credited with inventing the extortion racket, Don Vito Cascio Ferro, the Godfather in the years following the First World War. 'You have to skim the cream off the milk without breaking the bottle,' he would advise trainee racketeers. 'Try a new system. Don't throw people into bankruptcy with ridiculous demands for money. Offer them your protection instead, help them to make their business prosperous, and not only will they be happy to pay but they'll kiss your hands out of gratitude.'[30]

Don Vito coined a picturesque term for his invention, christening it '*ù pizzu*' in Mafia jargon, after the word for a bird's beak. Some six decades on, Don Vito's successors still believe that '*fari vagnari a pizzu*' ('wetting the beak'), as they like to call collecting extortion money, is a favour they are doing the community:

> A friendly relationship develops between the man who collects the monthly sum and the businessman, who sees that the local Mafioso is a normal individual . . . and because there is a guarantee that, if there is a robbery, those in the Mafioso environment will intervene so that he recovers what has been stolen. Or else if someone cheats him there is a whole network which forces [the offender] to pay up.[31]

This soldier boasted that he had found jobs for several of his acquaintances by turning to victims of the extortion racket. 'There's no problem: you talk with the owner and you tell him: "Give one, two, three, or any number of people a job." Probably the factory-owner will need two weeks, or a month, to sack somebody else or to create the job, but there's always a way.'[32]

Extortion is a practice which is becoming increasingly widespread in Italy, and what statistics there are demonstrate that the Mafia has honed this racket to a fine art. In the provinces of Palermo, Catania, Trapani and Caltanissetta, where extortion is most firmly entrenched,

80 per cent of traders are threatened by clans, and it is estimated that almost three-quarters pay up.

Using the account book of Palermo's Madonia clan as a rough guide, the average sum paid by anything from a small family shop to a big chain-store is £4,000 a year. For Palermo and the surrounding province, extortion alone brings to Cosa Nostra an annual income of over £40 million.[33]

The Ministry for Public Works

The Mafia state's rule over the Sicilian economy does not stop at extortion rackets. Of far greater weight in its budget is the role it has carved out for itself as sole arbiter of how billions of pounds' worth of taxpayers' money is spent, again elbowing aside the Italian State.

Cosa Nostra has claimed a generous share of the billions of pounds which the Rome government has poured into Sicily since the Second World War in pharaonic infrastructure and building projects. Italy's Mezzogiorno has long been the poor relation of the prosperous North. In 1861, the first premier of a united Italy, Camillo di Cavour, observed shortly before his death: 'It's not their fault, poor people. They've always been governed so badly.' Rome's interventionist policies, showering the problem with money, have played into the hands of its Mafia counterpart. Much of the money has been channelled by the Mafia, which decides which companies should be awarded the public contracts generated by such spending.

The first Mafioso to give investigators a clear understanding of this hugely profitable practice, probably the biggest single source of revenue for Cosa Nostra, was a supergrass from the small town of San Cataldo in central Sicily. Magistrates described Leonardo Messina as 'not a simple criminal labourer, but a real and proper manager of a criminal holding'.[34] His confessions triggered 'Operation Leopardo', the biggest anti-Mafia operation of 1992, which led to 241 arrests.

Thanks to the complicity of politicians, businessmen and officials of local or regional authorities, 'Public sector contracts in Sicily are directly administered by Cosa Nostra's public works ministry.'[35] This was no empty boast by Messina. Clans pull the strings behind the scenes from the very start of the proceedings.

Through its network of spies, some of whom sit in on local council deliberations, a Mafia family is often the first to know of forthcoming tenders for public contracts. The clan wastes no time. It meets to decide which of the companies likely to bid should be awarded the contract. A man of honour is appointed as 'trustee', with the task of seeing the tender through to a successful conclusion.

Messina, who repeatedly played this role, would call on each of the firms likely to compete. He dictated at what level each should price its bid, to ensure the company chosen by his clan won the tender. Once the contract had been awarded, Messina intervened again. This time he would impose the choice of suppliers and sub-contractors, and the recruitment of security guards and other staff. The company's staff department was often required to overlook any criminal records. To ensure compliance, the Mafiosi resort to arson, dynamite attacks or even murder.

Almost invariably, however, there is no need for force. Companies comply with the *diktat* of the local clan, in part because the latter seeks to ensure that firms are rewarded if they quietly wait their turn. Even companies from northern

Italy or abroad have learnt their lesson. They routinely pencil in an extra 10 per cent or so on their costs to budget for the Mafiosi's demands.

Some businessmen are so close to Cosa Nostra that the latter feels it would be an insult to levy protection money on them. The Costanzo brothers of Catania, among the richest entrepreneurs in the city, employed the local clan's soldiers as security guards. A member of the clan explained:

> For entrepreneurs like the Costanzo brothers and others like them, having the Mafia on their side meant . . . being able to work in peace and make a lot of money without running the risk of having motor vehicles damaged, or strikes, or demands for kick-backs which even the most low-ranking Mafioso feels he has the right to make of anyone who invests on his territory.[36]

Grateful for the efficient protection the men of honour provided, the Costanzos bought them a large reserve outside Catania where they could go hunting.

Palermo, October 1957

The Grand Hôtel et des Palmes, as its sonorous name indicates, attracts the better-heeled visitors to the Sicilian capital. Refurbished in the florid Art Nouveau style, it is the oldest hotel in Palermo and boasts a prime city-centre location in one of Palermo's main avenues, halfway between the opera house and the main theatre. One suite is named after the composer Richard Wagner, who wrote part of the opera *Parsifal* there. Years later, the cast of *The Godfather III* set up camp in the hotel's august surroundings.

For four days in October 1957, the Grand Hôtel hosted

a party of publicity-shy Sicilian and American gentlemen whose decisions were to shape the future of organised crime in their countries. The Mafia state was nurturing its foreign relations, and was about to take a step which helped to prompt its radical remodelling.

The men who took part in this meeting were the heavyweights of Cosa Nostra from both sides of the Atlantic. They included the Sicilian Godfather Genco Russo, bosses from New York's five families, including Joe Bonnano (better known as Joe Bananas) and Frank Coppola, and the Italo-American gangster Lucky Luciano.

It was to take the investigators several years to find out what the bosses had been discussing. Partly because the Italian police underestimated the importance of the meeting at the time, as it did that of the Mafia itself, only an incomplete list of participants was ever drawn up. Just one sentence of the animated deliberations filtered out, picked up by an eavesdropping waiter who overheard Genco Russo growl a maxim: 'When there are too many dogs after a bone, happy is he who can keep well away.'

The 'bone' the bosses were fighting over was drug trafficking, then in its infancy. Both Mafias felt they needed to regulate the flow. At a dinner given in his honour by his friend Luciano, Joe Bonnano suggested that the Sicilian Mafia – then a loose association of autonomous clans – should set up a ruling commission. One of its first tasks was to improve co-ordination with American gangsters. The Cupola was born.

It was to pave the way for the Mafia's participating heart and soul in the drugs trade. The Sicilians' involvement had previously been sporadic. For a decade, from 1947 to 1957, Lucky Luciano dealt in what at the time were considerable quantities of heroin, including 450 kilos in one year, which had been produced by big pharmaceutical companies based in northern Italy. The heart of the operation was Milan. In 1957, police discovered a heroin refinery there which had been operating for the previous three years.

Luciano, in partnership with Don Calò Vizzini, also set up a factory in Palermo, using a cousin as a strawman, to make sweetmeats and sugar-coated almonds, both traditional presents at weddings. But Luciano was forced to close it hastily after it had been up and running for only five years when a newspaper alleged that the sweets had heroin and not almonds at their centre.

Throughout the 1950s, however, the Sicilian Cosa Nostra's presence in international drug trafficking remained marginal. Lucky Luciano, one of the main dealers, did not even live in his Sicilian homeland and preferred to operate from Naples. Police investigations did target bosses like the Godfather Genco Russo, and Palermo's Gaetano Badalamenti and Tommaso Buscetta. But their involvement was minor. At the time, Sicily and southern Italy served only as transit points for heroin produced in France and bound for the United States. The main drug-dealers were Corsican gangs, who controlled the drug routes from Indochina and other neighbouring countries.

In the 1960s the Mafia discovered heavy drugs. From refining the raw product imported by the Corsicans, the Sicilians came to play an increasingly important role in shipping the refined heroin to the United States. As the influence of the Corsicans dwindled, the Mafiosi eventually worked directly with dealers in producer countries.

By the mid-1970s, the Sicilian Cosa Nostra could claim to have a near-monopoly in the field of international drug trafficking. Gradually it came to control one of the most important heroin routes – the one that unites the producer countries of south-west Asia (the Golden Crescent of Afghanistan, Pakistan, Iran and Turkey) and

The Italian State struggles to impose itself on Sicily's rugged landscape - a new military road makes its way up Mount Pellegrino above the island capital Palermo. *(Popperfoto)*

Obeying a law of its own, Agrigento sprawls across the hills above the Valley of the Temples on the south coast, spoiling the backdrop to the majestic ruins of the fifth century BC Temple of Concorde. *(Roberto Bettini/Olympia)*

Street theatre in Palermo - Sicilians in animated conversation.
(Popperfoto)

Sicilian peasants take a break from picking olives to chat with a police patrol. *(Sintesi)*

Carabinieri police flag down passing cars at a roadblock outside Corleone, the town made notorious by the clan of Salvatore 'The Beast' Riina. His bloody rise to power earned his hometown the nickname 'Tombstone' across the Atlantic. *(Sintesi)*

Pomp and circumstance - Mafiosi in their Sunday best pay their last tribute to the 'capo di tutti capi' Calogero Vizzini in his fiefdom of Villalba after he died at the age of 77 in July 1954. *(N. Scafidi-Italpress/AGF)*

The flamboyant bandit Salvatore Giuliano, well-groomed despite living rough on the run, fixes the camera with a seductive stare. His happy band killed an estimated 430 people in the Palermo area.
(Associated Press)

After terrorising the townsfolk of Mazzarino with a mafioso extortion racket run from their monastery, the not-so-holy Capuchin monks face an early judgement in court in 1962. Second from right in the dock is one of the ring leaders, Father Carmelo, 80. *(N. Scafidi-Italpress/AGF)*

The Godfather is dead, long live the Godfather. Dr Michele Navarra falls at the hands of his rebellious lieutenant Luciano Leggio, who with his acolytes fired 112 bullets to overthrow his mentor on 2 August 1958. *(N. Scafidi-Italpress/AGF)*

A flimsy shield for a lone emissary of the State - the Autobianchi car in which Carabiniere General Carlo Alberto dalla Chiesa and his wife were gunned down on 3 September 1982, only five months after he was named head of the anti-Mafia fight in Palermo. A bodyguard in an escort car was also killed. *(G. De Bellis)*

Leggio, with raised eyebrow and brandishing a cigar, makes a convincing imitation of a celluloid don with a threatening attitude. The cigar is a pose - Leggio smoked them only in court for the benefit of the press. *(G. De Bellis)*

The State graciously lends a bodyguard to the Mafia - a plainclothes policeman, a pistol held behind his back, watches over Michele 'The Pope' Greco as he walks out of Palermo's Ucciardone jail. He left the prison briefly in February 1991 because of a legal bungle. *(Associated Press)*

'The Beast' behind bars - momentarily cowed, Riina has little of the Godfather about him shortly after his arrest on 15 January 1993 ended 23 years of impunity. *(AGF)*

'They don't want me to marry her? Well then, I'll kill people.' The object of Riina's love, Antonietta Bagarella, together with one of their daughters, watches her husband in court. *(Sintesi)*

The dapper don, Tommaso Buscetta, violates the *omertà* law of silence to testify before the mid-1980s maxi-trial in Palermo, helping the State to inflict one of its heaviest legal triumphs over Cosa Nostra. *(Associated Press)*

'The Mafia doesn't forget and it doesn't forgive' - the symbol of Italy's fight against the Mafia, judge Giovanni Falcone was murdered on 23 May 1992 when a huge bomb exploded as his convoy sped past. His wife and three bodyguards were also killed by the blast. (*Nimmo Chianura/AGF*)

Judge Paolo Borsellino, with Falcone one of the architects of the maxi-trial, suffered the same fate as his friend and colleague two months later when a car-bomb killed him and five bodyguards. (*S. Annaloro/Italpress AGF*)

Euro-MP and former Palermo mayor Salvo Lima, described by informers as the Mafia's intermediary with ex-prime minister Giulio Andreotti, lies dead on a Palermo pavement on 12 March 1992. Lima paid for his failure to deliver the court acquittals he and Andreotti had allegedly promised the Mafia. (*N. Scafidi-Italpress/AGF*)

'God's Banker' Roberto Calvi, who was found hanging from Blackfriars Bridge in London on 18 June 1982.

A Sicilian supergrass has alleged that a man of honour, Francesco di Carlo, strangled Calvi because he owed money to the Mafia. *(Sintesi)*

'I say to those responsible: Repent. One day the judgement of God will come' - on an anti-Mafia crusade in May 1993, Pope John Paul pays a visit to Malaspina jail in Caltanissetta where many men of honour are detained. *(Sygma)*

A lasting rebellion? The murders of Falcone and Borsellino prompted a host of demonstrations, including this rally sponsored by trade unions. But investigators say eyewitnesses are still reluctant to testify on Mafia crimes. *(Bozzo/Italpress AGF)*

the big metropolitan markets of the United States and Europe.

The Sicilians soon almost completely dominated the heroin market in the United States. They supplied an estimated 80 per cent of the market in New York, using morphine base from Asia treated in clandestine laboratories in and around Palermo. In 1979, Cosa Nostra was running at least five heroin laboratories in Sicily, each capable of producing up to 50 kilos a week. French chemists abandoned Marseilles, previously the capital of heroin refining, to come and work in Palermo.

The profits to be made were staggering. The price jumped the highest once the Palermo laboratories had refined the morphine base into heroin. The supergrass Gaspare Mutolo, who claims to have organised the biggest imports of morphine base which Cosa Nostra had ever managed (400 kilos a time), would buy the raw material from Thailand at a price of 13,000 dollars per kilo, in quantities of 500 kilos or so, and would sell it at up to 130,000 dollars once it had been refined. The morphine base was brought in by sea, and a laboratory was installed on board ship.[37]

Latest estimates put the turnover of the drugs business currently managed by Italian organised crime at some £5 billion a year.[38] This is despite the fact that Cosa Nostra families are believed to be losing ground in today's global drugs trade. American and Italian police estimate that Italian drug-traffickers now supply under 5 per cent of the American market, which itself is said to be shrinking.

Cosa Nostra as an organisation has always taken a back seat in drug trafficking. From the outset, it acted as a controlling or co-ordinating body. Unlike in Colombian cartels, the members of Cosa Nostra rarely handle the drugs and hardly ever deal in small quantities at street-level. The Mafiosi and the drug-dealers at the end of the chain are two distinct groups.

When the Sicilian bosses first started importing morphine base from the Middle and Far East — using international routes previously reserved for tobacco smuggling — they used accomplices, often foreigners, outside their organisation. Even when the Sicilians were throwing themselves into drugs, the business did not concern Cosa Nostra as a whole. Only individual men of honour participated, acting with the authorisation of their *capofamiglia*, and a majority of clans have steered clear of drugs.

It was the clan from Corleone which put Sicily on the drugs map, eliminating the Old Guard Mafiosi who had wanted to stick to traditional crimes. The Corleonesi rationalised drug trafficking. Informers say the clan's Riina started his involvement in drug trafficking in the early 1970s. Because Riina was not very wealthy at the time, he would ask other Mafiosi to enter into partnership with him for individual ventures.

Mobsters used the proceeds of kidnappings or extortion rackets to invest. In the case of Mutolo's imports of morphine base, the clans were required to participate with a minimum quota of 300,000 dollars. The various clans used Francesco Marino Mannoia, who was later to turn informer, as their expert chemist. Nicknamed 'Mozzarella' because of his pale face, he would refine the morphine base into heroin at one of the Mafia's laboratories. In the two years from early 1979 to late 1980 (when he was arrested), Mannoia refined some 600 kilos of morphine, earning some £2,500 for every kilo he worked on.

In the early 1980s the clans of central Sicily were also allowed to invest in drug trafficking — a privilege which until then had been the jealous preserve of the Palermo families. Apart from investing, each family was allowed to take delivery of the drugs and sell them on their own territory. Recently the authorities of Cosa Nostra have stripped the clans of this privilege. 'They don't want our people becoming addicts, because several of our sons have got involved and they have consideration for the sons of others,' according to the supergrass Messina.[39]

Because the clans were involved on an autonomous basis, drug trafficking sparked an overhaul of the traditional Cosa Nostra structure. The seeds of change had already been sown by tobacco smuggling, which meant the Mafia had to turn to outsiders – its criminal counterparts on the Italian mainland and further afield.

But drugs had a deeper impact, helping to forge horizontal links between the clans which sat uneasily with the established, strictly vertical, hierarchy. The secret society has become more fragmented. The high stakes of the drug trade, coupled with the ferocity of the Corleonesi's climb to supremacy, have spawned wars between clans unprecedented in their human cost.

Cousins in Crime

Early in the fourteenth century, three Spanish knights sailed from their homeland and dropped anchor on the windswept island of Favignana off Sicily. The three knights – with the improbable names of Osso, Mastrosso and Carcagnosso – isolated themselves from the rest of the world in underground caves and three decades later re-emerged, having drawn up the rules for three associations they wanted to set up.

Thus, says popular legend, were the foundations thrown

for the three main organised crime empires which hold sway over much of southern Italy – Cosa Nostra in Sicily, the Camorra in the Campania region around Naples, and the 'Ndrangheta in Calabria in the toe of Italy's boot.

Though the other criminal organisations are distinct and separate, Cosa Nostra has overpowered them. They are satellites to the Mafiosi's empire. The Sicilians have infiltrated their cousins on the mainland, and have managed to ensure the domination of their allies inside both. Cosa Nostra has thus built a formidable base for its spread throughout Italy and abroad.

'If all three Mafie are present in one region,' says a senior carabiniere officer, 'the "general" is always the Sicilian Mafioso, the "colonel" is always a Calabrian mobster and the "lance-corporals" and the "carabinieri" are always from Campania.'[40]

The Sicilians, brandishing their code of honour, despise their mainland counterparts because they allow their members to run prostitution rackets. 'That's why we have always seen the Calabrians as inferior, a sub-product. And as for the Neapolitans, we can't trust them further than we can throw them,' said one supergrass.[41]

Cosa Nostra first showed its superior strength to the Camorra in the 1970s, when the Neapolitans were running cigarette-smuggling rackets. Eager for a share of the profits, the Sicilian Cupola intervened to dictate the ground rules and Naples became 'an El Dorado for Sicily', in the words of one Mafioso.[42] The leading Camorra smugglers were enrolled into Cosa Nostra. This was a humbling turn of events for the Camorra, which could proudly trace its ancestry back to 1820 – the first maxi-trial of Camorra members, in which 1,200 mobsters stood trial, took place in 1863.

The Bay of Naples was sealed off to outsiders and a rota

system drawn up to avoid several smugglers' ships queueing in the Tyrrhenian Sea. The mobsters took it in turns to bring in cargoes, limited to 40,000 crates of cigarettes each. The Neapolitans would smuggle in a load, then it would be the turn of the Sicilian Mafiosi living in Naples, and finally of the Palermo clans.

The arrangement worked so well for the Sicilians, at least for some time, that one Palermo smuggler, Tommaso Spadaro, was able to compare himself in court to the multi-millionaire Gianni Agnelli, head of Italy's biggest company, Fiat: 'I was the Agnelli of this city . . . I was Fiat: I fed thousands of families with cigarette smuggling.'[43] But quarrels eventually wrecked the pact. 'It became impossible to ensure that all would honour their pledges,' explained a Sicilian informer. 'The Neapolitans, as usual, were too sly. At every shift, they tried to unload many more crates than had been agreed.'[44]

Camorra members have also been roped in by the Sicilian clans to help in their dirty work. The worst outrage which resulted from such co-operation was a bomb which went off on a passenger train on its way from Florence to Bologna in 1984. Sixteen people died. The bomb had been planted by a Sicilian boss, Pippo Calo', and four Neapolitan accomplices. Their aim was to ease police pressure on Cosa Nostra following the revelations of Buscetta.

Cosa Nostra plays on the divisions of the Camorra to impose itself. The Camorra has no equivalent of the Sicilian Cupola. The Camorra clans, believed to number 126 (with a total of 6,700 members), forge or break alliances among each other with ease. These clans hold sway over the Campania region by recruiting drug-dealers and others among the poorest families. The Camorra delegates to others the importation of drugs, but is directly involved in their distribution. In this way it succeeds in establishing total control over the territory and the daily life of those who live there. But its military power and wealth are far behind those of Cosa Nostra.

Even further behind are the clans of the 'Ndrangheta. Informers say its 144 families and 5,600 members have been totally assimilated by the Sicilians. In the 1980s, the Palermo bosses intervened to pacify the warring clans in the city of Reggio Calabria, on the Italian mainland across from Mount Etna.

The Godfather Riina asked the Calabrians to do him a favour in return and had a senior judge, Antonino Scopelliti, murdered shortly before he was due to act as public prosecutor before the Supreme Court against hundreds of Mafiosi. The judge, alone and without an escort, was ambushed and shot dead in August 1991 as he drove home from a beach while on holiday in Calabria. 'It's a question of courtesy,' explained an informer. [45] Scopelliti was murdered because he refused a Mafia bribe of some 5 billion lire (£2.5 million), and because he defied telephone threats from the bosses who urged him to 'adjust' the forthcoming trial in the society's favour.

The 'Ndrangheta, more lenient in such matters than its Sicilian counterpart, does allow kidnappings – so much so that it can be said to specialise in seizing victims from the wealthy industrial north of Italy and holing them up in hide-outs on the rugged Aspromonte mountains of Calabria until ransoms are paid.

Too weak to threaten Cosa Nostra's domination over the Mezzogiorno is a fourth secret society, the Sacra Corona Unita (Holy United Crown) based in the Apulia region in the heel of Italy. It was founded relatively recently, at the end of the 1970s after a meeting between Raffaele Cutolo, the head of the Camorra, and criminal groupings from Apulia who copied the model Cutolo had fathered. The society is less firmly implanted on its territory than the other criminal brotherhoods. Its 500 or so members, divided among seven clans, are involved in extortion rackets and cigarette, drugs and arms smuggling.

In recent years, Cosa Nostra has been forced to come to terms with a new challenge to its authority, on its own home ground. The threat has come from local gangs of common criminals headed for the most part by rebel Mafiosi, often men of honour who have been expelled from Cosa Nostra.

These rebels make up the 'Stidda' ('Star'). As its name suggests, this is a constellation of criminal groups. First revealed to police by informers in 1987, it is now a force to be found in many parts of southern Sicily and which is spreading throughout the island. An organisation parallel to Cosa Nostra, its groups are not as close knit as the latter's families. The members of the Stidda, the stiddari, have no code of honour to obey. Many have five dots tattooed between the index and middle finger of one hand, once a mark used for branding prisoners.

Cosa Nostra's war against the Stidda has been at its most violent in the area where the latter originated, near the towns of Agrigento and Gela on Sicily's south coast. The province of Agrigento has the lowest revenue per capita of any Italian province, and the highest number of unemployed (some 70,000, of whom 40,000 are between fifteen and twenty-nine years old). In Gela, the stiddari rebels' original aim was to control extortion rackets but they have become involved in drugs and arms trafficking. At first, the Mafia clans believed the attacks on their soldiers were the work of rival families. In the two years 1991–2, the war in Gela claimed more than 110 victims.[46]

Cosa Nostra is not invincible in the face of such threats. Clans have sometimes been temporarily forced out of their domains. When the men of honour of Catania sought to exterminate common criminals under the ferocious boss Santapaola, the gangs forged alliances among themselves and fought back. In late 1976, the Mafiosi lost the upper hand and had to flee the city for several months. But such examples are few and far between. The Mafia state has no intention of giving up control of the territory to its legal counterpart or to rival criminals.

4

THE PEASANT FROM CORLEONE

A Devil or a God

In the spring of 1974, a little church in the modest Palermo suburb of San Lorenzo was the scene of an unusual wedding. In many ways it was a ceremony like any other. The bride and bridegroom exchanged vows before a priest, and after the service presented their relatives and friends with boxes of sweets, a traditional gift. After the reception, the happy couple left the Sicilian capital and headed, like so many other newlyweds, for a honeymoon in Venice.

But the gilded invitation cards, some of which were to turn up years later, showed that this was no ordinary wedding. The bridegroom was a wanted man, soon to become the Godfather of Cosa Nostra: Salvatore 'The Beast' Riina. The officiating priest, Don Agostino Coppola, who married Riina to his schoolteacher bride, was also a man of honour. A local Mafia boss supplied the bouquets of freshly-cut flowers which decorated the church.

Interpol had listed the semiliterate Riina among its ten most wanted criminals, and Italian police had put a price of one billion lire (£500,000) on his head. That there was nothing to prevent the forty-three-year-old Riina marrying so publicly was typical of the immunity he enjoyed for nearly a quarter of a century as he deceived and murdered his way to establishing a dictatorship over Cosa Nostra.

His rule was to prove a watershed for the Sicilian Mafia. Riina turned it into a totalitarian state, giving pride of place to its military arm as he waged war inside Cosa Nostra and launched a series of terrorist attacks on the institutions of the Italian State. His strategy, which involved trampling on the traditional code of honour, dealt a death-blow to the legend of the Mafia as an 'Honoured Society'.

Riina's prowess at evading justice gave him a mythical stature in the criminal organisation. He was not arrested until January 1993 after twenty-three years on the run. The Mafiosi ascribed supernatural qualities to Riina: 'He is either a devil or a God; he is nowhere, but he is everywhere and hears everything,' one said of him.[1]

The residential neighbourhood of San Lorenzo where Riina celebrated his wedding was one of his Palermo fiefdoms: 'Riina controlled specific, very calm areas [of Palermo] . . . Sometimes policemen would come across a car with Salvatore Riina inside. But they couldn't stop him anyway because he was escorted by another three cars and those people would have done them in,' said the informer Salvatore Contorno years later.[2]

In his first court appearance following his arrest, Riina wasted no opportunity to ridicule the authorities. Asked about his time as a fugitive, he answered: '. . . nobody ever looked for me. I'd go to work in the morning.

Nobody ever stopped me. I'd take the train to Trapani [in western Sicily]. I'd take the bus. Nobody ever said anything to me.'[3]

Riina also made a typically veiled Mafia threat to the protectors who had helped him escape jail for so long, telling the magistrates: 'I am a modest person who has been able to live all these years thanks to the goodness of those who gave me work, people who really helped me . . . naturally I won't say their names because they could be arrested and they don't deserve it.'[4]

All the informers have stressed Riina's ferocious and treacherous character. Buscetta called him a tyrant. 'He's like an apple: good on the outside but with an ugly heart,' said Marchese, who turned informer after he was betrayed by Riina.[5] Marino Mannoia, who had refined heroin for Riina's clan, told the investigators: 'If you can't think with an evil mind, then it's impossible to really understand the cruelty of that terrible demon [Riina] who reigns over Cosa Nostra.'[6]

'He was suspicious, taciturn, incredibly ignorant,' Calderone said of Riina, whose Corleonesi clan had murdered his brother. 'But he had intuition, he was intelligent. Difficult to understand, but intelligent. Like an animal. His philosophy was simple: if somebody's finger hurts, it's better to cut his arm off, that way you make doubly sure.'[7]

Riina's police file sums him up as 'violent, aggressive, vindictive, bloodthirsty and unscrupulous [but of] above-average shrewdness and determination'. The section on 'sexual anomalies' has the one-word entry: 'sadist'.[8] Inside the Mafia itself, Riina was known chiefly as 'The Beast'. His other, kinder, nickname was *Totò ù curtu* ('Totò the Short One'). Riina is 5 feet 3 inches tall.

When Riina was arrested in January 1993, Italians discovered a paunchy old man with a plump face, heavy bags
under the eyes and tousled greying hair. He had difficulty
signing his own name when he registered as a prisoner.
(Riina's work permit, found by the police in August 1992
during a search of his mother's house, described him as
an illiterate farm labourer.) The carabiniere Colonel Mario
Mori, the first to make Riina admit his true identity, said
of him: 'He is obsequious – small with a face like a peasant
and an anonymous bearing, but his eyes have a hypnotic,
metallic stare.'

Corleone

Corleone is a small agricultural town buried in the
uplands thirty-four miles south of Palermo. 'Corleone'
means 'Lionheart', but the town fails to live up to its
flamboyant name.

Wedged into a hillside, the town and its surroundings
are an appropriate backdrop to local tales and legends of
banditry and Mafia battles. Two crags cast their shadows
over a warren of steep and tortuous narrow streets lined
by dirty grey stone houses. On one of the rocks is a
Saracen lookout tower. On the other is a former fortress,
used as a jail until it was taken over by Franciscan
monks. In Byzantine as well as Norman times, the town
was an important strategic point dominating the road from
Palermo to Agrigento on the south coast.

The landmarks outside the town are no less desolate,
and the landscape lends itself to malefactors. The dark
Ficuzza woods, once a Bourbon hunting reserve, are
notorious as ideal terrain for burying bodies, as well as

a good hiding-place for stolen cattle. Although stripped of many trees by age-old deforestation, the woods still cover parts of the slopes of the majestic Rocca Busambra, a limestone outcrop that dominates Corleone and the surrounding landscape of pasture and wheatfields. The caves and steep gorges of the Rocca have provided refuge to fugitives for centuries.

The town has a long history of violence. When the island rose against the occupying French forces in the Sicilian Vespers of 1282, Corleone notched up more murders of foreign soldiers than any of the neighbouring towns. The role played by the people of Corleone in that insurrection, as well as in the siege of Palermo in 1325, earned their town the nickname of '*l'animosa*' ('the fiery one').

Salvatore Riina was born there on 16 November 1930, the second of five children in a poor family of peasant day-labourers. He grew up in a feudal society which had changed little in generations. The landlords administered their properties from the capital Palermo, entrusting day-to-day supervision to the *gabellotti*, the authoritarian overseers who often exploited both their absentee landlords and the defenceless peasants.

As in most of central Sicily, the peasants preferred to cluster together in small towns and travel great distances to reach their fields, rather than live in villages. At the time of Riina's birth, Corleone boasted a population of 14,200.

In the late 1940s, the commander of the small carabinieri force in Corleone was a young captain, Carlo Alberto dalla Chiesa. He later rose to the rank of general before becoming a martyr of the fight against the Mafia. Dalla Chiesa described the poor peasant society into which Riina was born:

Until only a few years ago, the overwhelming majority

of the people . . . were dedicated to agriculture and pasture; and early in the morning the squares teemed with day-labourers who offered themselves for very little to the enterprising sharecropper or more unscrupulous *gabellotto*. Already at three or four in the morning, others, many others, were on their way on the backs of mules to small rocky plots in feudal properties very far away where they would arrive exhausted after a journey of a dozen miles.[9]

The young Riina never went to school in Corleone, spending his days toiling from dawn to dusk with his parents to earn his keep in the vast estates that surrounded the town. Contemporaries remember him as the small, taciturn boy they nicknamed '*Totò ù curtu*' – but only behind his back, because of his short temper. His father died in December 1943, when Riina was thirteen, killed by an American bomb which burst in his hands. The explosion also killed a brother of Riina's, and injured another brother.

It is not known when Riina swore loyalty to Cosa Nostra, in the ritual which made him a man of honour, or who acted as his Godfather at the ceremony. But already as a teenager he had drifted into bad company and achieved notoriety as a violent character.

In May 1949, at the age of eighteen, he committed his first recorded crime in a brawl over women with other young peasants of Corleone, which started during a religious procession through the town. Riina drew a gun and fired repeatedly, killing one man and injuring another. He was sentenced to sixteen years in jail and banned from holding public office. He was to serve only six years in prison, studying to acquire the basics of a primary school education.

Riina returned to Corleone in triumph. He had proved his mettle in committing his first murder, and had served less than half his sentence. His reputation boosted by these achievements, he was taken under the wing of the métayer Luciano Leggio, born the tenth child of a poor and illiterate peasant family, and one of the most violent lieutenants in the local Mafia clan. Years later, the supergrass Calderone described the cruel streak in Leggio's character:

> He liked killing. He had a way of looking at people which struck fear into everybody, including us Mafiosi. The slightest thing was enough to make him change his mood, and a strange light would appear in his eyes which silenced everybody near him. The wrong tone of voice, a word misunderstood, and then there would be a sudden silence. Everybody was struck dumb, and felt uncomfortable – you could feel death in the air.[10]

It was probably Leggio who recruited Riina into the organisation.

In the aftermath of the Second World War, the head of the clan holding sway over Corleone and the surrounding feudal estates was Dr Michele Navarra, director of the local hospital. Known to all as 'ù *Patri Nostru*' ('Our Father'), Navarra was a shrewd, cultured patriarch with a passion for cards and hunting.

Always impeccably dressed before venturing forth into Corleone's dusty streets, the corpulent Navarra collected honorary titles with assiduity. He was chairman of the local Christian Democrats, health inspector for the Corleone area and doctor for State railway personnel in the region.

Navarra was a Mafioso of the rural Old Guard, who presided over a host of rackets in the feudal estates –

chiefly cattle-rustling and the hiring of day-labourers for the landowners. His clan seized land belonging to several local barons, stole cattle which it slaughtered clandestinely to supply the Palermo market, and organised electoral support for Christian Democrat candidates. His men even dealt in a substance which was little known at the time – in 1949, 50 kilos of heroin were seized in the Corleone area, the first seizure of the drug in Italy.

Riina was not to stay long in Navarra's shadow. His early criminal career was to be tied inextricably to the struggle for supremacy in Corleone between Navarra and his lieutenant Leggio. Years later, that battle was to earn the town of Corleone worldwide fame through Mario Puzo's novel *The Godfather* and the blockbuster films of Francis Ford Coppola. Today, bars in Corleone sell a strong, local after-dinner liqueur named after the saga's main character, Don Vito Corleone.

Riina was swept along by Leggio's ambitions to unseat Navarra, quickly becoming the younger Mafioso's right-hand man and one of his fiercest killers. Leggio set up a front company in Corleone, ostensibly to breed cattle. His real purpose was the slaughter of stolen cattle, and his business earned him fat profits.

Leggio's increasing prestige and insubordination enraged Navarra, who attempted to have his former pupil murdered in June 1958. Navarra's men ambushed Leggio and Riina, bursting out of a cowshed where they had been hiding. They only succeeded in wounding Leggio slightly.

Just under two months later, Leggio took his revenge, giving Riina his first experience of Mafia murder on a grand scale. The investigators reported that Riina was at Leggio's side when, on 2 August 1958, Leggio and fifteen of his men ambushed Navarra as he drove home to Corleone from the nearby town of Lercara Friddi.

The killers pumped 112 bullets into Navarra and another doctor he had given a lift to. Navarra's death robbed him of what he would have seen as the ultimate accolade – he had just been nominated for one of Italy's highest honours, Knight of the Order of Merit.

Leggio had taken a risk in murdering Navarra without first seeking the approval of the Cupola ruling over the Palermo province. This was an early violation of Cosa Nostra practice which was to become a trademark of the Corleonesi, and of Riina's later strategy. The Cupola summoned Leggio to account for his action, but failed to punish him.

In the ensuing settling of scores which lasted until the end of 1963, 140 Mafiosi died and many more disappeared as Leggio and Riina purged the Corleonesi clan of Navarra's henchmen. The younger face of Cosa Nostra emerged victorious, and bosses of Sicilian origin in New York's families across the Atlantic thought up a new name for Corleone – 'Tombstone'.

A Foothold in Palermo

The bloody reports from Corleone failed to impress the most powerful bosses of Cosa Nostra, caught up by their own rivalries in the Sicilian capital. Palermo, traditionally the head of the Mafia serpent because its clans have always carried the most weight in the organisation, knew little and cared even less about the Corleonesi.

According to Buscetta, their ignorance was part of the Corleonesi's strategy. The clan never boasted about its real strength, preferring to lull the veteran Palermitans into a false sense of security and encouraging the illusion that they had nothing to fear from the men from the uplands. The Corleonesi also kept the names of their members secret from other clans – another violation of time-honoured Mafia practice.

The Palermo chieftains despised the boorish Leggio, Riina and the other men of honour from Corleone who were seeking a foothold in their city. The new boys were snootily referred to as the '*viddani*' (the 'villains', or peasants).

But the elders were soon forced to sit up and take notice. The Corleonesi rapidly won notoriety as unscrupulous innovators. They were among the first to carry out a massacre in the centre of Palermo (in 1969) and to break the ban on kidnappings agreed by all the Mafia clans (in 1972).

The Corleonesi at first prudently bided their time. Palermo was in the throes of a war between rival clans which climaxed in 1963 with an explosion of unprecedented force.

The carabinieri had been called to the neighbourhood of Ciaculli to tow away a car with a flat tyre. The seven officers who examined the car found a fake explosive on the back seat. An unsuspecting officer then opened the boot. All seven men were blown to pieces by the explosion that followed – the boot had been loaded with two hundred pounds of dynamite. Investigators believe the bomb had been intended for the head of the Palermo Cupola, Salvatore 'Little Bird' Greco.

The explosion sent shock waves through the ranks of the Mafia, and prompted a crackdown by the authorities. In the ten weeks that followed, 10,000 policemen were sent to Sicily and carried out some 1,200 arrests. Greco dissolved the Cupola and fled to Venezuela.

'Cosa Nostra did not exist any more in the Palermo

area after 1963. It was completely knocked out,' said Calderone.[11] The Mafia did not start operating normally again until 1969, when several trials ended in acquittals for many of the Mafiosi.

The Corleonesi's plan to establish themselves in Palermo suffered a setback in December 1963 when Riina was arrested at a police road-block. Only six months later, Leggio was also arrested. Both men were charged with several murders. Leggio had been found in the home of his girlfriend Leoluchina Sorisi in Corleone. One of her previous lovers, the local labour activist Placido Rizzotto, had been murdered by Leggio himself sixteen years earlier.

Riina was sent to Palermo's Ucciardone jail, then packed with men of honour who had been rounded up following the Ciaculli bombing. His stay cannot have been too unpleasant. The forbidding appearance of the converted Bourbon fortress belies the soft regime that prevails inside its thick walls. For years the Ucciardone was run in effect by its inmates.

Awaiting his trial, Riina whiled away the time discussing the affairs of Cosa Nostra with fellow-mobsters. He borrowed few books from the prison library but recommended the tales of the Beati Paoli sect to his cellmate Mutolo. The restless Riina pledged: 'When I get out of here I will make so much money that I will walk on a carpet of 100,000-lire banknotes.'[12]

Mutolo, who turned informer years later, described him as already commanding great respect: 'I was very deferential because I had understood he was an important person when I saw how the other prisoners queued up to greet him. I spent some time with him playing draughts and I'd use little tricks to try and let him win every time.'[13]

Leggio, Riina and sixty-two other men of honour were called to stand trial for the murders of Corleone's boss

Navarra and several of his allies. The trial was held in Bari in south-east Italy for security reasons. The public prosecutor, whose case had been supported by two eye-witnesses (a rare feat when Cosa Nostra is in the dock), asked for three life sentences and a total of 343 years in jail to be handed down.

Leggio pleaded that he was being persecuted by a police officer who had invited him 'to offer his wife the possibility of having some fun; and I, for moral reasons, did not take up such an invitation.'[14]

Ever the gentleman, Leggio would name no names. The first witness for the prosecution called to confront Leggio was so terrified that he had to be given psychiatric treatment. The second, at a glance from Leggio, refused to give evidence.

Once they had withdrawn – supposedly in strict isolation from the outside world – to consider their verdict, the members of the jury received an anonymous letter. It told them: 'We want to warn you that if one gentleman from Corleone is condemned you will be blown up, you will be destroyed, you will be torn apart, as will your relatives. We think we have made ourselves clear . . . A Sicilian proverb says: a man forewarned is a man half-saved.' The letter ended with a large cross at the bottom of the page.[15]

On 10 June 1969 the jury acquitted Leggio, Riina and all the other men of honour of both murder and criminal conspiracy charges. Riina was sentenced to a year and six months in jail, and told to pay a small fine, for having stolen someone's identity papers. He was freed on the spot as he had already amply served his time in the Ucciardone.

The jury took the view that there was insufficient evidence to convict Leggio of killing nine people and attempting another murder, and Riina of committing six murders and attempting two others. The verdict shocked

Italy. In true Mafia style, Leggio and Riina had succeeded in manipulating the course of justice. It was one of the earliest examples of how the Corleonesi were to challenge the institutions of the Italian State.

On the evening of their triumphant acquittal, Riina and Leggio went to stay at the Hotel Nuovo in Bitonto, near Bari in the heel of Italy. Riina nursed his mentor, who was suffering from a bladder infection, ordering fresh fish for Leggio's diet. Less than a month later, the police in Palermo demanded Riina be exiled, describing him as 'sly, domineering and bloodthirsty, capable of conceiving, organising and committing any crime to consolidate the prestige he has always enjoyed among criminals'.[16]

Riina was called before a tribunal in Palermo, which exiled him for four years to the village of San Giovanni in Persiceto (population: 5,000) outside Bologna in central Italy. Riina signed the register of offenders under special surveillance, was handed the order sending him into internal exile and granted a couple of days to settle his affairs in Corleone.

And that, on the morning of 7 July 1969, was the last the police saw of him for over twenty years. Riina never did register at the police station of San Giovanni.

A Troublesome Priest

Informers say it was in his first years as a fugitive that Riina, his prestige enhanced by the Bari ruling, settled in Palermo for good. In recognition of his growing stature among the Palermo mobsters, he was assigned an important task in the capital shortly after he went on the run.

The 'villain' from Corleone was given command of a

squad of five men of honour to murder Michele Cavataio, an upstart Mafioso threatening the authority of the Palermo bosses. Cavataio had planted the Ciaculli bomb which devastated Cosa Nostra six years earlier.

Riina's mission turned into a bloodbath. He made his killers wear the uniforms of carabinieri officers. They stalked their prey to the offices of a Palermo builder, burst in and immediately started firing. Cavataio was shot dead as planned, but so were four others.

Among those killed was Calogero Bagarella, brother of Riina's fiancée Antonietta. Riina took the body in the boot of his car to the cemetery of Corleone, where he buried it in a vault belonging to another family. Riina wore a black tie in mourning for several days afterwards. The raid sparked a chorus of disapproval from Sicilian families, who accused the Palermitan clans of making treacherous peace overtures to Cavataio before killing him.

When Riina moved to the Sicilian capital, he worked side-by-side with all the Palermitan families, although he never forgot the interests of his Corleonesi clan. At the beginning of the 1970s, Palermo was dominated by three main groups – a first 'moderate' faction led by the families of Stefano 'The Falcon' Bontate, Gaetano Badalamenti and Salvatore Inzerillo; a second wing led by Leggio; and a third headed by the Greco family from Ciaculli.

Riina, on the pretext of seeking refuge as he was on the run, set up a network of allies within many clans. He asserted his control over towns in the province of Palermo, and began to infiltrate the Sicilian capital itself by striking up friendships with influential men of honour belonging to different clans. At the same time, Riina also penetrated clans in a similar way in other Sicilian provinces – Caltanissetta, Trapani, Catania and Agrigento – as well as Naples.[17]

His method was always to seek to cause or fan feuds inside families, in such a way as to recruit discontented men of honour. He set the younger generation against the Old Guard, only to purge the ranks of the young soldiers much later. 'We were a bit infatuated,' said one supergrass, 'because getting rid of the old [Mafiosi] we thought we would be in power, we would be the new representatives, the new bosses, acting in our interests. But it didn't turn out that way.'[18]

The ambitious Riina also sought to undermine the authority of his tutor. The arrogant and aggressive Leggio repeatedly clashed with other men of honour, including the chieftains Bontate and Badalamenti. But Riina put on a more conciliatory front to rally round himself those who had been put off by Leggio's tantrums.

Riina gave the impression of being humble and docile. He could even lay claim to an aura of pope-like dignity: 'He's like a preacher when you talk to him,' Gaspare Mutolo told the anti-Mafia commission. 'You remember Pope John, that handsome face . . . Forgive the comparison; I'm trying to explain.'[19]

In 1970 the Palermo bosses tried to impose some kind of order on the clans which had been disbanded following the police crackdown seven years previously. Riina was appointed to a new governing triumvirate alongside the 'moderates' Bontate and Badalamenti. Riina was named to the triumvirate as Leggio's representative – at the time Leggio was forced by a second arrest warrant to stay away from Palermo. He lived under a false name in an exclusive private clinic in Rome.

By this time Riina, at the age of thirty-nine, had become one of the most powerful bosses in Palermo. A decade earlier the families of the Sicilian capital had dismissed the Corleonesi as uncouth peasants from the provinces. Now they were forced to acknowledge their strength. Riina's appointment was also an endorsement of his status inside the Corleonesi clan, as second only to Leggio. And it invested Riina with the power to mediate between Sicily's most powerful families.

Ninetta

The myth of Riina as a fugitive impossible to catch began to take shape. That myth was strengthened by the arrests in the early 1970s of the bosses Bontate, Badalamenti and Leggio. But it was consecrated by a marriage to Antonietta Bagarella, known to all as 'Ninetta', which Riina celebrated while on the run.

Alongside her beloved, Bagarella had been active in the Corleonesi clan. A svelte, dark-eyed primary school-teacher, she like Riina was born and bred in Corleone. In 1970, aged twenty-seven, she made the front pages of the Italian newspapers when the Palermo police chief requested she be exiled from Corleone. Few women had ever been linked to the male chauvinist world of the Mafia, and only one, the sister of a Mafia boss, had ever been sent into internal exile.

According to the police, Bagarella was no less than the brain of the Leggio band. She was the only one in the gang of illiterates to boast a diploma. She had begun to study literature and philosophy at university, but gave up after the first year and qualified as a PE teacher instead. With two brothers in the Corleonesi clan, her tasks were many and varied. She ran errands, acted as a messenger and organised Leggio's stays in hospital (Pott's disease, or bone tuberculosis, partly paralysed him).

But the Palermo prosecutor Pietro Scaglione objected that Bagarella was 'not socially dangerous' and shelved the police request. Her boyfriend, however, found the controversy a bit much to take. Riina told Calderone at the time: 'I don't want other women, only Ninetta. They don't want me to marry her? Well then, I'll kill people.'[20]

The following year, the Palermo police reiterated its accusations against Bagarella. When the schoolteacher appeared in court, she said she was the victim of persecution: 'My only fault is being in love with Salvatore Riina. I have loved him since I was thirteen years old and he was twenty-seven. I saw him when I was going to school and he has never been out of my heart since. Is it a crime to be in love with a fugitive? The only thing I want is to marry him. I do not want ours to remain a platonic love.'[21]

To defend herself, Bagarella collected signatures among the mothers of Corleone for a petition proclaiming her innocence and good character. She managed to enlist the backing of the priest Emanuele Catarinicchia – who, like her, taught at the Institute of the Sisters of the Sacred Heart – and even appealed to the Court of Human Rights in The Hague.

Bagarella was not exiled but ordered not to move from Corleone for the next two and a half years. She was also forbidden to leave her home between 7.30 pm and 7 am. When in 1975 police again appealed for new measures to be taken against her, they found she had disappeared.

In the meantime, the two fugitives had exchanged vows. After nine weeks on the police's wanted list, Bagarella had married Riina, the man she saw as 'good, affectionate, a victim of injustice, a man who deserves all my love'.[22] They had become engaged in July 1969, just before Riina had gone into hiding. The priest who celebrated the wedding five years later, on the afternoon of 16 April 1974, was the mobster Father Agostino Coppola, cousin of the New York boss Frank 'Three Fingers' Coppola.

A carabiniere captain, Giuseppe Russo, found hand-written invitations for the wedding of 'Totò e Ninetta' four years later in a flat in Palermo used by Bagarella and one of her brothers. He also found a snapshot of a smiling, slightly overweight Riina feeding the pigeons in St Mark's Square in Venice during his honeymoon.

Dubbed the Mafia's First Lady by the Italian press, Bagarella was to give birth to four children – Maria Concetta, Giovanni, Giuseppe and Lucia – in Palermo's expensive Noto private clinic. Their births were legally registered at the clinic under their mother's maiden name and their father's name. The children were all baptised.

The Riinas, unbeknown to the police, sent their offspring to private schools. Only after Salvatore Riina's arrest in January 1993 was it discovered that the whole family had lived comfortably in the heart of Palermo for much of the time he was wanted by police. They had settled in a six-bedroom villa in a plush residential complex shaded by palms and pine trees. Their neighbours, rich building entrepreneurs, let the Riina children have the run of their swimming pool on hot summer days.

The Riinas, however, had failed to register their marriage with the local mayor. This enabled the authorities to declare the wedding null and void three months after the Godfather's arrest. Anxious to give his union with Ninetta a legal status, and to set an example in respecting the Mafia code of honour's marital obligations, Riina was eventually granted permission to stage a civil wedding in Palermo's Ucciardone jail.

The Corleonesi's Challenge

When the two other members of the Palermo triumvirate, Bontate and Badalamenti, were arrested in May 1971, Riina enjoyed an almost free hand because both recognised him as Leggio's lieutenant and entrusted him with the government of Cosa Nostra. For the Corleonesi, this was a chance to make their mark. They did not waste the opportunity and set about breaking all the rules which the staid Palermo families had preached for generations.

One of the unwritten rules was that men of honour could kill each other but should refrain from murdering magistrates or politicians. Threats only were in order. But in May 1971, the Corleonesi carried out the first murder of a judge since the Second World War.

Leggio and Riina shot dead Palermo's public prosecutor Pietro Scaglione as he left his wife's graveside in the Capuchin cemetery of the Sicilian capital. Leggio, because of his long illness, was partially paralysed by this time. But, determined to play a part, he shot Scaglione from the seat of his car.

Still in command a year later, the Corleonesi dealt another blow to the Palermo rule-book. Riina was the first to break a ban on kidnappings in Sicily, seizing in August 1972 Luciano Cassina, the son of a Palermitan builder, Count Arturo Cassina, without seeking prior approval from other clans.

Riina did not hesitate to negotiate over the telephone

with Cassina, while he held his gun trained on the count's son Luciano who knelt before him.[23] Father Coppola, the priest who was later to celebrate Riina's wedding, collected the ransom. Breaking with the past practice of sharing out ransom money among the clans, the Corleonesi kept the profits for themselves.

The violation of the kidnapping ban incensed Bontate and Badalamenti. It was in particular an affront to Bontate, who was linked to Count Cassina and who had inherited the duty of safeguarding the equilibrium between Mafia, business and politics in Palermo from his father. Leggio placated the pair, saying bygones should be bygones as the ransom had been paid and the hostage freed – in February 1973, after seven months in captivity.

But the Sicilian families decided to reaffirm the ban on kidnapping in the island, this time on pain of death. They argued that such activities led to excessive repression by the police. Leggio was told to restrict his clan's hunting ground to northern Italy.

The Corleonesi had no intention of abandoning such a lucrative activity, and this gave Riina one of his earliest opportunities to forge ties with other mobsters in Cosa Nostra's cousins on the Italian mainland. Leggio moved to Milan, Italy's business capital, to identify potential victims. He sent Riina to negotiate with the heads of the Calabrian 'Ndrangheta so that they would agree to hide the captives on their territory.

Only a few months after the ban decreed by the Palermo bosses, the Corleonesi struck again. In July 1975 they kidnapped Luigi Corleo, father-in-law of Nino Salvo, a powerful man of honour close to Bontate and Badalamenti, who with his brother Ignazio had a monopoly as tax collectors for the government in Sicily. The aim of the kidnapping was to demonstrate the Corleonesi's strength to the Salvos and their allies within the Mafia. But it went wrong despite the intervention of Badalamenti and the payment of a large ransom. No trace of Luigi Corleo was ever found.

Riina's involvement in kidnapping was his first taste of real wealth. An accomplice, Stefano Giaconia, commented later: 'Before the kidnapping, before he discovered money, Riina did not appreciate it. But after the kidnapping he'd got very fond of it.'

He began to invest the ransoms he had been paid into drug trafficking. According to the supergrass Calderone, it was in the early 1970s that Riina launched himself into heroin trafficking, asking other families if they would like to contribute financially to a particular venture. 'I can tell you that in 1966 or 1967, Totò Riina was crying when he told me his mother could not go to visit him in jail, because she could not pay the train ticket! . . . Then [the Mafiosi] all became billionaires, all of a sudden, in a couple of years, through drugs.'[24]

Riina's increasing stature did not pass unnoticed. His mentor Leggio had begun to worry about the power that Riina was accumulating. Seeking to bring him down a peg, Leggio sought to favour his other lieutenant from Corleone, Bernardo 'The Tractor' Provenzano, despite his having a low opinion of the latter's intelligence. A mobster later quoted Leggio as saying: 'Provenzano shoots like a god, it's a shame he's got the brain of a hen. Riina on the other hand would like to take bites which are bigger than his mouth.'[25]

Leggio went so far as to spread the word among the Palermo bosses that Riina drank and therefore talked too much. Riina got to hear of this through his network of spies, but Leggio's arrest put paid to his plotting.

On 16 May 1974, carabinieri police burst into the Milan

flat where Leggio was in hiding, nursed by a woman who had taken him in without knowing his true identity. Nonplussed, he told the men who arrested him: 'It's just as well it's you who got me. I know you are gentlemen and among gentlemen we understand each other.'[26] Buscetta has hinted that Riina himself may have betrayed Leggio to the authorities. Leggio was jailed for life for killing Navarra.

As a result of Leggio's arrest, Riina and Provenzano were appointed in his stead to a new Cupola. The two were supposed to take turns on the council, with Riina due to sit on it for the first two years. But Provenzano, elbowed aside by Riina, never did get his turn. Riina gradually supplanted Leggio too, not only at the head of the Corleonesi clan, but also at the head of the Mafia itself. Riina thus brought to fruition the Corleonesi's strategy of hegemony launched by his mentor.

Much later, according to the turncoat Gaspare Mutolo, Riina even foiled a plan by Leggio for his escape during a transfer from one prison to another. Riina made sure the plan failed, telling Mutolo and others who wanted to free Leggio to mind their own business.[27]

Leggio cut an increasingly pathetic figure as he languished in jail. Trying to live up to the silver-screen image of a Cosa Nostra patriarch, he had boxes of long, fat cigars sent to him at the time of the mid-1980s maxi-trial in Palermo, where he had a cage all to himself, unlike the other mobsters. He would light them only when he was due for an appearance in the courtroom, to try to impress the television crews and photographers. He also sported a fat gold and diamond ring. Back in his cell, he dedicated himself to painting the rough countryside of his former power-base, working from memory or using postcards sent by his relatives. Leggio's lawyers said his inspiration was Vincent Van Gogh.[28]

Leggio died of a heart attack in November 1993, aged sixty-eight. He was rushed to hospital after collapsing in his cell, but doctors were unable to save him. Relatives and friends buried him without ceremony in his home town of Corleone after the local officials banned them from holding a funeral service. Leggio was laid to rest in the family vault – only yards away from the man he murdered to become the head of Corleone's clan, the gentlemanly Dr Michele Navarra.

5

THE GODFATHER

The Rout of the Patriarchs

In the early 1970s, Leggio was not the only one worried about Riina's increasing standing. The Old Guard governing Cosa Nostra soon became aware of Riina's infiltration of the clans in Palermo and the surrounding province.

Between 1974 and 1976 the Palermo bosses held meeting after meeting to discuss how to slow Riina's rise. Some pressed for his murder. But Michele 'The Pope' Greco, an urbane figure popular with the city's wealthier classes, tended to try to placate the more extreme clan chiefs, arguing against any physical clash with Riina. Increasingly, Greco came to host these meetings at his estate in the district of Ciaculli.

As the other bosses were to find out only much later, Greco, the secretary of the Cupola, was in fact Riina's mole at these gatherings. Making full use of his stooge's reports, Riina launched a Machiavellian strategy to eliminate his enemies. He consistently worked to prepare the ground for the demotion or killing of his opponents, exploiting their mistakes in order to make his actions seem only 'fair play' in accordance with the rules of Cosa Nostra.[1]

The supergrass Calderone, one of the many who lost out to Riina, summed up his strategy: 'His devilish plan was to eliminate opponents one by one, every time a suitable opportunity presented itself, in a formally correct way so that not even the victims' closest friends could react, being formally in the wrong.'[2]

In the words of another informer:

If you talk to Salvatore Riina, you'll ask yourself: 'Is it possible that this is Salvatore Riina?' He is a very educated person, with such a gentle expression. He was the first person to invent the method, before killing someone, of inviting him for a meal, of making him eat and relax, of making him enjoy himself. After eating, you would strangle him and that would be the end of it . . . You eat, you have fun, and then you kill. That is the novelty introduced by Salvatore Riina.[3]

Riina's Corleonesi demonstrated how little respect they had for the established hierarchy when in 1977 they murdered the carabiniere colonel Giuseppe Russo as he searched for bodies in the woods of Ficuzza outside Corleone. The area was within the remit of the Palermo provincial Cupola, but the Corleonesi acted without first seeking its approval as they should have done. Clans across Sicily protested in unison, furious that they had received no advance warning, which meant that their men of honour who had had nothing to do with the assassination were rounded up in random police checks.

An arrogant Riina used his stool-pigeon, Michele Greco,

to defuse the protests. Berated by angry bosses, Greco coolly quoted Riina as saying that no questions should be asked about the murder of a '*sbirro*' (an offensive Sicilian term for 'policeman').[4]

An irate Giuseppe di Cristina told Greco to his face that Riina was manipulating him like a puppet. A few days later Di Cristina narrowly escaped an attempt on his life in which two other people were killed.

In his bid for supremacy, Riina was pitted against the 'moderate' faction led by Stefano Bontate, Gaetano Badalamenti and Salvatore Inzerillo. They specialised in penetrating state institutions and delivering votes to corrupt politicians in exchange for public works contracts and immunity from prosecution.

The faction's most powerful leader was Bontate, head of a family from Santa Maria del Gesù on Palermo's outskirts. He was the embodiment of the Old Guard, which had built its power on collusion with corrupt right-wing politicians who needed votes to keep the Communists out of power in Sicily. Heavily involved in cigarette smuggling, he drew the line at Cosa Nostra getting involved in drug trafficking (like the fictional Don Vito Corleone of Puzo's *The Godfather*), and was also opposed to the murder of magistrates and policemen.

Bontate, a citrus fruit dealer by trade, was a boss of great charisma, much respected by men of honour. Nor did he lack panache. On one occasion, Bontate was an hour late for an appointment with other men of honour in a motel on the Palermo–Catania motorway. Arriving in his Porsche Carrera, Bontate apologised: 'Forgive my lateness, but I had to change a burst tyre and I had to strangle Stefano Giaconia.'[5]

Giaconia was a promising Palermo mobster who had committed the offence, in Bontate's eyes, of allying himself with Riina. Bontate added: 'That cuckold made me worry until the very last. After I'd killed him, we burnt his clothes, and while they were burning there was an explosion. It was a .22 calibre pen-pistol that Giaconia had on him.'

The first victim in what became an extermination of Riina's rivals, including Bontate, was Di Cristina, dubbed 'The Tiger of Riesi' (a town near Caltanissetta in central Sicily). A leading drug-trafficker, he was shot dead in a residential district north of Palermo's city centre on 30 May 1978. Released on bail shortly before his murder, he had been about to take delivery of a new armoured car. In a cynical violation of the families' territorial sovereignty, Di Cristina was executed on the territory of his friend Salvatore Inzerillo, who shortly afterwards was also killed by the Corleonesi. Some 10,000 people – half the population of Riesi – followed Di Cristina's coffin to the cemetery. Schools and offices were deserted, cinemas closed for two days, and the local street-sweepers were ordered to drop their brooms and carry the dozens of wreaths paying tribute to the patriarch.

Di Cristina, following the first failed attempt on his life in November 1977, had contacted the authorities in a desperate attempt to enlist the help of the police in defeating the Corleonesi. He told the carabinieri that Riina and fellow-Mafioso Bernardo Provenzano were the most dangerous of Leggio's killers, having each carried out at least forty murders.

Ostensibly Di Cristina was killed because he had talked to the police, but the real reason was that he was one of the closest allies of Riina's next targets – Bontate and Badalamenti.

'The elimination of Di Cristina was the first step in a lucid plan, carried out with ferocious determination by the Corleonesi, to eliminate, one by one, all the most powerful allies of Stefano Bontate, so that the planned elimination of Bontate himself would not prompt any reactions,' the magistrates wrote in one indictment of Riina.[6] 'And Stefano Bontate's mistake, in this tragic game of chess, was that he did not understand his opponents' perverse plan in time.'

On 23 April 1981 Riina's Corleonesi finally set their prize target a trap. Bontate was ambushed as he drove home in the rain late at night after celebrating his forty-second birthday with friends. As he waited at traffic lights on Palermo's ring road, a powerful motorcycle drew up level with his car. Riding pillion, the famed killer Pino 'Little Shoe' Greco opened fire with a .12 calibre 'lupara', or sawn-off shotgun. One of the bullets shattered Bontate's skull.

Police also found bullets fired from a kalashnikov, one of that weapon's first appearances in Palermo. Bontate had been betrayed by his jealous brother Giovanni. Incensed by a series of provocations from the ambitious Riina, Bontate had signed his own death sentence when he finally lost his patience during a Mafioso summit and burst out: 'I'm going to wait for a meeting of the commission and then I'll kill him [Riina] with a couple of rounds in front of everybody.'[7]

The killing of Bontate, for which Riina was given a life sentence *in absentia* at the Palermo maxi-trial, was the signal for a carnage masterminded by the Corleonesi. Some 300 Mafiosi were either murdered or disappeared without trace in the two years it took Riina's clan to purge the Palermo families. In 1982 in the Sicilian capital alone, 151 people were slaughtered, another 91 disappeared – victims of the so-called 'lupara bianca' ('white shotgun'). An additional twenty-three failed murders were also recorded.

The butchery has been dubbed the 'Mafia War' of 1981–82. But it would be more appropriate to describe it as an extermination. Riina's potential rivals were given little opportunity to fight back.

'A war is when two or more families arm themselves

and know that one groups fights against another,' said one informer. 'There was never such a Mafia war in Palermo. There was a massacre . . . There was only Totò Riina's strategy of terror. We had got to the point of being scared of talking even among friends because we would think: "He's not here, but he hears everything.'"8

Bontate's ally Salvatore Inzerillo, the boss of Passo di Rigano – one of the biggest and militarily one of the strongest of the Palermo clans – struggled to counter Riina's rise. He told Buscetta he had ordered the murder of Palermo's public prosecutor Gaetano Costa because 'I had to do something big. I had to show my opponents that my family was strong and powerful. That I could order anybody I wanted killed, and when I wanted, just like the Corleonesi.'9

Inzerillo knew the Corleonesi had him in their sights but he foolishly believed he had time on his side. Riina had passed 50 kilos of heroin on to him to send to his contacts in New York. Inzerillo thought that as long as he had not handed over payment to Riina – some four million dollars – no one would harm him.

But less than three weeks after Bontate's murder, on the morning of 10 May 1981, nine men of honour lay in wait for Salvatore Inzerillo outside the home of his mistress. Half an hour after midday Inzerillo walked out. He was caught in a hail of cross-fire from a kalashnikov and a pump-action shotgun before he could open the door of his new armour-plated Alfetta car.

The killers fired from inside a van, through its windscreen. The van's driver, Giuseppe Marchese, told magistrates years later that he heard the bullets whistle past his ears and this stunned him. He said he was so close he could see some of the bullets leaving sparks.10

To be sure of its effectiveness, should Inzerillo manage to get into his car, the hitmen had successfully tried out the kalashnikov against the armour-plated windows of a jewellers' shop the previous night. Inzerillo was sold to Riina by ambitious subordinates in his own clan who wanted to take his place. Riina had shrewdly fanned their aspirations.

Only Badalamenti managed to survive Riina's purge of the moderate faction. He had secretly plotted to kill Francesco Madonia, a clan chief close to the Corleonesi who had hosted Riina's wedding in his district. Badalamenti's scheming was obviously a violation of Cosa Nostra rules and Riina exploited this, engineering punishments which were disproportionate to the offence.

Badalamenti was stripped of his post as representative of the Cinisi family in 1977 and the following year was expelled from the Mafia. He managed to escape to Brazil. According to Calderone, Badalamenti had during their first days in Palermo been like a father to Riina and Leggio's other lieutenant Bernardo Provenzano. It was typical of the Corleonesi to turn against those to whom they had debts of gratitude.

After the murders of Bontate and Inzerillo, Salvatore Riina was at the age of fifty the Godfather of Cosa Nostra, having successfully challenged the traditional dominance of the Palermo patriarchs. He now commanded a military organisation of some 5,000 sworn soldiers, and thousands of accomplices ready to do its bidding.

The Purges

The assassinations of the so-called moderate leaders marked a historic turning-point for the secret society. It was transformed from a formally 'democratic' organi-sation racked by concealed internal conflicts into a new organisation shaped by Riina's thirst for absolute power.

The new Godfather's Corleonesi, according to a magistrates' indictment, 'transformed Cosa Nostra into a "dictatorship", based no longer on the search for consensus but exclusively on terror, be it internally or in its relationship with society and the State.'[11]

Riina purged even the Corleonesi's allies of those he felt he could no longer trust. The result was a tight-knit squad totally subjugated to Riina's will. 'Napoleonism' had contaminated the Mafia's leadership, said the Sicilian writer Leonardo Sciascia.

It was after they had got rid of their three main enemies that Riina and the Corleonesi launched what the magistrates branded their 'systematic extermination not only of all the men of honour who were definitely their enemies, but also of all those who, even just potentially, did not supply guarantees of absolute trustworthiness'.[12] Riina's rivals were killed, as were their relatives, their friends and even those who might have helped them in some way or given them temporary refuge.

The ages of their victims meant nothing to the Corleonesi. Weeping over the body of his father Salvatore, sixteen-year-old Giuseppe Inzerillo swore to seek revenge. He pledged he would kill Riina with his own hands. That pledge was enough for the Corleonesi.

Buscetta testified: 'Giuseppe was intercepted and seized by Pino "Little Shoe" Greco, who did not kill him straight away. First Greco cut his arm clean off with one blow of his axe and while the boy was fainting he shouted in his ear: "That way you won't shoot Riina." He then put the gun to his head and fired.'[13]

Salvatore's brother Santo insisted on a Mafia summit to find out why the chieftain had been killed. The meeting was held in a warehouse. The bosses sat round a table with Santo, urging him repeatedly not to try and find out too much. Santo's uncle Calogero di Maggio, sensing the elders' patience was running out, sought to placate him.

But Santo went too far. He demanded an explanation, shouting and beating his fists on the table. At a sign from one of the bosses, Santo was surrounded and immobilised by three men while a fourth strangled him with a cord. Di Maggio was strangled at the same time.

The two bodies were stripped, trussed up like dead goats ('*incaprettati*' – a favourite Mafioso treatment of corpses in which the body is bent double with a cord linking the neck, wrists and feet), and bundled into two big rubbish bags which were heaved into a car boot. The bodies were finally burnt on a large grill in a country estate outside Palermo. Several bodies had been disposed of in the same way by the estate's owner, with some of the remains being fed to a pig. Two other brothers of Salvatore Inzerillo, his father, an uncle and two cousins were also killed by the Corleonesi.

Not even hospital wards were safe from Riina's butchers. When the wife of Natale Badalamenti, a member of a rival clan, had to be operated on for appendicitis, he spent a night with her in hospital. As Badalamenti slept, seven killers dressed as doctors burst into the ward. Drawing the guns they had hidden under their white coats, they shot Natale in front of his wife.

Natale's son Agostino, aged twenty-five, buried his father and fled to what was then West Germany. But in February 1984 he was stabbed a dozen times and then shot dead. His left cheek was slashed with a knife from ear to mouth, in a sign of contempt for the victim and possibly to punish him symbolically for threatening reprisals.

One of the last acts of the bloodletting of 1981–2 was particularly treacherous even by Cosa Nostra standards. At a Christmas lunch late in 1982, Riina and his informer

Michele Greco played host to some fifty men of honour from various Palermo families on Greco's Favarella estate, a sprawling property of orange, lemon and mandarin groves in Ciaculli.

Rosario 'The Terrorist' Riccobono, who headed the clan from Palermo's fashionable seaside resort of Partanna Mondello, was one of the most pampered guests. Riina had wanted to kill Riccobono five years previously in reprisal for his murder of a mobster close to himself. But Greco had persuaded Riina to bide his time, arguing that the murder of such a popular boss would only isolate the Corleonesi. Now that he was consolidating his position as Godfather, Riina could no longer tolerate a well-liked boss like Riccobono, who was head of the only Palermo family which Riina had failed to infiltrate.

At their Christmas lunch, Greco and Riina plied their cronies with plentiful food and wine laced with seasonal goodwill. The guests were thrown off guard. After the partying, they dozed off for their afternoon siestas. Three assassins, one of them Pino Greco, strangled Riccobono as he slept, while he whispered to him sotto voce: 'Saruzzu, a' to' storia finisci cca' ('Saro, your story ends here').[14]

Outside, eight other soldiers were killed in the same way, hunted down as they strolled through the estate after lunch. Several of Riina's men had hidden in the grounds during the feast, waiting to carry out his instructions. Some of the bodies were then dissolved in two 200-litre metal barrels filled with sulphuric acid. When rain diluted the mixture and made it less potent, one mobster was sent to buy some more acid. Several bodies were buried in the grounds of the Favarella estate.

It was to be Riina's night of the long knives. Their task accomplished at the estate, several men of honour drove off to hunt down members of Riccobono's family. Three members of rival clans were shot dead in a bar. Over the next forty-eight hours, more than a dozen others were murdered and many disappeared.

Pino Greco's own story ended just three years later, in the autumn of 1985. Formerly one of Riina's most faithful lieutenants, Pino Greco was idealised by the younger Mafiosi. They venerated him as a ruthless and infallible killer. Starry-eyed soldiers would swap tales of Greco's latest exploits and hope one day to emulate him.

One favourite story told how Greco murdered Alfio Ferlito, a member of a rival clan. Ferlito was in carabiniere custody at the time, and Greco staged his attack while officers were escorting Ferlito from one jail to another. On Palermo's busy ring road, Greco jumped on to the bonnet of the car in which Ferlito was travelling, a Mercedes, and brandished a shotgun. He let fire a hail of bullets through the windscreen, caring little that passers-by could see him. Ferlito, the three carabinieri escorting him, and the driver, were all shot dead. 'He acted that way to show he was ferocious and brave,' explained an informer.[15]

Pino Greco rose through the ranks to sit on the Palermo Cupola as the representative of several families. Greco antagonised Riina by not paying even lip-service to the old rules of Cosa Nostra, often sending his deputy to sit in for him at Cupola meetings. Riina first prepared the ground for Pino Greco's elimination by organising several murders in Greco's territory of Ciaculli, without first informing him. Then Riina accused Greco of failing to control events in his own territory.

Acting on a decision endorsed by the Cupola in secret, Riina sent two members of Greco's own Ciaculli family, whose dissatisfaction with their boss had been expertly fanned by Riina, to call at his house. As a hospitable and unsuspecting Greco prepared coffee for them, his friends shot him three times in the head. 'He had to die – he was out of his mind,' said one of the killers, Giuseppe Lucchese, as he stood above the body.

The Backlash

Greco's murder left Riina firmly in control of the Palermo Cupola. The Corleone peasants had completed their climb to the top of Cosa Nostra. An insignificant town in the hills south of Palermo had acquired world-wide fame because of Riina's exploits. In New York's Caffé Giardino on a muggy August day in 1987, the boss Joe Gambino was heard to tell a fellow mobster: 'Everything happens from Corleone and not from Palermo . . . not even a leaf can move if those from Corleone haven't been told.'[16]

Once he had eliminated his rivals, Riina swiftly over-hauled Cosa Nostra to establish a personal dictatorship. The composition of the Cupola at the time of Riina's arrest in January 1993 shows how successful his strategy was. Its members were either mobsters who had been his firm allies since the outset, or men he had used to worm his way into rival families.

Riina changed the organisation's strict hierarchical structure in which each family elected its bosses inde-pendently and ruled almost supreme over its own territory. Seeking to undermine the *capofamiglia*'s authority, he introduced a new figure. From the late 1980s onwards, he appointed 'ambassadors' to groups of families. Previously, a member of the ruling Cupola would have to go through a clan boss to hire the services of his men of honour. But Riina's ambassadors began to leapfrog the bosses, ordering soldiers to assist in a murder.

Riina had already flouted the established order by recruiting individuals whose entry he kept secret from other men of honour. Informer Giuseppe Marchese was initiated in 1980 (when he was only seventeen) on the personal orders of Riina, who kept his membership secret so that Marchese could be employed exclusively by Riina and his uncle Filippo Marchese, the boss of Palermo's Corso dei Mille clan. Marchese enjoyed the absolute trust of Riina for a period, and became one of the few to be told where Riina was hiding.

But Riina was to turn against his faithful lieutenant. In 1989 he ordered Marchese to kill his cellmate at the Ucciardone prison, Vincenzo Puccio (a representative of Ciaculli), because Puccio was plotting to have Riina murdered. Puccio's plan to help a group of inmates escape from the jail through a tunnel, and then launch a war against Riina, had been leaked to Riina by members of Puccio's own clan. Riina told Marchese not to worry about getting a heavy sentence for Puccio's murder because witnesses would say Marchese had acted in self-defence during a row.

At about 6 am one May morning, as Puccio slept, an obedient Marchese split his head open with a cast-iron frying pan. Two hours later, a brother of Puccio, Pietro, was shot dead in Palermo's Rotoli cemetery. Marchese's self-defence plea collapsed because the prosecutors argued that the two murders were obviously linked. Marchese had planned to say that he and his cellmate had quarrelled over what to watch on television − a soccer match or 'Colpo Grosso', a quiz game in which housewives strip to score extra points.

Marchese was given a life sentence. 'Riina made promises to me that he would intervene to fix the trial, but he did nothing. I didn't even get house arrest. So now here

I am,' said Marchese when he renounced Cosa Nostra.[17] In October 1993, Riina was sentenced to life in jail for ordering the murder.

Riina's treacherous methods prompted an unprecedented backlash. A wave of men of honour turned their backs on Cosa Nostra – to save their skins, and because they could not reconcile their idealised concept of the organisation with Riina's methods. By January 1993, the police had 270 Mafia turncoats on its books. The mobster Leonardo Messina explained why he decided to betray his oath of affiliation:

At the beginning I was fascinated by the values which such an affiliation gave me. I felt the sense of security which came from the respect of the rules which constituted the traditional essence of Cosa Nostra. But as time passed, however, I realised the traditional principles had been undermined in today's organisation. Understand me, Cosa Nostra has always been a bloodthirsty and criminal organisation, but in the past, a member risked being killed by another member only if he violated those rules of behaviour that had to govern the conduct of each man of honour.[18]

In July 1992, a month after the murder of judge Falcone, Riina's lawyer Nino Fileccia went on Italian state television to say his client had never left Sicily during his years on the run and moved at will on the island. It was a humiliating slap in the face for the Italian government, which had supposedly been hunting Riina for more than two decades.

The interview may also have been a last-ditch attempt by Riina to reaffirm his power, which had been weakened by the stream of defections from the Mafia. Riina's aim, according to the informer Mutolo, was 'to say that he is there and he can strike if he wants to: it's not as if, being abroad, he was dead.'[19]

If Mutolo was right, the interview was one of the Godfather's last gestures of defiance.

The Beast is Caged

On the morning of 15 January 1993 Riina was picked up by his driver outside a villa in a residential neighbourhood north of Palermo's city centre. Unknown to the two men, unmarked carabinieri police cars followed them through the sluggish rush-hour traffic. As Riina's Citroën slowed down to a crawl at a roundabout, the carabinieri forced the driver to stop.

When asked for his papers, Riina played for time, staring fixedly at the young carabiniere captain and saying: 'You're making a mistake, I'm not this Riina, I don't understand what you're saying.'[20] He handed over a false identity card. Worried that Riina's bodyguards might come to his rescue, the captain ordered him and his companion to lie face down on the ground, their hands behind their backs.

Then, with a blanket thrown over his head and several guns trained on him, the handcuffed Riina was rushed in a car to military headquarters. A trembling Riina, fearing he had been ambushed by rival mobsters, asked who his captors were. He relaxed when they identified themselves.

Shortly after arriving at the Bonsignore barracks opposite Palermo's Norman palace, Riina finally admitted his identity.

The sixty-two-year-old Godfather magnanimously praised his captors, in the style of a true Cosa Nostra boss. 'Yes, I am Salvatore Riina. *Bravi*, congratulations!'[21]

The Italian State had finally caught up with Riina after twenty-three years, six months and eight days. In Rome, the cabinet of Prime Minister Giuliano Amato burst into applause when the news broke. Some investigators were more cool in their reactions. The anti-Mafia magistrate Giovanni di Lello, who had worked with Falcone in Palermo, made the damning comment: 'It's happened now because they decided to look for him now.'

The supergrass Buscetta, whose family had been decimated by the Corleonesi, exulted at his enemy's capture: 'The arrest of the boss of bosses is the first miracle of 1993. It's a beautiful thing . . . I have lived with hatred for Riina. God is great, and today Riina will pay.'[22]

Riina was betrayed by one of the many men of honour who had rebelled against his dictatorship. It was his former driver, Baldassare di Maggio, who gave himself up to the carabinieri in northern Italy and decided to reveal Riina's probable whereabouts.

Di Maggio was flown to Palermo and told police whom to shadow. He also pointed out several buildings where he had gone in the past to pick up Riina. A week later, police showed Di Maggio a video one of their surveillance teams had recorded. He recognised the Godfather's wife Antonietta, and two of their children. The trap was set with the informer hiding in a van outside Riina's refuge.

In common with his predecessors as Godfathers such as Genco Russo and Don Calò Vizzini, Riina's appearance was an unassuming one. The photograph published by police after his arrest showed a sad, handcuffed old man with a paunch, a round face topped by greying hair, bags under the eyes and heavy jowls. He was dressed casually, wearing an open-necked shirt, a checked jacket and brown corduroy trousers but sported a smart green cashmere scarf.

The police made him pose for photographs below a portrait of General Dalla Chiesa, the man who had written a report on the Mafia of Riina's native Corleone in the aftermath of the Second World War. Riina turned to glance at the picture but lost none of his composure.

The contents of Riina's pockets and of his black leather 'Le Sac Georgette' handbag reflected his activities as God-father – a small Casio calculator for the businessman who dealt in millions of dollars, Polaroid snapshots of wife and children for the man of honour devoted to his family, and a picture of St Joseph, of the kind used in Mafia initiation rituals. Police also found a packet of cigars, some cash and a lucky charm.

The Palermo magistrate Guido lo Forte was among the first to question Riina after his arrest. 'Riina's manners are very controlled,' he said. 'He is courteous and has the aspect and the manner of an old country gentleman. He would stand up every time I walked into the room. But behind this simple exterior, I saw acute intelligence and a very high degree of self-control.'[23]

In his first court appearance, Riina cut a very different figure from the photograph of a boorish, uneducated peasant released by police shortly after his arrest. Flanked by six tall carabinieri who underlined his small stature, Riina breezed confidently into the courtroom near the Ucciardone jail, smiling and waving at the cameras before giving a quick ceremonial bow to the court.

Riina handled questions with verve, rarely giving straight answers and asking questions instead – a performance watched by eight million Italians when it was later broadcast on state television. Riina faced charges of ordering the murders of three Sicilian politicians – Mattarella, La Torre and Reina – between 1979 and 1982. 'I am not a member of the Mafia. I don't know what Cosa Nostra is. I only heard people talk about it on television and in the newspapers,' he said.

Riina asked the judge to forgive his Sicilian accent, saying: 'I am a poor illiterate . . . I'm only a working man, all home, work, family and church, as they say in our parts.' He said he was self-taught and had been given lessons by his schoolteacher wife. Asked if he was indeed the 'boss of all bosses' of Cosa Nostra, Riina said he earned his living working for a construction company which paid him 400,000 lire (£200) a week, on which he had to provide for a family of six.

But six months later police seized assets worth 60 million dollars held in the names of Riina, his relatives and his acolyte Provenzano. They included property, farms, apartments, bank deposits and holdings in eleven private companies. And in March 1994 magistrates confiscated another 96 million dollars' worth of assets including 165 villas and flats, 600 acres (240 hectares) of land, 60 cars and lorries, 317 commercial properties and stakes in 33 companies – all part of Riina's wealth.

Riina jumped at the chance to discredit the men of honour who had betrayed the Mafia. He also asked to confront his accusers directly in court – according to the informer Mutolo, this was a message to his men of honour, an appeal to them to retaliate against the turncoats.

RIINA: Your excellency . . . at one time there were anonymous letters. Now that the letters are thrown in the rubbish these informers have been created . . . These gentlemen informers are managed . . . can you tell me by whom? . . . Today they don't write letters, they talk and talk because one gets out of jail, gets money, wages, they get villas by accusing others . . .

PUBLIC PROSECUTOR LO FORTE: You said that all informers obey a common logic. So why should they accuse you, giving such precise accounts?

RIINA: I am the lightning rod of these people. I am 'The Beast', they unload everything on to me because they get more money, they are better believed . . .

LO FORTE: Why should they accuse somebody who is unknown?

RIINA: I am not an unknown because there are news-papers and television programmes which make me out as big and tall, not realising that Salvatore Riina is small and short.[24]

And he cheekily stood up to prove it.

There were other reasons for Riina's notoriety. In the mid-1980s Palermo maxi-trial, Riina was accused of fifty-two murders, only half a dozen fewer than the most bloodthirsty of the men of honour in the dock, Filippo Marchese. In his absence, the court found Riina guilty of thirty-nine murders, sentenced him to life in jail and fined him some £95,000.

Like Don Calò and Genco Russo before him, Riina had won respect within the criminal organisation by collecting a series of acquittals at trials in various Italian cities – in Bari for Mafia conspiracy, in Genoa for the murder of public prosecutor Scaglione, and in Reggio Calabria for the murder of judge Terranova.

By April 1995, however, Riina had nine life sen-tences to his name. His victims included Michele Reina, the Christian Democrat provincial secretary in 1979, Piersanti Mattarella, the Christian Democrat president of the regional government in 1980, and in 1982 both General Dalla Chiesa and Pio La Torre, the regional secretary of the

Communist Party. He was also found guilty of some thirty
or so killings, chiefly of rival men of honour, between 1981
and 1991. And prosecutors accused him, along with forty
other Mafiosi, of the murder of judge Giovanni Falcone.

Corleone Takes a Cautious Breath

The Godfather was put away in the Ucciardone. He was
allowed no physical contact. His lawyer Mario Grillo
complained that in eight months he had been able to
shake Riina's hand only once, and that was soon after
his arrest. 'Riina has been buried alive,' he said. 'He
is in a windowless cell, and surveillance cameras record
his every movement, even when he goes to the bathroom.
He is without doubt Italy's most closely guarded jailbird.'
But Grillo added: 'Despite these conditions, he is not
downcast.'

The prison authorities, fearing someone might attempt
to poison Riina, asked him to cook his own meals, and he
agreed, preparing his food in a corner of his cell. He was
later transferred to a specially-built 215-square-foot cell on
the island of Asinara off Sardinia. The sinister fascination
of the Godfather exercised a powerful attraction on some
members of the opposite sex, and Riina received dozens
of love letters in jail from Italy and abroad. But, true to
Cosa Nostra's code of fidelity, he took no notice of them
for the sake of his companion Ninetta.

The anti-Mafia investigators believe Riina's arrest has
not ended his rule as Godfather. It is standard practice
for a boss to appoint one of his lieutenants to act as his
deputy while he is in custody. Among those who may have

taken on that role is the brother of Riina's wife, Leoluca Bagarella. He was forty-nine at the time of Riina's arrest and had served thirteen years in jail on drug-trafficking and criminal conspiracy charges, but was freed before serving his full sentence in December 1990.

Bagarella went on the run after marrying the sister of the informer Marchese, in a wedding which was celebrated in the luxury Palermo hotel Villa Igea. Bagarella was thought to be the head of Riina's '*gruppo di fuoco*' ('firing group'), made up of some fifty men of honour from the Corleonese clan who have infiltrated different families, ready to eliminate potential rivals if the need arises.

If Bagarella did take a turn at the helm, it was a brief one. In June 1995, police acting on tip-offs from informers challenged him as he drove alone through Palermo. He first tried to speed away but soon became stuck in heavy traffic and gave himself up, shouting he was unarmed. Prosecutors accused him of playing a key role in Falcone's murder and of masterminding bomb attacks on churches and museums in Florence, Milan and Rome in 1993.

Another candidate for the post of Riina's deputy could be the thirty-four-year-old Pietro Aglieri, nicknamed '*ù signurino*' ('the little gentleman') because of his elegance. Aglieri, the head of the clan of Santa Maria del Gesù in Palermo, has been accused of a series of murders and of drug trafficking. Together with Riina and twenty-two other bosses, he is also charged with ordering the murder of the Euro-MP Salvo Lima in 1992.

Provenzano, a native of Riina's home town of Corleone, may also have stepped into Riina's shoes. Fifty-eight years old, he was sentenced to life in jail *in absentia* during the Palermo maxi-trial, but this was cut to ten years on appeal. Informers have said he took care of Cosa Nostra's financial affairs, but for several years reports suggested he might have been murdered. In April 1994, however, Provenzano quashed these rumours after more than twenty years on the run. He sent a handwritten letter by registered post to a court in Palermo, naming two lawyers to defend him against charges of murdering a fellow-mobster. Unable to resist a touch of humour, he sent his missive in the name of a specialist in nervous illnesses, who lived only yards away from Palermo's Ucciardone jail.

Riina's home town of Corleone reacted with mixed feelings to the news that its most famous son no longer freely walked the streets. The local monthly newspaper *Città nuove* (*New Towns*), which had taken a courageous anti-Mafia stand, headlined its editorial: 'Hopes and fears'. The article ran:

> Once more we have seen two Corleones, the democratic and civilised one which has rejoiced, and that which is subservient or accomplice to the Mafia . . . We are with the first . . . The 'silence' of so many old people who have lived with the Mafia for years and who remember with terror the dozens of people killed in the 1960s is understandable. We understand the concerns of so many housewives, brought up in the Mafioso sub-culture, who confusedly ask themselves: 'Who will protect us now?' We answer only that the democratic institutions of the State and our clear consciences must protect us.[25]

The day after Riina's arrest, Captain Francesco Iaccono, commander of the carabinieri in Corleone, knocked at the door of the house from which Riina's wife Antonietta had disappeared nineteen years earlier. Iaccono, who has the job Dalla Chiesa held during the late 1940s, was acting on a warrant to search the house for Antonietta's brother Leoluca Bagarella.

'When we opened the door we found Riina's wife and their children,' says Iaccono. 'They had only just come back. She was not very well dressed, with a brown skirt of cheap material and a dark sweater. We asked her a few questions and she attacked the Mafia informers, saying her husband was a victim. She said: "He is a good man, I would wish it upon all women to have a husband like mine."'[26]

Antonietta's return was seen as a sign that Riina remains in command. She could visit and talk to him freely in jail, and could obviously be used as a go-between relaying messages to Riina's mobsters. For the town of Corleone, Salvatore Riina was still very much alive, despite his arrest. The locals' fears were understandable. In an account given before Riina was caught, the supergrass Antonino Calderone shows how much power the Godfather had. But he also highlights the price that Riina had to pay. It could well serve as an epitaph:

Today Totò Riina is up high, at the top of the mountain. Tomorrow he could find himself on the ground, in the dust, shot at and with his head eaten by dogs . . . And yet Riina is as powerful as Jesus Christ because he has supreme power. He decides on a man's life. With a nod he can take away or spare the life of anyone. He is above everybody. But at the same time he is reduced to a miserable condition because he cannot go for a walk, he cannot move, he cannot sleep, he cannot sit in a garden of orange trees in the evening and enjoy the cool air and the smell of blossom . . . He is submerged in the terror of being murdered. And when he dies and looks back on it all, what can someone like him say he had? He will see a life always on the run, a life in hiding, always alone. An existence of tension and fear, a life of tragedy.[27]

6

THE FRIENDS OF
THE FRIENDS

Uncle Giulio

Thousands of 'friends' protected Riina during the years
he spent establishing his dictatorship over Cosa Nostra.
Recent testimony by several supergrasses has exposed the
extent to which his empire penetrated the Italian State. The
secret service tipped him off when police were about to
raid his hide-out, leading politicians helped him to 'adjust'
verdicts when his soldiers were in the dock, a Supreme
Court judge overturned unfavourable sentences and the
mayor of Palermo allowed himself to be manipulated by
the clans. Even the Roman Catholic Church was for a
long period at best complacent towards the Mafia, with
many priests giving refuge in their churches to men of
honour.

The linchpin between Riina's 'state within a State' and
its Roman counterpart, according to the informers, was

none other than the most powerful figure in post-war Italian politics, the Christian Democrat statesman Giulio Andreotti. The men of honour knew him simply as 'Zu' Giulio' ('Uncle Giulio'). It was an affectionate nickname for a man Cosa Nostra saw as its miracle-worker in Rome, the politician Mafia bosses would turn to as a last resort when facing the threat of a life sentence.

Seven times Prime Minister, thirty-three times minister, Andreotti had served in every parliament since the war and held office on and off since he was twenty-eight. He had held key portfolios including Defence, the Interior, Finance, the Budget, the Treasury, Industry and Foreign Affairs. Among the most abiding of European statesmen, Andreotti had been in government at the time of Stalin, de Gaulle and Truman, and was still Prime Minister of Italy in April 1992 at the age of seventy-three. A devout Catholic who attends mass early every morning, he was for decades the Christian Democrat politician closest to the Vatican, befriending popes and archbishops. Henry Kissinger paid tribute to him as no less than 'the leader who has made the biggest contribution to the post-war history of his country'.

A bespectacled, stooping figure with hunched shoulders and protruding ears, he was dubbed 'Beelzebub' by his enemies. Over the years, a myriad of caricatures of him gave pride of place to the devil's horns and tail. In the country that gave the world Machiavelli, Andreotti was renowned for his cunning, and embodied Italy's Byzantine political system. He was also notorious for his sharp wit and typically Roman cynicism. 'Power wearies only those who don't possess it' was the most quoted of his caustic one-liners, which he collected in a best-selling anthology.

In May 1992, when he was hoping to crown his distinguished career with the one post he had never held –

President of the Republic – the supergrasses shattered the career of the senator-for-life. Their evidence is a detailed account of how Cosa Nostra has not only infiltrated the Italian State, but in many ways has made pawns of even its most eminent statesmen.

No fewer than eight ex-Mafiosi lined up to denounce Andreotti as 'the most powerful political patron of the Mafia'.[1] They charged that the man who had seven times led the West's fifth industrial power had had secret meetings with Riina and several other bosses, and had helped to 'adjust' Mafia trials. They also accused him of using the criminal organisation to establish his Sicilian electoral power-base and to murder the courageous carabiniere General Dalla Chiesa (the hero of Italy's victory over terrorism and appointed to fight Cosa Nostra), and a journalist who threatened his political career.

Andreotti's first reaction to the plethora of allegations was embittered. 'I am deeply distressed but not surprised. I was waiting for their vendetta and in a certain sense it is better this way than with a *lupara*,' he said shortly after the Palermo magistrates warned him he was under investigation. He denied all the charges.

Andreotti's secret association with Cosa Nostra is alleged to have spanned nearly a decade and a half from the late 1970s until 1992, a year before the supergrasses made their claims public. At the heart of their accusations was Andreotti's alliance with Sicily's Christian Democrat overlord, the former Palermo mayor Salvo Lima. This would have been an alliance worth hundreds of thousands of votes to Andreotti. Lima, who also served as a deputy in the Rome parliament before moving on to the European parliament, was allegedly not only Andreotti's viceroy in Sicily but also his link with Cosa Nostra – in an island where the secret society held sway over much of the electorate.

The supergrasses testified that Lima was himself a Mafioso, 'very close to the men of honour, their inter-mediary with the Honourable Andreotti for the needs of the Sicilian Mafia'.[2] In 1979, according to the informer Francesco Marino Mannoia, Lima was present at one of Andreotti's first meetings with the Palermo bosses, in a hunting reserve in Sicily. At the time, Andreotti had just left prime ministerial office and was chairman of the parliamentary foreign affairs committee.

In the hunting reserve he allegedly met Stefano Bontate, then one of the most powerful of the Sicilian capital's Mafioso patriarchs, and the Christian Democrat cousins Nino and Ignazio Salvo – two men of honour who enjoyed a monopoly on tax collection in Sicily. Andreotti by no means always held the upper hand in his relations with the Mafia. It was at this first meeting that Bontate complained to him about the behaviour of the Christian Democrat Piersanti Mattarella, president of the Sicilian regional government, who had at first enlisted the Mafiosi's electoral support but then sought to distance himself from Bontate's clan.

A few months later, after Mattarella had been murdered by the Palermo clans, Andreotti returned to seek an expla-nation for the killing. In a heated exchange punctuated by shouts, Bontate threatened: 'It is we who command in Sicily, and if you don't want to completely wipe out the [Christian Democrats], you must do as we say. Otherwise we shall withdraw the votes not only from Sicily, but also from Reggio Calabria and the whole of southern Italy. You can count only on the votes of the north.'[3]

Andreotti may well have been relieved when Bontate fell from grace and was subsequently eliminated in the purges spearheaded by the Corleonesi clan. It was alleged that he subsequently wove much closer ties with an even more powerful boss, the Godfather Salvatore Riina, no less. In 1987, Riina was anxious to ensure a favourable outcome to the maxi-trial of several hundred Mafiosi taking place in Palermo. The informer Baldassare di Maggio, who was later to deliver Riina to the police, accompanied the Godfather to Ignazio Salvo's Palermo home where Andreotti, then Italy's foreign minister, was waiting. According to the supergrass, Godfather and ex-prime minister were already acquainted:

> When we arrived, the people present got up and greeted us. I shook hands with the two deputies and kissed Ignazio Salvo . . . Riina, however, greeted all three with a kiss . . . Riina insisted to me that the event must stay absolutely secret. He made the gesture of someone locking a door with a key . . . I interpreted the kiss that the Hon. Andreotti and the Hon. Lima exchanged with Salvatore Riina as a mark of respect 'as long as things go well'. My impression was that the three already knew each other.[4]

Other supergrasses have claimed that Riina in the late 1980s sought to use Andreotti as an intermediary to influence the pinnacle of Italy's judicial system, the Supreme Court in Rome. This time, Riina's objective was the acquittal by the court of the hundreds of Mafiosi who had been given heavy sentences, nineteen of them for life, at the Palermo maxi-trial.

Riina's lieutenants were so confident his manoeuvre would succeed that they repeatedly reassured those Mafiosi worried about the Supreme Court's impending verdict. 'No problem, everything has been arranged,' the bosses told Messina, who later turned informer and became the first to dare to accuse Andreotti.[5] 'Uncle Giulio', they said, his viceroy Lima and even a Supreme Court judge, Corrado

Carnevale, had thought of everything and had given Cosa Nostra watertight guarantees. Carnevale, nicknamed 'sentence-killer' because of the many Mafiosi convictions he managed to overturn, 'constituted a guarantee not just because of his ideas relating to the law [but] also because it was said he could be manipulated'.[6]

Riina's attempt failed and despite his lieutenants' confident forecasts, the Supreme Court rejected the men of honour's appeals. But the Palermo magistrates investigating Andreotti's links with the Mafia said the affair highlighted the existing 'pact of peaceful coexistence and exchange of favours between Cosa Nostra and part of the political world, of which Andreotti's faction [within the Christian Democrats] was an essential component'.[7] The magistrates early in 1993 accordingly demanded that Andreotti's parliamentary immunity be lifted so that he could be investigated on suspicion of Mafia conspiracy.

There was worse to come. The supergrasses shortly afterwards alleged that Andreotti had asked Cosa Nostra to murder General Dalla Chiesa. The leader of the successful battle against the terrorist Red Brigades in the 1970s, Dalla Chiesa was sent as civil governor to Palermo in 1982 to lead the fight against the Mafia. That September, only four months after he had arrived in Sicily, Dalla Chiesa, his wife and their only bodyguard died in a hail of bullets when they were ambushed in Palermo.

Supergrasses have alleged that Dalla Chiesa was murdered on Andreotti's orders because he knew too much about political manoeuvres to prevent the possible release of the former Christian Democrat Prime Minister Aldo Moro, who had been kidnapped by the Red Brigades in March 1978. 'The General had become too much of a nuisance,' explained Buscetta.[8] Leading figures of Moro's party had been told where the former premier was being held but did nothing to save him, because he had begun to turn against them in letters sent during his fifty-five days in captivity. Nearly three months after the Red Brigades had seized him and killed his five bodyguards, Moro was found dead in the back of a Renault Five in Rome's historic centre. His captors had fired five bullets into him.

This was not the first time Andreotti had been accused of using the Mafia to remove someone who threatened his political future. In 1979, three years before Dalla Chiesa's murder, the journalist Mino Pecorelli was shot dead outside the offices of his small magazine in Rome. The magazine specialised in peddling inside information on politics and the security services, and Pecorelli also knew too much about Aldo Moro's mysterious death. Informers said Pecorelli's killing was organised with the help of the Salvo cousins, friends of Andreotti and members of Cosa Nostra.

According to the supergrasses, Andreotti gradually became estranged from his Mafia contacts – so much so that the bosses turned against him. In summer 1992, Mafiosi including Bagarella, Riina's brother-in-law, met at a hide-out in Palermo. Bagarella told his acolytes that Andreotti should be killed because he 'no longer has either the strength or the will' to obstruct the government's anti-Mafia measures. Cosa Nostra tried to draw up a plan for an attempt on Andreotti's life, but gave up because he was too well protected and it was not as strongly implanted in Rome, where Andreotti lived, as in Palermo. Instead, the Mafiosi decided to try and murder one of Andreotti's two sons. But this idea was also later cast aside.[9]

The host of accusations were far more serious than any of the clouds that had previously overshadowed Andreotti

during his fifty-year career. On previous occasions, magistrates had no fewer than twenty-six times sought to have
his parliamentary immunity lifted so that they could pursue
their investigations against him on suspicion of corruption
and links with shady financiers, but their requests were
turned down every time.

In May 1993, shortly after the Palermo magistrates
requested his immunity be lifted on suspicion of Mafia
ties, Andreotti called a news conference at the foreign
press club in Rome hoping no doubt to salvage what he
could of his battered image abroad. He had lost little
of his caustic humour, making several witticisms which
caused laughter among his tense audience. Only once did
he betray some nervousness, when he lost his patience with
a journalist who listed the names of Mafiosi associated with
his Christian Democrat Party.

Denying all the charges, Andreotti said he was the
victim of a smear campaign designed to punish him for
the crackdowns he had initiated on the Mafia while in
government. 'Objectively there is a conspiracy when I
see that a whole series of elements are woven together
without a shred of evidence . . . [When turncoats] say
I supposedly went to the home of [Ignazio] Salvo, who
was then under house arrest and therefore under police
guard, to meet Totò Riina and kiss him, then I ask myself
. . . if there is not someone who has hatched all this,'
he said.[10] On the allegation that Bontate had given him
a dressing-down, Andreotti quipped: 'I am quite humble,
but I would never have allowed the Mafia to tell me that
they were in charge.'

Summoned earlier by the Senate panel due to rec-
ommend whether or not his immunity should be lifted,
Andreotti had denied ever having met either the Salvo
cousins, Bontate or any other Mafia boss. He hit back at

the magistrates, accusing them of 'professional dishonesty' and 'working in a sinister way'. He told the panel: 'We cannot allow the magistrature to govern.' The Senate lifted Andreotti's immunity from prosecution in July 1993 – the former premier had himself requested this, saying he wanted an opportunity to clear his name. The Palermo magistrates were given the green light to pursue their investigations of a man who was alleged to have 'made a positive contribution to the defence of the interests of [Cosa Nostra] and to the achievement of its aims'.[11] In March 1995 Andreotti was ordered to stand trial after the magistrates hardened the charges against the statesman in a 90,000-page dossier containing allegations from association with the Mafia to full membership of the organisation.

A Life in Cosa Nostra's Service

On the morning of 12 March 1992 the former Palermo mayor Salvo Lima set out from his home in a leafy neighbourhood of ornate Art Nouveau villas once typical of the Sicilian capital. Two members of the Euro-MP's political faction accompanied him as he drove towards the nearby Palace Hotel, where they were due to make final arrangements for a rally by Andreotti ahead of general elections.

A powerful motorcycle suddenly drew up level with Lima's car. A gunman riding pillion shot him in the chest. Lima stopped the car and tried to run away. 'They're coming back!' he shouted as he fought to free his coat, which was caught in the car door. Lima managed to wrench it free, but the gunman caught up with him and shot him at point-blank range through the head from behind. Lima collapsed on the pavement beside a rubbish bin.

In killing Lima, Cosa Nostra had decided to bite the hand that fed it. 'Either you stick to our understanding or we kill both you and your family,' Riina had warned Lima.[12] Andreotti's plenipotentiary, and the most powerful politician in western Sicily, Lima paid for his failure to deliver what he and Andreotti together had allegedly promised – the acquittal by the Supreme Court of the hundreds of Mafiosi sentenced in the mid-1980s Palermo maxi-trial. Two months previously, the court had not only rejected the mobsters' appeals but had also accepted the testimony of Buscetta that all the most serious murders of the Mafia wars had been decided by the Cupola, thus ruining any prospects of lighter sentences for the convicted bosses.

Lima served as a Christian Democrat deputy in three Rome legislatures, was elected three times to the European parliament, and served eight years as mayor of Palermo. His career epitomises how the Mafia uses politicians to assert its control over the territory and safeguard its interests, showing no hesitation in seeking to manipulate a leading statesman like Andreotti. Lima was the guarantor of the co-existence of Cosa Nostra and the Italian State which the latter had tacitly accepted in Sicily.

It was during his years as mayor of Palermo, from 1958 to 1963 and again from 1965 to 1966, that Lima made his greatest contribution to Cosa Nostra's accumulation of power and wealth. He had started his political career as the organiser of sports events staged by the Palermo branch of the Christian Democrats. At the age of twenty-eight, he became the borough surveyor of the capital, and he was elected mayor for the first time only two years later. Lima launched an unprecedented building boom in the Sicilian capital, which was later dubbed 'The Sack of Palermo'. He fathered a pharaonic plan to extend Palermo northwards – into the domain of the local boss Angelo la Barbera, and therefore to the latter's benefit. As a result, the urbanisation of Palermo progressed at a frenetic pace. Bulldozers razed avenues of Art Nouveau villas. Huge blocks of flats were erected to house thousands of families on land where little or no provision had been made for adequate sanitation, and where people often had to manage without street-lighting or services such as local shops or bus routes. In the decade from 1951 to 1961, the number of residents in Palermo jumped by a hundred thousand.

The Mafia was involved in this rewarding enterprise from the outset. It concluded a pact with Lima and with construction firms which became a model for many areas of the Mezzogiorno. Lima affirmed himself as the ultimate arbiter of relations between the Mafia and political interests. He monopolised and developed the existing system of political patronage, under which various Christian Democrat notables had until then granted favours (such as a public works contract) to local entrepreneurs or Mafia bosses in exchange for votes, money or other services. Even the wholesale food markets of Palermo were placed under Mafia 'protection'. Cosa Nostra played a big role in the building boom as shady entrepreneurs bought land adjacent to the city perimeter and stifled the most luxuriant part of the 'Golden Shell' bay with huge blocks of flats. Of the 4,000 building licences granted by the city hall in 1956–63, 2,500 went to just three individuals who were strawmen for companies controlled by Cosa Nostra – a bricklayer and two retired workers.

As early as the 1960s, Lima's ties with the Mafia were investigated by Dalla Chiesa, who was then a carabiniere colonel. Lima's name was mentioned 162 times in reports

published by the Rome parliament's first anti-Mafia commission. But this did nothing to slow his political career.
The boss La Barbera helped Lima to get elected mayor in
1958, and was in charge of his personal security. Much
later, the informer Marino Mannoia revealed that Lima
had several times met the patriarch Stefano Bontate in
a Palermo bar, the Baby Luna, on days when it was
closed to the public.[13] Palermo's public prosecutor, Pietro
Giammanco, quietly shelved the testimony because, he
explained, it did not refer to the content of the conversations. After Bontate's death, Lima swiftly became
a political reference point for other bosses of Cosa Nostra,
including Riina.

Because of Lima's importance, only a few privileged
Mafiosi were allowed to approach him. Those who were
given the Cupola's permission to do so turned to him
for a host of favours, big and small. The supergrass
Calderone told how he once met Lima in Rome to ask
for the transfer from Catania of the city's over-zealous
police chief. An obliging Lima passed on the request.[14]
The informer Buscetta, who was introduced to Lima by
the latter's father (a Palermo man of honour), said he and
Lima went to see an opera at the Sicilian capital's Teatro
Massimo together. Lima even sent him tickets for the whole
season as a gift.[15]

In return for his valuable co-operation, Cosa Nostra
swung its electoral clout behind Lima, enabling him
to score some impressive performances. His political
standing was so high that he was invited to take part
as mayor of Palermo in John F. Kennedy's presidential
election campaign. After he had served a second term as
mayor, he was triumphantly elected to the Rome parliament
in 1968. Although he had made no campaign speeches,
he was elected with almost 80,000 votes — a classic

sign of Mafia support. He was elected to the European parliament in 1979, but there was no loosening of his ties with the electorate or of his involvement in Sicilian affairs. In 1984 he was re-elected to the European parliament, with 246,000 voters giving him first preference under the Italian system, yet another avalanche of votes.

The slaughter of Lima revolutionised Cosa Nostra's relations with State institutions. He was killed because he symbolised a political class which, after a long-standing relationship of peaceful coexistence and exchange of favours, no longer safeguarded the Mafia's interests. His murder, said the anti-Mafia commission, carried a grave message: 'Killing the old mediators, either to punish them, or because they are no longer needed, is a terrible admonition to all the politicians who have been close to Cosa Nostra. After such murders, relations between the Mafia and politicians cannot be taken for granted.'[16]

Cosa Nostra on the Campaign Trail

Controversies over leading figures such as Lima and Andreotti are only the tip of the iceberg as far as the Mafia's infiltration of the State is concerned. The organisation has long penetrated Sicilian, and Italian, public life. This fifth column is a precondition for the Mafia state's political strategy – the occupation and governing of the territory, to be carried out in competition with the legitimate authorities. The relationship between the Mafia on the one hand and political forces and institutions on the other make it not just a criminal organisation but also an instrument of corruption and conditioning of society.

Ever since fledgling Mafiosi rigged a plebiscite on Italian unification in the novel *The Leopard* ('Voting, 512; Yes, 512; No, zero'),[17] the ballot-box – which gives life to the institutions of the State – has been at the root of this infiltration.

One candidate was particularly blunt in his appeal for Mafioso electoral support. Vittorio Orlando, who had as Prime Minister represented Italy at the Congress of Versailles following the First World War, ran for a seat in the poor and Mafia-infested town of Partinico near Palermo in 1948. The posters he put up bore the slogan: 'Vote Orlando, The Friend of The Friends'. He was elected. Some years later, a Sicilian historian, Virgilio Titone, professor at Palermo University, suggested that all elections should be suspended in western Sicily (its traditional fiefdom) for at least ten years as an effective remedy to fight against the Mafia. He argued that the Mafia could exist only in a democratic-liberal political system. The professor's advice went unheeded.

Before the 1992 general elections, the Mafia was estimated to be the fourth political force in southern Italy. A survey by an authoritative business magazine showed that the clans directly controlled more than a million votes and influenced a total of almost six million voters. In Palermo alone, a city of 600,000 residents, some 250,000 votes were tainted.[18] The electoral weight of a single Mafia family can be considerable, as the supergrass Calderone explained:

The politicians have always come to look for us because we have a lot, a huge amount of votes at our disposal. To get an idea of how much weight the Mafia has in elections, just think of the family of Santa Maria del Gesù (in Palermo), a family of 200 members. It's a terrifying strike force, especially if you consider that each man of honour can dispose of another 40–50 friends and relatives. There are between 1,500 and 2,000 men of honour in the province of Palermo. Multiply that by 50 and you get a fat bundle of 75,000–100,000 votes to steer towards friendly parties and candidates.[19]

Cosa Nostra has no particular political ideology. It does not make abstractly ideal or disinterested choices but acts according to its own interests. It is not uncommon for the organisation to back candidates from different parties at the same time in a single election, given that its aim is simply to profit from pacts with successful candidates. Since the war the Mafia has been chiefly liberal, separatist and Christian Democrat.

The informer Messina, who participated in various electoral campaigns, has revealed how the Mafia endorsed candidates. Clan bosses whose dominions fall within a given constituency hold a meeting, a kind of 'convention', to hear a candidate recommended to them by their superiors at regional level. The politician presents his manifesto, and lists what he would do for the clans if elected. If the hearing is successful, the candidate gives each of the bosses sums of money of between 5 and 30 million lire (£2,500 and £15,000).[20]

Almost invariably the Christian Democrats, a popular conservative movement backed by the Roman Catholic Church and for four decades the biggest party in Sicily, attracted the most support from Cosa Nostra. 'It was the members of the party who had most protected the Mafia,' explained the informer Sinagra.[21] 'The basic rule was that electoral propaganda for the Communists and the Fascists was banned. But we were allowed to vote occasionally for other parties, but only on a personal basis, in return for personal favours, and always without any propaganda.'

The Mafia's ties with the Christian Democrats were dictated by necessity. Since the Second World War there have been some fifty different governments in Italy, based on various coalitions, but in effect they were with a few exceptions merely cabinet reshuffles. The Christian Democrats always dominated. Party men, especially in the South, were the backbone of a system in which the structure of society and the economy was governed by an exchange of favours for political loyalty. The party's 1992 election manifesto boasted it had helped secure 200 trillion lire (£100 billion) in government funds for the South over the last forty years. Much of that money had gone into Mafia pockets as payment for the votes needed to keep the Christian Democrats in power.

When in 1987 the clans of Palermo chose to show their displeasure with the Christian Democrats, who had failed to block anti-Mafia investigations by magistrates in the capital, the effects were impressive. Party support crumbled overnight. On the eve of the June general elections, the clans spread the word that voters should rally behind the Socialists, who had adopted a critical stance towards the magistrates. In the neighbourhood of Ciaculli, home to Michele Greco, the inhabitants showed themselves to be model voters, turning out en masse to rally behind the Socialists, whose count leaped from 5.6 to 23.5 per cent of the vote. At the same time, they delivered a stinging rebuke to the Christian Democrats, whose score plummeted from 62 to 38.8 per cent. Shortly after the results were announced, the surprised magistrates asked the police to investigate.

By expertly manipulating the electoral system, Cosa Nostra exercised control over the formation not only of local councils but also of provincial councils, regional assemblies and the Rome parliament. Until the introduction of a new system in the April 1992 general elections, voters were ordered to rank Cosa Nostra's chosen candidates on their ballot papers and to follow precise instructions. Post-war proportional representation allowed voters to choose up to four candidates from a given party, ranking them in order of preference. In many areas of Sicily, Cosa Nostra imposed a particular ranking on voters and ensured that its wishes were respected by checking the ballot papers after the vote. Some voters were ordered to write down the full names of the candidates, others just the surname, and yet others the number allocated to the politicians. During the public vote-tallying, the clan's emissaries would identify anyone who had failed to obey their instructions.

Another ingenious and far simpler tactic was for the Mafioso boss to steal a blank ballot paper before the vote and fill it in himself. The paper is passed on to a voter, who goes to the polling station and takes another ballot paper from the returning officer. But he discreetly keeps the new form and votes with the ballot filled in by the clans. The Mafioso fills in the new blank form and the procedure starts again. This tactic survived the change to a first-past-the-post electoral system in early 1992.

Those who dared to rebel against the imposition of the Mafia line were few and far between, and there was rarely any call for intimidatory violence. Bribes helped. In Catania in the run-up to 1991 regional elections, voters were encouraged to obey the clans' instructions with a host of rewards – money, petrol vouchers, theatre tickets, even food parcels. The latter were made up of 5 kilos of pasta, 2 litres of olive oil, a 5,000-lire note, and a 'voting suggestion'.[22]

Playing out its traditional role as a mediator, the Mafia

tells people that if they vote for a particular candidate they will get something in return – possibly a job – and that the Mafia will guarantee that this actually happens. People are more likely to believe a mobster promising a favour than a politician. 'I act without motives; whoever asks me a favour, I think of granting it because nature commands me,' the Godfather Genco Russo once told an interviewer. 'People ask how they should vote because they feel the duty to ask advice, to show a sense of gratitude, of recognition; they feel in the dark and want to follow those who did them good.'[23]

In return for Mafia support, politicians are expected to pay the clans money, help them win public contracts, intervene to 'adjust' Mafiosi trials or find jobs for anyone recommended by the clans. According to the anti-Mafia commission, 90 per cent of the 8,887 people taken on by the Sicilian regional government in 1943–63 were given jobs on the basis of personal recommendations and not after passing tests.[24]

Politicians can become members of Cosa Nostra, but only if they have the requisite qualities for a man of honour. If they are not members of the Mafia, they count for very little. 'Inside Cosa Nostra there's a strong mistrust of them, because they are faithless, they don't keep their promises, they always pull a fast one. They are people without principles,' the informer Calderone sniffed.[25]

It is always the Mafiosi who give orders to the politicians, never the other way round. 'The Mafia doesn't make alliances with anyone,' judge Falcone told the author. 'It doesn't seal pacts, it doesn't sign treaties. What it does is to use people, it only looks after its own interests. If these happen to converge with those of other organisations, or of other people, it uses them, even if they are politicians.'[26]

Successful but ungrateful candidates who later turn their backs on Cosa Nostra are punished. The informer Messina, who claims to have controlled 500 votes in the small town of San Cataldo, once slapped a regional councillor in the face because he had failed to stick to his campaign pledges and had refused to receive the local boss at his home.[27]

The Spider's Web

The manipulation of politicians is vital to Cosa Nostra because it can use them as intermediaries with corrupt policemen, secret service agents or investigating magistrates. However, Cosa Nostra usually turns to politicians as a last resort when it has no other channel at its disposal, because politicians must then in turn appeal to others – the Mafia prefers to make its requests as direct as possible. Just as in the late nineteenth century the Sicilian landowners guaranteed the impunity of their Mafioso managers and private armies (the *gabellotti* and *campieri*), so today vast sections of society cover for the mobsters – including part of the supposedly anti-Mafia front. Judges acquit Mafiosi for mere formalities, lawyers submit false evidence, doctors cure mobsters' wounds without telling the authorities, and priests give refuge to fugitives. Calderone called it a spider's web of complicity:

Cosa Nostra's ruse has always been to be the association of men of honour, something secret and for the few, but to remain at the same time linked to normal life, to people's professions and trades. There are all sorts inside the Mafia. Apart from judges and policemen, there are people of all kinds, infiltrated in every corner of society. The Mafioso is like a spider. He spins spiders' webs of friendships, acquaintances and obligations.[28]

Few have been as skilful as Riina. He allegedly succeeded in entangling not only Andreotti and Lima, but also Bruno Contrada, the number three in Italy's civilian secret services (SISDE). Contrada, according to evidence given by four informers, was the Mafia's highest-placed spy and passed on to Riina and other bosses such as Stefano Bontate and Michele Greco classified information about investigations, holding clandestine meetings with them.

News of Contrada's arrest, and the weight of the accusations against Contrada, sparked widespread outrage because of his thirty-five-year career in some of the most sensitive anti-Mafia agencies and his role in investigating some of Palermo's most notorious murders. Contrada had headed the SISDE in western Sicily, and was the service's deputy director when he was arrested on Christmas Eve 1992. He had previously headed Palermo's flying squad and had served as chief of staff to the national anti-Mafia High Commissioner. Contrada could also boast of his membership of a para-religious chivalrous order, the Knights of the Holy Sepulchre, based in Monreale outside Palermo. Founded in 1209 at the time of the crusades, it has turned into a kind of secret masonic lodge whose members – Mafia bosses, politicians, businessmen, magistrates, churchmen – form a sinister network.

According to the informer Marchese, Contrada tipped off Cosa Nostra in early 1981 that the police were about to raid Riina's refuge. Marchese rushed to the villa to warn Riina, who got into his white Mercedes with his family and sped away.[29] On another occasion, Contrada allegedly blocked a police raid in 1985 on a hotel in the resort of Cefalù on Sicily's north coast, where Riina was attending a wedding reception. Several years earlier, the Palermo boss Saro Riccobono boasted of his relationship with Contrada to his fellow-Mafioso Gaspare Mutolo: 'Contrada is our man. If the police arrest you, call him, and if they take you to the police station, say that he knows about you.'[30] To his irritation, the Mafiosi gave Riccobono the nickname '*sbirro*' (a pejorative local word for 'policeman') because of his friendship with Contrada.

Already in 1980 the Palermo police chief Vincenzo Immordino had written a note saying Contrada was doing precious little investigative work on crimes whether big or small, and had taken away from him an investigation into a suspected Mafioso drug-trafficker, Rosario Spatola. The police chief went as far as to keep Contrada in the dark when Spatola's men were rounded up. But Contrada's career progressed without hindrance, and it was twelve years before he was arrested.

On occasions when Contrada's protection failed to prevent the arrests of Riina's henchmen, the Godfather had another card up his sleeve. This ace was the Supreme Court judge on whom the Mafiosi had counted for their acquittal after the Palermo maxi-trial. Judge Corrado Carnevale was a Sicilian whom Cosa Nostra trusted as 'a very intelligent person, whom we greatly admired,' according to the supergrass Mutolo. 'We thought Carnevale was subtle and cunning . . . For us, Carnevale in the Supreme Court was a trademark and a guarantee.'[31] Another informer alleged that Carnevale was a friend of the Mafioso boss Francesco Madonia, of Vallellunga in central Sicily.[32] The judge said he did not know Madonia and was not aware of the accusations against him.

In the seven years before an official investigation was launched in September 1992, the Supreme Court judge had quashed or reduced sentences on hundreds of Mafiosi. His most notorious verdict (in June 1992) overturned the convictions of four Cupola bosses, one of whom was Michele Greco, and denied that Cosa Nostra was a single, tight-knit structure grouping various clans. Again and again, the leniency of his judgments was put down to either magistrates' insignificant procedural errors or the assumption that the word of supergrasses alone was not enough to convict a suspect.

Apart from freeing dozens of Mafiosi, such acquittals discouraged many leading informers from revealing all they knew to the authorities. There was little point, protested Buscetta:

> Whether the accused is condemned or not doesn't interest me, but what does concern me is when a court manages to pass sentence and then the trial goes to Rome and we're told the trial is to start from scratch again. In cases where I don't understand anything, I ask: 'What is happening? Has anything new happened?'. The answer is that the Italian State doesn't want to fight the Mafia. That is my humble opinion.[33]

If the informers' evidence is to be believed, Carnevale was not alone in the Italian judiciary in defending the interests of Cosa Nostra. In October 1993 five senior Sicilian judges were officially notified that they were under investigation over allegations of Mafia association. They included Giuseppe Prinzivalli, who presided over a Palermo court which acquitted eighty Mafiosi, including Riina and Greco, at a 1989 mass trial. Another of those under investigation, the former Palermo appeals court judge Pasquale Barreca, was lambasted in 1991 by the then Justice Minister Claudio Martelli after the escape of a clan boss he had allowed out of prison for hospital treatment. A few days later, it emerged that informers had named four other judges, accusing them of ties to Cosa Nostra – Palermo's chief public prosecutor Pietro Giammanco, his predecessor, the president of the Palermo appeals court, and a former investigating magistrate.

Cosa Nostra has a long history of harnessing members of the judiciary to its cause. When the Godfather Vizzini died, Giuseppe Guido lo Schiavo, attorney-general in the Supreme Court, wrote this heartfelt tribute in a legal periodical:

> It has been said that the Mafia despise the police and the magistracy, but this is incorrect. The Mafia has always had respect for the magistracy and for justice; it has submitted to its sentences, and has not obstructed the judge in his work. In the pursuit of bandits and outlaws . . . it has openly sided with the forces of law and order . . . Today Don Calogero Vizzini's successor is making his reputation, and in time he will succeed to his predecessor's authoritative position in the secret conclave. May his labours increase the respect in which the laws of the State are held, and may they be for the social betterment of all.[34]

The Mafia will stop at nothing to ensure that its members remain unpunished. This impunity underscores the prestige of the Mafioso, and his ability to influence the Italian State. Anybody willing to help the Mafia to achieve this will be exploited to the full. When in December 1970 a Fascist war hero, the 'Black Prince' Junio Valerio Borghese, offered to pardon Mafia crimes in exchange for the organisation's support in an attempted coup d'état across Italy, the Cupola jumped at the opportunity. He promised the new regime would revise a host of verdicts, including a life sentence given to Riina's mentor, the Corleone chieftain Luciano Leggio.

The Prince told the Catania boss Nino Calderone that the Mafia's role would be to help the conspirators to install their men as civil governors in several regions of Sicily. Men of honour were to await orders for attacks on town halls, carabinieri barracks and other targets.[35] In Rome, the plan was to occupy the offices of the RAI state television and the Interior Ministry. But Calderone and other clan chiefs were worried by the Prince's request for a list of the Mafiosi to be deployed, and by his demand that they should wear an armband so that they could be recognised like the other plotters.[36]

Worse, the Prince wanted the Mafiosi to behave like policemen and arrest officials who refused to be dismissed – unthinkable for an organisation which despised police as servants of the State. Calderone retorted that the Mafia had never arrested anybody but that if the Prince so desired, Cosa Nostra would kill the opponents of the coup instead.[37] The Mafiosi doubted the coup would succeed, but they concluded that they had nothing to lose from supporting it on their own terms. In the weeks leading up to the event, Mafiosi set off many bombs in Palermo which, as Buscetta explained, were intended to 'destroy the credibility of the Italian government'.[38] But the coup was aborted shortly after forestry guards, Borghese's main troops, entered the Interior Ministry. The Prince had failed to win wide enough support within the military and police forces, and Cosa Nostra itself gave him only lukewarm support on the day of the attempt, refusing to supply him with a list of its members.

Borghese's intermediaries with the clans were Palermo freemasons, one of whom was a man of honour, Carlo Morana. This was not the first time – or the last – that Cosa Nostra used freemasonry as a formidable instrument to extend its power and obtain favours. Masonic lodges, with an estimated 5,000 members in Sicily, are a meeting place for all. According to the informer Leonardo Messina: 'Many men of honour, that is those who manage to become bosses, belong to freemasonry . . . It's in freemasonry that you can make contact with businessmen, with institutions, with the men who administer power.'[39]

In 1977, freemasons suggested to the Cosa Nostra bosses that they affiliate two Mafiosi from each Sicilian province to a secret lodge, whose existence would have been kept secret from other masons. The proposal was accepted, and in Palermo Bontate and Greco were recruited. But, as ever, the oath of allegiance to the Mafia predominated for the men of honour. Their aim in undergoing the freemasons' initiation ritual was to penetrate the brotherhood's secrets without revealing anything in return.[40] More than a decade later, an informer testified that Riina and the rest of the Cupola were freemasons.[41]

Men of Honour, Men of the Cloth

As the midday sun beat down on an open-air mass in Agrigento's Valley of the Temples, Pope John Paul suddenly raised his voice, which shook as he brandished a crucifix. 'God once said "Do not kill." Man, any man, any group of men, the Mafia, cannot change and trample

on this most sacred law of God. The Sicilian people . . .
cannot always live under the pressure of a civilisation of
death.' The tens of thousands of faithful gathered beneath
the ancient Greek temples of the Sicilian coastal town burst
into applause. Virtually shouting, the Pope admonished
in prophetic tones: 'And these men who are guilty of
disturbing this peace, those who have on their consciences
the weight of so many human victims, must understand
– must understand – that they cannot be allowed to kill
innocents. In the name of the crucified and risen Christ
. . . I say to those responsible: Repent. One day the
judgement of God will come.'

The climax to a three-day visit to Sicily in May 1993
which turned into a fiery crusade, Pope John Paul's
diatribe was the Roman Catholic Church's strongest-ever
condemnation of the Mafia. It was a plea to turn the
page on decades of co-existence in Sicily between the
Church and the organisation which has borrowed many
of its trappings. Again and again archbishops and priests
attempted to minimise, when not actually abetting, the
Mafia's penetration of society. As early as the late nineteenth century, Catholic groups and associations had forged
ties with Mafiosi in an alliance against the fledgling Italian
State, which was at the time expropriating Church property.
In the ensuing decades, many Mafiosi fugitives have found
refuge in churches, or have been patronised by the clergy
in other ways.

The men of honour's blood ties with men of the cloth
sometimes foster friendly relations between the two. The
Godfather Vizzini, to name only one, had two brothers who
were priests and two uncles who were bishops. An uncle
of Leggio was a priest in Corleone. Church patronage can
include a host of favours. In December 1993, magistrates
launched an investigation on suspicion that a priest in

Monreale outside Palermo, Mario Campisi, had helped the boss Leoluca Bagarella, Riina's brother-in-law, while he was on the run. Investigators had intercepted several calls by Bagarella made from a mobile telephone which belonged to Campisi, the secretary to the archbishop of Monreale.

The priest who married Riina and his bride Ninetta, Father Agostino Coppola, was also a Mafioso and according to informers, he collected the ransom in a kidnapping masterminded by Riina. In some remote Sicilian towns, Catholic feast-day celebrations are today still sponsored by the local Mafioso chieftain.

'Objectively the Church does have its share of blame because in the past it did not do all it could to make the faithful aware of the gravity of the Mafia,' said Palermo magistrate Francesco Morvillo.[42] 'Nobody has been immune to the negligent or malicious behaviour which has allowed Cosa Nostra to become so powerful. All institutions – the Church, the State – and even the people are guilty, without exception,' he said.

Such ties have been generated to an extent by the Church's links with the Christian Democrats, for several decades after the Second World War the country's largest party and the pillar of a system built on political favours. For the Church, the Christian Democrats' struggle against Italy's sizeable Communist Party was the overriding priority. The unity of the Catholic vote in Mafioso neighbourhoods, achieved with the complicity of local clan bosses, has enabled Christian Democrat candidates to triumph at the ballot-box.

The Church's reaction to the investigation of Andreotti's alleged Mafia ties was typical of its unwillingness to distance itself from the party. For over half a century, Andreotti could boast close relations with

168   A DISHONOURED SOCIETY

several popes and also with top Vatican officials. Bishop Doigi Tettamanzi, head of the Italian bishops' conference, insisted that no one should gloat over the accusations because they still had to be proved: 'When a brother is accused of a wrong, everybody must demonstrate regret and perplexity, and not rejoice in the slightest.'[43]

Cardinal Ernesto Ruffini of Palermo, a man known for his extreme right-wing views and who ruled over the Sicilian Church from the end of the Second World War until his death in 1967, set the tone early on. Born in the Veneto region around Venice and the brother of a Christian Democrat government minister, Ruffini denied in 1954 that the Mafia even existed. In a pastoral letter, he branded two campaigners against the secret society, Danilo Dolci and Michele Pantaleone, slanderers of Sicily in their talk of the Mafia. When the secretary of state of Pope Paul VI, shocked by the car-bomb in Ciaculli which killed seven police and army officers in 1963, sent a secret letter to Ruffini asking the clergy to shake off its torpor and combat the Mafia, all he obtained was an indignant answer. The Mafia was 'an invention of the Communists', Ruffini retorted.[44]

Much later, it emerged that not only had Ruffini doggedly sought to play down the Mafia in his public pronouncements, but he had also forged ties with Palermo clan bosses – including, appropriately enough, Michele 'The Pope' Greco. Seeking to clear his name in a 1987 trial, Greco testified that he was friendly or at least acquainted with the cream of the Sicilian capital's high society. Greco related how he had on one occasion wanted to build a church in Ciaculli. One of his friends, a former public prosecutor of Palermo, at his request lobbied Ruffini to press the request for permission to build the church.

Greco proudly reported: 'A few days went by and I was given the answer. The Cardinal was willing to come. We fixed the day and the time and we agreed they would all come for lunch to my house, including the Cardinal. Everybody turned out to wait for the Cardinal, there was also a band. When the Cardinal arrived he was given a warm welcome.'[45] Despite his name-dropping, Greco was sentenced to life in jail as a member of the Mafia's Cupola.

Ruffini's opinions on Cosa Nostra helped a small band of Capuchin monks from Mazzarino, then one of the biggest towns in central Sicily, to reconcile their Mafioso actions of the late 1950s with their faith. For two years four friars from the local convent, assisted by its gardener and three unemployed delinquents, terrified the town. The monks ran an extortion racket, collecting money from locals while at the same time claiming they were doing so on the behalf of others. One of the ringleaders, the eighty-year-old Father Carmelo, a prophet-like figure with a full white beard, black-rimmed round glasses and a high forehead, clashed with his friend Angelo Cannata, a landowner and the wealthiest man in town. The two met after Cannata received an anonymous letter demanding a payment of 10 million lire, to be handed to Father Carmelo within a week. 'I'll pay at the most 200,000 lire!' exploded Cannata. 'What if the Mafiosi don't accept?' asked Father Carmelo. Cannata retorted: 'That's God's problem.' 'God? God?' exclaimed the friar. 'My son, do not take the name of God in vain. We are talking about money and Mafiosi!' Cannata stood by his refusal to pay, and was shot dead in his vineyard two weeks later.[46]

The four friars were arrested and tried for having acted as messengers between the Mafia and its intended victims, as well as for murder. They were acquitted at their first trial but sentenced to thirteen years in jail in an appeals court. Cardinal Ruffini absolved the friars, saying they had only been 'imprudent' and were the victims of a conspiracy: 'It was all a Communist and masonic plot and there is no measuring the publicity which has been given all over the world to the calumnies against these poor friars, to the disgrace not so much of Sicily as of our holy religion.'[47]

The death of Cardinal Ruffini in 1967 paved the way for a change in attitude towards the Mafia on the part of the Sicilian Church leadership. Under the guidance of the Sicilian-born Salvatore Pappalardo, who had been appointed archbishop of Palermo in 1970 and made a cardinal in 1973, Sicilian bishops began denouncing the ills of the Mafia. But they did not analyse the reasons behind the society's growth, nor did they denounce the system of political power which supported it.

In an event which would have been unthinkable under Ruffini, Pappalardo in 1981 celebrated a special mass in Palermo Cathedral for all the victims of the Mafia. In his homily, Pappalardo urged Sicilians to mobilise against the violence of the Mafia. Cosa Nostra was no longer taboo, and to denounce it was no longer deemed an insult to Sicily as it had been in Ruffini's day. Pappalardo's efforts culminated a year later, following the murder of General Dalla Chiesa. At the funeral ceremony, Pappalardo accused the government in Rome of abandoning Palermo to the mercy of the mobsters.

For the first time a prelate had stopped short of appealing for Christian forgiveness for the Mafiosi killers and offered no prayers for their repentance. Never before had a Sicilian bishop publicly lampooned the national government for failing to act. The Mafia took note of the severity of Pappalardo's attack, and its men in Palermo's Ucciardone jail boycotted the traditional Easter mass which he celebrated in the prison chapel. Pappalardo's speech appeared to mark the launch of a new campaign of Church intervention. Shortly after Dalla Chiesa's death, Sicilian bishops again pronounced the excommunication of those who were guilty of theft and murder. This summarised a text drawn up in 1944 and repeated in 1952, but this time the crimes were highlighted in a context which referred to a Mafioso killing. An informer acknowledged the changes: 'The Church understood before the State did that it should distance itself from Cosa Nostra. Before, in a way, Cosa Nostra seemed to help people and the Church lent itself to that role. For some years now the Church has refused any contact whatsoever.'[48]

But the revolution in the Church's dealings with the Mafia was a gradual one. The new excommunication cannot have had much of an effect, and again the Church was reducing the Mafia to its criminal manifestation. In the years that followed his speech at Dalla Chiesa's funeral, Pappalardo chose to intervene alone on particular occasions to denounce the moral gravity of the Mafia's crimes and to appeal for the help of the State and the political classes. But he was slow to speak of the ties between the Mafia and politicians, which were at the root of the brotherhood's web of influence. In 1986, on the eve of the first maxi-trial of several hundred Mafiosi in Palermo, Pappalardo even showed signs of backtracking. In comments which echoed his predecessor Ruffini's attacks on those who slandered Sicily, he shocked many when he said: 'We risk being crushed by the publicity which the trial will attract . . . [It is] a spectacular and oppressive mise-en-scène.' He added that he feared Sicily would be overwhelmed by 'more or less morbid attention'.[49]

It was only much later, after bombs killed the judges Falcone and Borsellino in 1992, that Pappalardo denounced the links between Cosa Nostra and the Italian State. 'Palermo demands an end to the turbid interweaving between Mafia and unscrupulous businessmen, an end to collusion between administrators and politicians and Mafia bosses, which has so discredited the institutions and the men who represent them.'[50]

For years the Church's battle against the Mafia was left to individual parish priests who stood out as exceptions to the rule of co-existence. The indefatigable Father Turturro, whose church of Santa Luisa stands opposite the main gates of the Ucciardone jail, set up an association, 'Paint Peace', and turned the church into a centre for local children, teaching them about the Mafia. He would invariably on All Saints Day gather toy guns from the children and then make a huge bonfire of the weapons. Priests such as Turturro were exceptions and therefore vulnerable figures. He was given a police escort after he was threatened by Mafiosi.

But not all mobsters shunned the dedicated priest. One twenty-two-year-old man of honour sought him out and confessed in tears that he had participated in five murders, including Falcone's. 'A lad came to me in church and told me weeping: "Father, I have killed many times, can I ever be forgiven?"' Turturro told his congregation at Christmas midnight mass in 1993. 'Now that boy is living shut up at home for fear of being killed.'[51] When the magistrates questioned him, Turturro refused to give any details, invoking the secrecy of the confessional. But his sermon sparked a storm of controversy, with Church figures accusing him of violating canon law in mentioning his meeting with the Mafioso.

On the eve of Pope John Paul's visit to Sicily in May 1993, a group of activist priests and Roman Catholic intellectuals wrote an open letter to the Pontiff. They urged him to call for the dismissal of bishops, priests and members of the laity who were tied to the 'politico-Mafioso system' by family links, imprudent friendships or other interests.[52] Such a network was 'not only humanly shameful and injurious to the credibility of the Catholic Church, it also constitutes a scandalous barrier to the evangelisation of the Sicilian people.'[53]

Their appeal did not fall on deaf ears. The Pope, during his previous visits to the island, had disappointed Sicilians in failing to take a clear stand against the Mafia. When he addressed Palermitans in November 1982, only weeks after the murder of Dalla Chiesa, he never even mentioned the word 'Mafia'. But on the first day of his third visit to Sicily, he broke his self-imposed silence and launched his unprecedented offensive in Agrigento's Valley of the Temples. During his tour of the island, the Pope denounced what he called 'a culture of death' oppressing the Sicilian people. The Mafia was the Devil out to ensnare man-kind into doing its will. In an address to priests in the western port of Trapani, he urged the clergy to take a front-line stand against Cosa Nostra: 'Do not just proclaim your faith in words, but follow that line of conduct which inspires and convinces the people.'[54] He also met the parents of Rosario Livatino, a thirty-eight-year-old Agrigento magistrate who had been shot dead by the Mafia in 1990.

Pope John Paul's crusade overhauled the Roman Catho-lic Church's position on the Mafia, which until then had rarely gone beyond episodic condemnations. For the first time, a pope had publicly urged his clergy to take a clear stand and campaign against the Mafia. Cosa Nostra's answer was swift and extreme. Its victim was one of the few churchmen who had not waited for the strong words of the Pope to wage their own battle. Four months after the Pontiff's visit, Father Puglisi, from the Mafioso district of Brancaccio in Palermo, was shot dead on the evening of his fifty-second birthday, with a single bullet fired at point-blank range into the back of his neck. He was the first priest who had campaigned against the Mafia to be slaughtered by the brotherhood.

The son of a cobbler, Puglisi ran a social centre where he gathered the Mafia's potential young recruits and taught them that violence was wrong – an act of courage in the drab and industrial neighbourhood dominated by mobsters. A few years previously, one of Puglisi's predecessors, Rosario Giue, intervened to stop locals who were planning celebrations of a special kind for a Catholic feast day – they wanted to mark the victory of the Brancaccio clan over its rivals. A small and humble figure of steely determination, Puglisi openly denounced the Mafiosi from his pulpit. Two months before his murder, Puglisi refused to hire local companies linked to the Mafia to restore his church. A few days later, someone set fire to the door of the building. He had also received several anonymous telephone calls threatening him with reprisals for his actions. In one of his last Sunday masses, Puglisi had appealed to the Mafiosi: 'Let us talk together, I would like to meet you and understand the reasons why you stand in the way of those who try to help and teach your children lawfulness and mutual respect.'

Puglisi's murder was a clear warning to churchmen to stay out of the Mafia's way. It was a message addressed to the humble parish priests of the Sicilian capital, the true driving force of the Palermitan Church's commitment against the Mafia in the absence of a firm stand by Archbishop Pappalardo. The work of priests like Puglisi, and the virulence of Pope John Paul's attack, made Cosa Nostra feel threatened by the Church for the first time in decades. A powerful institution which until then had lain inert was at last showing signs of rallying its forces against the Mafia.

Puglisi was not the only Italian priest to be slain for taking a stand against organised crime. Cosa Nostra's Neapolitan cousin, the Camorra, was quick to follow suit. In March 1994, seven months after Puglisi's killing, another crusading priest, Giuseppe Diana, was murdered in his church in the poverty-stricken town of Casal di Principe north of Naples. The thirty-six-year-old churchman was shot three times in the face by two men who walked into the sacristy, in the ugly concrete church of San Nicola di Bari, one Saturday morning as he was putting on vestments before Mass. A nun who had been praying nearby rushed into the sacristy to find the priest lying in a pool of blood under a font.

The Camorra killed Diana not only because of his public stand against the society but also because he had denounced its network of allies. The priest had organised a petition against the Camorra, and testified before investigating magistrates only four days before his death, naming the local politicians and businessmen he suspected of having links with the Camorra. Some 20,000 mourners attended his funeral.

7

TENTACLES SPREAD INTO EUROPE

Operation 'Green Ice'

Two well-groomed men and their blonde female companion are enjoying ice-creams at the expensive Tre Scalini café in the Piazza Navona, a picturesque square with baroque fountains in the heart of Rome's historic centre. It is Friday and the vivacious city has quietened down for the weekend as Romans relax in the welcome coolness of a September evening. As he strolls away with his friends after paying the bill, the leader of the group suddenly feels the barrel of a gun pressing against the small of his back. Three strangers bundle him into a waiting car, seven others take his companions and the cars roar off, scattering the pigeons who plague the Piazza.

This was the beginning of operation 'Green Ice', in which police dismantled a vast drugs and money-laundering ring spanning fifteen countries in September 1992, arresting

201 people. The biggest of its kind and the climax of a ten-month investigation, the operation revealed the strength and ambitions of Riina's Cosa Nostra – a pact with the Colombian cartels, the world's biggest producers of cocaine, to give the Corleonesi clan a monopoly over the distribution of the drug across Europe. Months, if not years, before Green Ice, investigators and some politicians had warned European governments that the Mafia 'Octopus', as it is dubbed in Italy, was set to spread its tentacles across the continent. The imminent creation of the single market in what was then the European Community, with its lifting of border controls, would be a golden opportunity for the Mafiosi. In fact, the Mafia had long ago crossed borders to set up rearguard bases, oversee drug and arms trafficking, run protection rackets and murder its rivals in various European countries including Germany, France and Britain. The lifting of border controls, however, has undoubtedly played into the hands of the Mafiosi.

The prize catch in Rome's Piazza Navona was Ospina Vargas, a thirty-eight-year-old Colombian, described by Italian officials as the biggest cocaine distributor in the world for the drug cartels of the South American country. Arrested along with Vargas was the associate he had brought over to Italy to introduce to his contacts in Cosa Nostra as his agent for Europe, Pedro Felipe Villaquiran. Their blonde companion was Bettein Martens, forty-one, who was responsible for the recycling of profits made from the sale of the drug in Europe. Investigators had recorded Vargas' negotiations with the Mafia on his first visit to Italy: 'It's time we did things seriously. I will expand exports, I will send all the cocaine that is needed, but then we need an organisation able to manage the distribution and I want nothing to do with dilettanti; I want people who know the job, people who can be trusted.' He insisted: 'I want to do business only with Riina's Corleonesi; they must be the guarantors of the affair.'[1]

The plan was for the Corleonesi to buy the cocaine in New York through the Bonnano family who would act as their representatives. In a coalition that also included a Neapolitan Camorra clan and a family of the Calabrian 'Ndrangheta (the junior partners), Riina's men had secured a monopoly over the import and wholesale distribution of Colombian cocaine in Europe. Cocaine shipments were sent from Colombia to Italy, the Netherlands and Spain, hidden among cargoes of frozen fish, bananas, flowers and leather goods. Laundering the illicit profits was also part of the pact between the Sicilians and the Colombians. Emissaries from Corleone assured Vargas that the Sicilian clan could shift and launder any amount of money, however large. Payments were sent to Colombia through fifteen different front companies (including an animal rights group) in Italy, Venezuela and the United States, and through US, Swiss and Austrian bank accounts. Among the companies closed down by the Green Ice investigators was a wine-export company based in Corleone. The police raids worldwide resulted in the seizure of 65 million dollars in cash, as well as securities and other valuables.

The ring was so vast that Green Ice spanned three continents. Named after the phrase used to describe laundered and frozen dollars, it was spearheaded by the US Drug Enforcement Agency (DEA) and an élite unit of the Italian police (the SCO). In the USA, 167 people were held by police, including a top official of Colombia's central bank, the head of its foreign affairs division, Rodrigo Polonia Gonzales Camorga. In the past, he had represented his country at many international conferences on various topics, including drug trafficking. If investigators are right, he must have been a particularly well informed speaker. Thirty-four people were arrested in Italy, including four Sicilian businessmen operating in Palermo who had organised a 300kg shipment of cocaine from South America. Other members of the ring were arrested in Costa Rica and Spain. In central London, customs officers arrested two Americans and seized a 22-cubic-metre pile of banknotes (worth some £2 million) from a lock-up garage.

Green Ice showed that the Colombian cartels were taking advantage of the financial unification of western Europe to attempt a major expansion on the Old Continent. But in doing so, they were only following in the footsteps of the Sicilian Cosa Nostra.

The Octopus Reborn

As investigators wound up the operation, Liliana Ferraro, who had succeeded the murdered judge Giovanni Falcone as director of penal affairs at the Justice Ministry in Rome, sounded a warning note: 'Green Ice is under way in Italy, France, London, Sao Paulo in Brazil, New York, Canada and Santo Domingo . . . these are things that evidently have a global dimension, that cannot be neglected. Perhaps people now realise that the problem is not purely Italian or Sicilian.' Ferraro, who had worked with Falcone for a decade before his death, said the inquiry was an example of the kind of international co-operation needed to combat those who believed that greater European unity would provide organised crime with ample opportunity to launder money. 'Civil society in Europe is faced with a choice: to defend itself or be occupied.'[2]

It is a choice which has not yet been made, and time is running short. Long before border restrictions were lifted on 1 January 1993, Cosa Nostra's entry after the Second World War into cigarette smuggling and then drug trafficking had transformed the 'Honoured Society' into a crime multinational, and many Mafiosi into managers of a highly competitive business which knew no borders. The seemingly indestructible epicentre of Cosa Nostra remains Palermo – like a hydra, the society can count many heads but has only one immortal one. According to the anti-Mafia commission, Cosa Nostra's spread abroad is not a migratory movement but a colonial-like expansion:

> Palermo and Sicily remain the territory of Cosa Nostra. It is no coincidence if in the capital of the island, the political heart of the regional government and the place where colossal regional and state financial resources are distributed, Cosa Nostra has set up and maintained a structure of control over the territory which can be found in no other locality. In Palermo . . . the Mafioso organisation is present with a multiplicity of 'families' which have divided the city among themselves so as not to leave any part of the territory uncovered and uncontrolled.[3]

Remaining true to its roots, and drawing strength from its tightly-controlled fiefdom, Cosa Nostra evolved into a superpower of crime. Its sheer efficiency stems not so much from the huge army of criminals and collaborators at its command as from the uncompromising hierarchical structure which enables it to launch unitary strategies across different countries. Organised criminals from other continents acknowledged this early on, and realised it was in their interest to privilege the Sicilian Mafia. They could exploit the fast channels of communication inherited from cigarette trafficking and pioneered by the likes of Lucky Luciano, use the Sicilians as mediators to knit relations with the American Cosa Nostra, and – not least – rest assured they were dealing with an organisation ruling supreme over its territory.

Few have been as quick to realise this as the cocaine-producing cartels of Colombia. With the North American market now deemed saturated, Europe is potentially the cartels' largest market and commands the highest prices for their product. The US Drug Enforcement Administration (DEA) estimates that cocaine fetches 44 per cent more on the European market than in the USA (£26,000 a kilo against £18,000). In recent years Sicily's Cosa Nostra has shifted its drug operations from the heroin trade to the cocaine-smuggling routes between South America and Europe. As part of this strategy, it has also on several occasions exchanged Asian heroin for Colombian cocaine.[4] Investigators believe Cosa Nostra has forged an alliance with the Colombian cartels in order to supply an expanding European market. In return, Cosa Nostra has helped the Colombians to break into the New York heroin market and to launder drug profits. At the same time, the Mafia has reduced its own share of the US heroin market.

Four years before Green Ice, the Mafioso boss Francesco Madonia, a member of the Cupola and the head of a ruthless Palermo clan, had forged a pact with two drug-traffickers of the Colombian Medellin cartel to try to guarantee himself a monopoly over cocaine distribution in Europe. Falcone learnt months after its arrival in Sicily in January 1988 of a 600-kilo load of cocaine aboard the Chilean cargo ship *Big*

John. The ship had been chartered by Madonia's Palermo clan and the Colombian Medellin cartel. They injected the cocaine into the Italian and European markets. 'We have proof of the start of direct contacts between Colombian drug-traffickers and the Sicilian Mafia,' said Falcone as he described the alliance in his last public address before his death. 'These contacts are extremely dangerous because of the possible risk of tight alliances between criminal organisations of remarkable economic power and great operational capability . . . We must fear, given what is happening today, an offensive on the cocaine market managed by a Mafia/Colombian alliance which would have a truly explosive and terrifying effect.'[5]

Falcone's warning was given at a time when the number of addicts in the USA was estimated to be falling but when the use of heroin and cocaine in Europe was increasing dramatically. The Medellin cartel had been willing to give the Madonia clan a monopoly over cocaine wholesale sales in Italy, but had balked at a European-wide exclusive. In the early 1990s, however, as Green Ice showed, the Colombian cartels were to have no such reservations. In a further sign of Cosa Nostra's supremacy, the informer Messina, the first to speak of the Sicilian organisation's colonies in several European countries, revealed the existence of a global Cupola-type council made up of representatives of all the world's criminal organisations. Saying he had first heard about the group in 1980, Messina said Riina had been the head of the global Cupola since November 1991.[6]

In a pattern bearing a striking resemblance to the Mafia clans carving up Sicily's territory among themselves, the criminal syndicates have apparently agreed on geographical areas of competence, on formalities for mutual assistance, and on ways of resolving possible

disputes. The biggest drug-traffickers exercise a power
which competes with the legal authority of governments.
According to the anti-Mafia commission, theirs is a state
within several states on a European, if not a wider, scale
– 'a real criminal 'counterpower' able to impose itself on
the will of states, to upset institutions and regulations, to
break the delicate economic and financial equilibrium and
destroy their democratic life.'[7]

Cosa Nostra's pacts, and its recent shift from heroin
to cocaine, proved wildly successful. In the past few
years, cocaine has invaded the European market, produced chiefly by the Colombian cartels. Between 1982
and 1991 seizures of heroin in Europe increased from
1,335 to 6,770 kilos. Cocaine seizures, by contrast,
jumped from 396 to 13,773 kilos.[8] In 1990, cocaine
was seized in eighteen different European countries – the
biggest consignments were found in Spain, the Netherlands,
Germany and Italy. The nationality of those who have been
discovered is revealing. Among the more than 2,000 traffickers identified, the biggest groups by nationality were
Colombian (with 377 individuals) and Italian (with 199).
In the six months following the lifting of border restrictions
in January 1993, the amount of cocaine seized by European
customs authorities rose by 42 per cent on the same 1992
period. The haul jumped from 6,914 to 9,800 kilos.

A Rude Awakening

The murder of Falcone in May 1992, followed by the
killing of his friend and colleague Borsellino two months
later, apparently stung western European governments

into a sudden realisation of the threat posed by the Mafia octopus. Italy and France jointly called for an 'extraordinary' meeting of Interior and Justice Ministers from the European Community. The first-ever anti-Mafia summit of the EC, held in Brussels that September, set up a Community-wide group of policemen expert in the fight against organised crime. It was high time the EC took the Mafia threat seriously. Only two years previously, on the insistence of the German Chancellor Helmut Kohl who wanted to highlight its spread abroad, EC documents made explicit reference to the 'Mafia' following a summit in Dublin.

Needless to say, it should not have taken the murders of Italy's leading anti-Mafia judges to jolt the EC governments into action, albeit limited, against Cosa Nostra's infiltration of their respective countries. But it was already too late. What European capitals did not seem to realise was that the infiltration was not simply a threat, but was already well under way. Much of the work of both judges, including the Palermo maxi-trial of several hundred Mafiosi in the mid-1980s, had highlighted how the Mafia's agenda for profit and power embraced whole continents – Europe, America and beyond. As early as 1984, Falcone had told the European parliament that the fight against Cosa Nostra was a task for the whole of Europe and not for Italy alone. He later met German federal police at their headquarters in Wiesbaden and repeated his message. His former boss Antonino Caponnetto told the author that Falcone confided to him: 'They didn't take me seriously.'9 Also following the Cosa Nostra trail beyond Italy's borders, Borsellino went to Mannheim in Germany to investigate Falcone's murder. He himself was killed shortly afterwards.

Italy's anti-Mafia judges were by no means alone in warning their lethargic European partners that progress towards unification was making the continent particularly vulnerable to penetration by Cosa Nostra and its allies. In April 1992, eight months before border controls were lifted, a special committee set up by the European parliament produced a report on the spread of organised crime throughout the twelve-member European Community. A disappointing document, it astonishingly falls for the Mafiosi's own propaganda and describes Cosa Nostra as originally an 'honourable' organisation which has grown into 'a dynamic, but criminal and bloodthirsty institution'. Neither does the report expose the real extent of the Mafia's spread into EC countries, limiting itself to a brief list of investigations such as those into its links with French criminal clans in Marseille, and with the US Pizza Connection drugs ring. Similarly, the Camorra and the 'Ndrangheta are also given brief, almost dismissive, treatment.

But the committee did at least underline the nature of the Mafia as a criminal institution spreading far beyond the borders of Italy: 'The power of the criminal organisations which control the drugs traffic is growing at an alarming rate. It is having increasingly serious effects on society and on the political institutions of [EC] member states. It is undermining the foundations of the legitimate economy and threatening the stability of the states of the Community.'[10] Cocaine seizures in Europe had doubled in 1990 against the previous year, totalling 12 tonnes. Greedy for easy money, criminal organisations outside the EC such as the Colombian cartels, as well as networks of organised crime within the EC such as the Mafia, were exploiting Europe's porous borders and creating their own single market. The report argued against abolishing all internal frontier controls from January 1993, saying selective checks aimed at high-risk traffic should be maintained between member states.

No matter. The parliamentary report died an unattended death, helped on its way to oblivion by a controversy over its majority recommendation for the decriminalisation of drugs which totally obscured the warnings of a Mafia threat. In September 1992, only four months before the scheduled birth of the single market, a report by the French Senate sounded the last warning bell. The growth of drug trafficking in the nine countries which had signed the Schengen free travel accord (all twelve EC countries except Britain, Denmark and Ireland) endangered democracy, and had swollen the number of addicts to an estimated 800,000 individuals – all victims in a drugs market with a European turnover of 392 billion francs and profits of 171 billion francs. More than half of all police arrests in Europe were for offences linked to drugs. The report concluded: border controls, whether within the Schengen area or in the wider EC, were about to be lifted without adequate compensatory measures, and this would further increase drug trafficking.

Years before the Maastricht Treaty on European union was signed, and without the long and difficult procedures which preceded its implementation, a European criminal market had already been formed, stretching beyond the Twelve, and unifying East and West. The only borders the Mafia knew were those it had set up itself to keep its enemies away from its own territories. Borders existed for the enemies of Cosa Nostra – anti-Mafia investigators – not for the organisation itself. The Sicilian Mafia, which had already spawned an offshoot in the United States, in recent years had planted clans – which were far from inactive – in several European countries including France, Germany and Belgium and laundered millions of dollars' worth of dirty money in fiscal paradises such as Monte Carlo and the Channel Islands.

Cosa Nostra was helped by the myopia of governments who believed they could take money from the Mafia, serving as havens for its dirty money, without taking in Mafiosi at the same time. A team of experts (GAFI) set up by the Group of Seven leading industrialised countries estimated in 1992 that the value of illicit drugs sold worldwide was in the region of $270 billion a year – a turnover which placed the drugs industry in second place after the weapons trade and ahead of the oil industry. The volume of laundered drug money invested in Europe and North America was put at one trillion dollars over a decade.

Switzerland in particular has been a haven for the biggest criminal syndicates, especially for those trafficking in drugs, for the past three decades. Already by the 1960s, the American Cosa Nostra controlled a bank in Geneva, the Banque de Change et d'Investissement. For decades banking secrecy laws meant that penal sanctions of up to six months in jail could be imposed on a bank employee who gave information about a client to a third party. When a new law did finally allow Swiss bank documents to be seized, an Italo–Swiss crackdown on a drug-trafficking ring led to 130 arrests in October 1993. Among those arrested were members of the Palermo Madonia clan and the Calabrian 'Ndrangheta. The ring was active in and around Italy's workaholic financial capital, Milan, laundering its annual billion-dollar profits through Swiss banks.

Mafia money deposited in Swiss bank accounts is often recycled and invested in neighbouring Germany or Austria. In a 1992 report, the United Nations International Narcotic Control Board observed laconically: 'for the moment Austria is still the only country in western Europe where it is possible to deposit money in a bank anonymously.'[11] In Germany the Mafia's illegal profits are invested in shares, in gold and increasingly in property or companies, often in the former East Germany. The German federal police (the BKA) estimate Cosa Nostra invested 27 billion marks in Germany in 1991, with no fear of prosecution because recycling money became a crime in Germany only in September 1992. According to a confidential report by Germany's secret services (the BND), drug barons are forcing indebted Western nations to be as dependent on their immense capital as addicts are on drugs. Part of the money has been invested in state bonds and has thus helped to finance the budget deficits of various countries, including Italy's crippling state debt.[12]

European governments ignored a string of danger signals. Even appeals from men of honour themselves fell on deaf ears: 'People mustn't be surprised if a Mafioso is arrested in Milan, or Turin, or elsewhere,' said the supergrass Calderone, meaning anywhere across the globe. 'They are about to open the frontiers: if Italy is big, think how big Europe is. That's why we have to think about the issue in time.'[13] Another informer, Messina, was among the first to speak of the '*decine*' (groups of about ten 'soldiers') which Cosa Nostra had deployed abroad. Messina himself travelled to Brussels to contact immigrants from his home town of San Cataldo because his clan wanted to set up a *decina* in the Belgian capital.[14] He said he knew of such groups in France and Germany. But there is much more to Cosa Nostra's spread throughout Europe.

Germany: Refuge and Rackets

The poor hilltop town of Palma di Montechiaro, near the

southern coast of Sicily, is at first sight an unlikely starting-point for a tour of the Mafia's European strongholds. Few Sicilian towns epitomise so well the island's detachment from the European continent. Its only claim to fame is the fact that it was founded in 1637 by Carlo Tomasi, one of the princes of Lampedusa and an ancestor of Giuseppe Tomasi di Lampedusa, who wrote *The Leopard*. The ducal palace in the town is often identified as the summer retreat of Donnafugata patronised by the book's fatalist hero Prince Salina, who watches passively over the end of an era as Italy drifts towards unification in the late nineteenth century. Today the squat, dirty-white palace of the Lampedusa family looks derelict and gloomy. According to a once secret report by Italy's anti-Mafia high commissioner, the town with its 27,000 residents is the sad symbol of the decay and self-destruction which pervades the novel:

> Whoever wants to experiment with a concrete example of a territory expropriated from the State has only to travel to Palma di Montechiaro and try to understand the tribal rules which govern it . . . On the eve of the year 2,000, a big open-air cesspit serves as a sanitation system and gathers the urban sewage, drawing it away and dispersing it on the ground, in unhygienic conditions which under other latitudes would have prompted the evacuation of the entire community. [15]

Since the mid-1980s, battles between rival Mafia clans 'which recognise only the law of violence and murder and see the State as a nuisance' have turned Palma di Montechiaro into one of the most lawless towns in the province of Agrigento. For locals, the butchery was only the latest confirmation that their salvation lay in emigration – thousands of them abandoned the town to its fate, fleeing chiefly to Germany, to wealthy cities like Mannheim, Berlin and Cologne a world away. Along with these emigrants went many Mafiosi, who soon dotted Germany with little colonies of Cosa Nostra.

The investigation into the killing of a young Sicilian magistrate near Agrigento in 1990 was to reveal how safe men of honour felt in their new German havens. The thirty-eight-year-old judge Rosario Livatino died as he drove to work in Agrigento from his home in nearby Canicatti one September morning. A car drew up alongside Livatino's and one of the gunmen inside shot at the judge before he could stop. High on cocaine, the assassin missed his target. Livatino struggled out of his car and jumped over the guard-rail at the edge of the road. The hitmen chased him down the escarpment, firing a machine-gun and pistol and drowning his pleas not to shoot. They caught up with him and shot him one last time through the mouth.

The day he was murdered, Livatino was due to decide what measures to take against the clan bosses of Palma di Montechiaro. His executioners were members of the town's *Stidda* families, made up in part of bosses expelled from Cosa Nostra. The murderers had settled in Germany and had made a short trip to Sicily to carry out their task. The informer Giuseppe Croce Benvenuto explained that the *Stidda* clans had decided to kill Livatino to assert themselves in the long-running war against the families of Cosa Nostra.[16] An eye-witness recognised two of the gunmen as Domenico Pace and Paolo Amico, both from Palma di Montechiaro, and they were arrested a month after the murder in the quiet German town of Leverkusen near Cologne, where they both worked washing dishes in the Ai Trulli pizzeria. The two had carried out the killing on behalf of another family to whom they owed a favour.[17]

The pizzeria itself had already come to the attention of the police. According to German federal police, four years previously it had hosted a party for members of rival Sicilian clans who had declared themselves ready for a reconciliation. The meal ended with one of the guests being burned alive.[18]

For Sicilians like the killers of Rosario Livatino, the personal liberties enshrined in Germany's constitution are a great attraction. The police in Germany have far fewer legal instruments available to help them catch up with fugitives than in Italy. The lack of a law making Mafia association a crime, as in Italy, has forced the police to release any suspected Mafioso who can prove he has a fixed abode. But the use of German towns as refuges is only part of the story of how Sicilian criminals have settled in that country. Germany has become a key base both for the laundering of dirty money by Cosa Nostra and – since the collapse of Communist regimes – for the infiltration of eastern European markets. The integration of Europe, Germany's central location and its strategic border with the former Soviet bloc have turned the country into a focal point for organised crime. German business is so worried by its spreading influence that it has appealed for state protection. In January 1994, the Chamber of Industry and Commerce told Chancellor Kohl that companies and business associations needed the help of police and intelligence services to ward off criminal gangs. The government should give business its intelligence, the Chamber demanded.

As in the United States at the beginning of the century, the first to feel the impact of the Sicilian Cosa Nostra's implantation are the Mafiosi's own countrymen. Following the blueprint for success in their homeland, the men of honour first seek a foothold in their new territory

by levying *Schutzgeld*, or protection money, among the
bars, restaurants, shops and other small businesses run
by Italian immigrants. Worst hit are the southern and
western areas of Germany – especially the Rhine–Main
area, the Ruhr, the Rhine–Neckar and Munich, capital of
the strongly Roman Catholic Bavaria. In Frankfurt, some
80 per cent of Italian restaurants are believed to pay sums
which vary from 1,000 to 5,000 marks a month. In Munich,
more than half the owners of such restaurants are victims of
the racketeers.[19]

As in Sicily, the law of *omertà* holds firm. Most of the
victims, whether Italian or German, prefer quietly to make
provision for the regular payments in their books and not
alert the authorities. One Italian who opened a games
hall in Frankfurt and who twice turned away mobsters
demanding protection money received a human tongue
in the post – gruesome advice to keep quiet and not
go to the authorities. The racket is so extensive that
Josef Geisdorfer, head of anti-Mafia investigations for the
Bavarian state police, admitted in July 1992: 'There are
essentially no more blank spots on the German map where
the Mafia or the Camorra are not active.'[20] In 1989–92,
the German federal police launched 118 investigations into
Italian organised crime.[21]

Cosa Nostra's rival clans regularly settle their differences
on German soil. In 1984, Agostino Badalamenti was
murdered in Solingen in what was then West Germany
because he was related to the Palermo chieftain Gaetano
Badalamenti, who had sought to prevent Riina from establishing a dictatorship over the Mafia. In April 1992,
another enemy of Riina's Corleonesi clan was given a taste
of Mafia justice in Germany. Gioacchino Schembri, owner
of a Mannheim pizzeria, was beaten up by an envoy from
Palma di Montechiaro. The hitman was Gaetano 'The

Fly' Puzzangaro, who was later accused of the murder of judge Rosario Livatino.

With steady revenue assured chiefly by protection rackets and drug trafficking, the Mafia went further and sought to bribe and corrupt local officials. In 1992, German police recorded 450 cases of corruption in which Mafioso interests were involved. One out of six of these cases involved government officials and one out of twenty involved investigating magistrates.[22] Alarmed at the scale of such offences, the BKA chief Hans-Ludwig Zachert said the sudden, uncontrolled expansion of organised crime threatened to corrupt both politicians and the police in eastern Germany. If nothing was done, sophisticated Mafia-style gangs would control up to 40 per cent of all crime in Germany by the year 2,000.[23]

France: Mafiosi on the Riviera

Early in February 1983 the Mafioso Antonino Calderone was desperate to put an end to a lifetime in the service of Cosa Nostra. His brother, the boss of Catania in eastern Sicily, had been murdered by rivals – the heaviest price Antonino Calderone was to pay for his devotion to the criminal cause. Years later, he told of his state of mind as he sought a way out, one which many other men of honour who have sought refuge abroad would recognise:

> I was a hunted animal who looks up at the skies and sees big clouds, clouds which get bigger and bigger and more threatening, and who hopes to have enough time to find a refuge before the storm. I wasn't thinking any more, I

wasn't living any more, I was scared of everybody but I
didn't know where to go. My whole life had been spent
in Catania and Sicily, inside the hallucinated world of
Cosa Nostra and its plottings. Beyond it there was only
darkness.[24]

Calderone fled first to a hostel run by priests in
Switzerland, then spent some time in the French town
of Menton near the Italian border before settling in Nice.
Eager to blend into French society and avoid contact of
any kind with his former acolytes, he opened a small
laundry in the city centre in 1984. He lived discreetly
and happily, even managing to earn enough to start
saving money. But he was arrested two years later.

Few of the Mafiosi who have settled on the French
Riviera are as eager as Calderone to build themselves a
new and honest life. Most emissaries of Italian organised
crime, whether members of Cosa Nostra, the Camorra or
the 'Ndrangheta, are too busy looking for ways to launder
and invest profits from drug trafficking or other illicit
activities. In a Franco-Italian operation in May 1993
codenamed operation Green Sea, police dismantled a
Cosa Nostra–Camorra ring of thirty-nine people who dealt
in cocaine and the laundering of profits in Italy, France and
Germany. The network lent money to financial companies
and forced managers to either pay huge sums in interest or
hand over their businesses. The same tactic was applied
to the gamblers who flocked to the casinos on the French
Riviera. Foolish or desperate enough to accept loans in
cash at interest rates of 20–25 per cent, many of these
punters fell into a vicious circle and ended up having to
work for the ring. In this way, the ring acquired a host
of shops, hotels and small companies along France's Côte
d'Azur and Italy's Ligurian coast.

The Green Sea police raids brought to a sudden halt the career of a Neapolitan who had pioneered the colonisation of the French Riviera by both the Camorra and Cosa Nostra. Michele 'The Madman' Zaza, a heavily-built, alert fifty-year-old with an aquiline nose, owed his nickname to notorious foolhardiness in the face of danger. He frequently boasted of friends in high places, saying he had helped out financially several Christian Democrat and Socialist ministers in Italy who had publicly campaigned against organised crime. The head of the Camorra's Nuove Famiglie (New Families) grouping which emerged in the early 1980s, Zaza had been co-opted by the Sicilians so that he would serve them better. He was arrested in the Green Sea operation along with the Camorra boss Carmine Alfieri and the leader of Cosa Nostra's Fidanzati clan. The latter welded the alliance between the two syndicates. Police burst in on Zaza at his luxurious villa in Villeneuve-Loubet near Nice, fearing he might flee when he learnt of the other arrests. A Palermo judge had previously issued an international warrant for his arrest on several charges including Mafia association and drug trafficking.

Zaza had until then been relatively fortunate in his dealings with French and Italian justice. The king of cigarette contraband in the port of Naples, he had moved to France to try and extend the traffic to Marseille. Arrested in March 1989 in his villa on the Riviera where he lived with his wife and children, he was sentenced by a French court in July 1991 to just three years in jail for cigarette trafficking. The sentence, and the charge itself, infuriated the Italian investigators who had linked him to a drugs ring which included the clans of Ciaculli in Palermo, Barbarossa in Naples, and Gambino and Bonnano in New York. The Italian investigating magistrates asked for Zaza's extradition so that he could face a double murder charge, but this was not granted. The French trial did however uncover Zaza's attempt to create on the Côte d'Azur a criminal organisation using the usual Mafioso techniques of corruption of officials and the hijacking of companies. During the investigation, Zaza and his henchmen tried to corrupt a policeman, a doctor and several examining magistrates. Benefiting from a French law which facilitates the release of prisoners who have already served half their sentence, Zaza was released in November 1991 and lived in his villa until his rearrest in May 1993. He was finally extradited to Italy in March 1994, to face charges of Mafia association, drug trafficking and cigarette smuggling. But Zaza's death four months later in July robbed Italian magistrates of their chance to bring him to book for serious offences. Fifty years old, he died of a heart attack in a Rome hospital after he was suddenly taken ill in the maximum security Rebibbia jail on the city's outskirts.

According to a special commission set up by the French parliament to study the spread of organised crime in France, Zaza's activities were the best example of Italian organised crime's attempt at colonisation. The commission was the first of its kind to be formed in a European country other than Italy, and the first to investigate Mafia incursion after the EC's dismantling of its internal borders. It reported in February 1993 that Zaza was only one of many 'worrying signs of a growing Mafia presence in France'.[25] Although the presence of Colombian cartels, Japanese yakuzas and Chinese triads had been signalled to the commission during its three-month investigation, it chose to focus on the Mafia, branding it the most immediate threat for France and the most sophisticated model of criminal organisation. France was deemed to be vulnerable to intrusion by organised crime because the country's various police and customs services spent more time obstructing each other than fighting it, and because there was too little information available about the criminal syndicates based in Sicily and southern Italy.

For the time being, the report said, the Mafia did not have a generalised territorial disposition in France. But it did single out one attempt and named a fifty-eight-year-old Sicilian, Giacomo Pagano, who was then living in Grenoble at the foot of the French Alps, as one of those responsible for the spread of Cosa Nostra into France. The informer Messina had identified Pagano as the head of a *'decina'* in the French town, a colony of the clan ruling over the latter's small home town of Sommatino (population: 8,000) outside Caltanissetta in central Sicily. Officially, although he drove a Mercedes, Pagano's income was limited to the unemployment benefit he drew every week. But the report said he had contaminated the local economy through several companies. The Italian police believed Pagano, who had previously been convicted of procuring and receiving stolen jewels, acted as the link between Germany and Italy in a ring which involved illicit profits and the use of the Grenoble area as a logistical rear base for Cosa Nostra.[26] The investigators believed Pagano was involved in drugs (and possibly arms) trafficking as well as an extortion racket, and may also have sheltered a Mafioso fugitive for several months.[27]

The naming of Pagano by the parliamentary commission sparked an irate reaction from the state prosecutor in Grenoble, home to several thousand Sicilians, who protested he had been forced to abandon police surveillance operations after criminals were tipped off that they were under suspicion. The report's authors retorted that the names had already appeared in Italian newspapers. The French authorities expelled Pagano shortly after the report was published on the pretext that his residence permit was out of date, and handed him over to the Italian police. But the Italians were forced to release Pagano because no measures had been ordered against him. Nothing more was heard of Pagano until his arrest in a suburb of Brussels in December 1993 after Caltanissetta magistrates finally issued an international warrant for his arrest on a charge of Mafia association.

Spared a partial territorial takeover by Cosa Nostra, France is however attracting an increasing slice of the Mafia's illicit profits. These are placed in bank accounts outside France, then laundered through front companies particularly in Switzerland, the Channel Islands and Monte Carlo, before being invested in legal activities in France. These include property and other concerns such as large tourist complexes, casinos, golf clubs, restaurants, private clinics, state-funded construction and development projects and waste-disposal firms. Falcone reported before his death that a third of the construction projects on the Côte d'Azur belonged to companies financed by the Mafia.[28]

Casinos are a traditional prey for Italian organised crime on France's Mediterranean coast. A Franco–Italian investigation in 1990 found that Cosa Nostra and the Camorra were seeking control of some of the biggest casinos on the Riviera, including that of Nice, Beaulieu and Menton on the Italian border, the tranquil resort favoured by the well-heeled elderly. Giuseppe Liguori, one of the managers of the front company Sofextour which planned to take over the Menton casino, was Michele Zaza's father-in-law. The Camorra aimed not only to recycle and reinvest its own capital, but also to do the same with funds belonging to other criminal gangs.[29] The mayor of Menton, Jean-Claude Guibal, refused to allow the takeover and received a series of threats – dead birds were squashed against the doors of his office, his car was sabotaged, and gambling chips were left on his desk as a warning to stop interfering in the buy-out of the casino.

One Sicilian company involved in two big French construction projects – the Channel Tunnel and the EuroDisney park outside Paris – had ties with Cosa Nostra. The giant Sicilian consortium Italimprese, active in public works projects across Europe, is based in Catania in eastern Sicily. Headed by the family of Mario Rendo, it had been mentioned by the prosecution in the Palermo maxi-trial of the mid-1980s. The Catania supergrass Calderone has described at length the links between local Mafia clans and the city's leading industrialists, including the head of Italimprese, Mario Rendo: '[They] were never victims of the Mafia, at least as long as I lived in the city . . . On the whole, they all took advantage of the reputation they had of being associated with us. Now they say they don't know us.'[30] The French commission noted that Italimprese was involved in practices which were illegal under labour laws and which were typical of money-laundering techniques. Although an Italian judge exonerated the consortium from all Mafioso collusion in 1991, he did acknowledge they had had business relations with Cosa Nostra.

The commission's report pulled no punches in spotlighting the Mafiosi's financial weight on the French Riviera and in other areas. It stated that 80 per cent of casino revenue on the Côte d'Azur was of Italian origin and that this might be an important recycling channel. A number of Achilles heels rendered France vulnerable to Mafiosi interests: fiscal paradises such as Andorra and the Franco–Dutch island of St Martin in the Caribbean. FBI investigators have proof of a visit in spring 1991 the Catania boss Santapaola made to the island. That evidence is a photograph of him meeting the suspected money launderer Rosario Spadaro, a poor immigrant from Messina who had settled in the Dutch part of St Martin and built himself a tourism and hotel empire worth an estimated one billion francs in 1992. The picture shows Santapaola and Spadaro, who was arrested in November 1994, in animated conversation on the latter's yacht.

For the first time, an official French report paid no heed to diplomatic niceties and described Monte Carlo as one of the most popular Mafia recycling centres. In the principality's forty or so banks – a third of which are local, a third are subsidiaries of French banks and a third are subsidiaries of other banks – deposits had increased by 40 per cent in a year and a half. These banks had in 1992 received close to 12 billion dollars in cash deposits which, the report said, came largely from Mafia funds.

Monte Carlo and the luxury hotels of the Côte d'Azur are also a favourite haunt of Italian crime bosses, who use them as discreet venues for their summits. In 1989, the suspected Camorra boss Nunzio Barbarossa and two cronies were arrested in a pizzeria in Nice near the luxury Elysée Palace Hôtel, where the previous day they had attended a meeting of some fifteen members of the Neapolitan secret society. Other bosses have sought refuge on the Riviera. One of the leading figures of the 'Ndrangheta, Domenico Libri, was arrested at Marseille airport in 1992 after flying in from Paris. Far from seeking retirement despite being over sixty, Libri was hiding in France on the run from Italian justice which had sentenced him in 1991 to ten years in jail for Mafia-style association. An innovator, he had invested far beyond the Riviera, building a network of property firms, service companies and public works projects which stretched as far as the Finistère region in the northwest of France and the prosperous Yvelines region west of Paris.

In January 1994 the investigators discovered that a senior lieutenant of the Godfather Riina was also hiding in southern France. In a dashing raid which must have been inspired by James Bond, French and Italian police using helicopters descended on a block of flats in the smart ski resort of Isola 2000 in the French Alps. Their prize was the forty-four-year-old Sicilian Gaetano Sangiorgi, a surgeon with boyish good looks who owned a clinic in Palermo. He was suspected of having acted as a key link between Riina and the Italian political world. For several months he had lived with his wife and two teenage children in a villa in the Riviera town of Biot before, suspecting he might be discovered, he sought refuge in the ski resort. Italian justice had issued an international warrant for his arrest on charges that he ordered the 1992 murder of his relative Ignazio Salvo, a Palermo tax-collector and man of honour who allegedly acted as an intermediary between Mafia clans and the former Prime Minister Andreotti. According to informers, Sangiorgi, the son-in-law of Ignazio's cousin Nino Salvo, hired four Mafia assassins to carry out the killing and was present at the murder – but a few minutes later he was comforting Salvo's widow. Three months after the slaying he gave the men of honour he had hired Cartier watches as tokens of his gratitude.[31]

Britain: Heroin and God's Banker

In May 1985, a routine check by a sniffer dog at Felixstowe

docks uncovered a consignment of 60 kilos of heroin from Thailand hidden in furniture bound for Canada. Although small by today's standards, the haul, worth £75 million, was the largest discovered in Britain that far. The investigation, codenamed operation Devotion, revealed that Cosa Nostra was using Britain as a staging-post for heroin bound for the Americas and that several leading Mafiosi and their underlings had settled there. For several years prior to the discovery, police had denied there was any Mafia presence in Britain.

The heroin haul put investigators on the tracks of a Sicilian businessman, Francesco di Carlo. A lover of relics from the past, he had paid for the restoration of the ornate Palazzo Ganci in Palermo, where the Italian director Luchino Visconti filmed part of *The Leopard*, including the glittering ball scene starring Burt Lancaster and Claudia Cardinale. Among his friends Di Carlo counted the owner of the palace, Prince Alessandro Vanni Calvello Mantegna di San Vincenzo. Di Carlo had settled in Britain in 1977 and lived an apparently quiet life in Woking, playing the stock exchange and exporting antique furniture.

But British police were to discover a more sinister side to the antiques dealer. Di Carlo was a man of honour, a one-time boss of a clan from Altofonte south of Palermo who had risen through the ranks to sit for a period on Cosa Nostra's Cupola. The rise of Di Carlo, known as 'The Butcher' in his home town, was cut short when rival clans ruled in 1980 that he had stolen 20 kilos of heroin from a shipment organised by the Mafia. The punishment could easily have been death. But Di Carlo, who protested his innocence and said the missing heroin had been stolen by the police, was spared because of his friendship with Riina. His punishment was to be '*posato*' ('dropped') by the secret society and banished from Sicily, but this did little to prevent his persisting in activities worthy of a man of honour.

Among the members of Cosa Nostra who were indulgent with Di Carlo was the Cuntrera–Caruana clan from Siculiana near Agrigento in Sicily. It had settled in Montreal in the 1950s and did not shirk trafficking in drugs with him. Apart from the heroin trade, Di Carlo had been able to build up a series of businesses and other smuggling interests. He could boast ownership of dozens of import-export companies based in the heart of the City of London – a hotel, a restaurant, an elegant pub, a travel agency and financial companies with branches as far away as the North and South American continents.

Di Carlo was jailed for twenty-five years in March 1987 for smuggling the heroin found at Felixstowe and a separate £3 million consignment of cannabis. Three accomplices were given similar sentences. The heroin route stretched from the Far East to Venezuela, and hashish was also shipped from the Middle East to Sicily. Di Carlo's trial did not purge Britain of Cosa Nostra. Judge Falcone, the architect of the Palermo maxi-trial then in progress and in which Di Carlo was being tried *in absentia*, said on the day of the Old Bailey verdict that as many as fifty Mafiosi could be working under cover in Britain, and that London remained a focal point for drug trafficking. A year after the sentence, an attempt was made to set up a duplicate network by a clan from Trapani in western Sicily which sought to establish contacts in Britain. But the attempt was frustrated by British and Italian investigators, who found out about it in time.[32]

As judge Falcone knew only too well, when the police arrested Di Carlo, his leading associates slipped their clutches. Key Mafiosi were based in Britain, some in luxurious exile in the Surrey stockbroker belt. Alfonso

Caruana, an even more senior member of the Cupola than Di Carlo, lived in a £450,000 manor in Godalming. He and his brother Pasquale fled to Venezuela before customs and police officers could catch them. Their escape left unresolved much of Cosa Nostra's entry into Britain – Di Carlo's heroin trafficking was only a part of a huge financial empire which the Cuntrera–Caruana clan was building across the globe.

By the early 1970s, the Cuntrera–Caruanas had left their native Sicily and succeeded in setting up an import-export company in New York. Their clients included all the biggest Sicilian and Sicilian–American drug-traffickers – Gaetano Badalamenti, Giovanni Spatola, Salvatore Greco and John Gambino. The company even had a subsidiary in the Venezuelan capital, Caracas. In 1975 the family's head, Liborio Cuntrera, moved to Britain, buying a house in Surrey for about a million dollars which he handed over in cash. Posing as a dealer on the stock exchange, he succeeded in organising the drug-trafficking ring which was to prove Di Carlo's undoing. Couriers lugged suitcases full of banknotes into banks in Montreal in Canada, where Di Carlo's correspondent Gerlando Caruana lived, and exchanged the money for cheques. These were then sent to banks in various European cities – Paris, Lugano, Brussels, London and Amsterdam. There the cheques were converted back into cash which eventually ended up in New York or Caracas. In the decade 1970–80, the annual heroin seizures in the United Kingdom increased from 20 to 220 kilos.

When Liborio Cuntrera died in July 1982, Pasquale and Alfonso Caruana replaced him as the London envoys of the clan. The three other Cuntrera brothers – Pasquale, Paolo and Gaspare – had over the past decade become thoroughly at home in Caracas, hobnobbing with élite society. A former president of the republic, Luis Herrera Campins of Venezuela's Christian Democrat Party, was the guest of honour at the wedding of one of their daughters. The brothers ruled over an empire consisting of some fifty companies of all kinds (hotels, services, property) worth an estimated 500 million dollars. Until 1985, when Di Carlo was arrested, they smuggled heroin into Britain. But the brothers' key role was a financial one, serving Riina among others. From the City of London to Cyprus, from Thailand to Venezuela and from Zurich to Montreal, dozens of front companies and bank accounts belonging to the Cuntreras have allowed Cosa Nostra clans to recycle hundreds of millions of dollars.

For several years the Venezuelan authorities, no doubt influenced by the Cuntrera brothers' friends in high places, successfully blocked Italian attempts to have them extradited. The US Drugs Enforcement Administration threatened to go into Venezuela and seize them. Italian justice finally caught up with them in September 1992. Judge Falcone did not live to see his repeated requests for the brothers' extradition finally granted – his appeals had been refused in 1983, 1985 and again in 1990. According to the investigators who led operation Green Ice, the brothers acted as the link between the Sicilians and the Colombian cartels which grew and distributed the network's cocaine.

The brothers' firm which laundered such huge sums for so many Mafia clans had survived despite fierce rivalry and wars between the families they served. Their role was so important, so professional, that none of the Mafia families could manage without them. Between 1980 and 1984, the brothers laundered some $70 million for crime organisations in Italy, North and South America. Computer data seized in raids on the Cuntreras' homes and offices showed the clan had plans to send cocaine and heroin into the ex-Soviet Union. Alfonso Caruana, believed to be the real financial brains of the clan, escaped capture.

If supergrasses are to be believed, Di Carlo was not only the mastermind behind the British heroin traffic. He was also the murderer of the Italian Roberto Calvi, the man known as 'God's banker' who was found hanging from Blackfriars Bridge in London on the morning of 18 June 1982. The sixty-two-year-old Calvi, who owed his nickname to his extensive financial dealings with the Vatican, was tied by a rope to scaffolding under the bridge. The pockets of his trousers and jacket had been stuffed with some 5 kilos of stones and bricks. A week previously, Calvi had fled an Italian investigation into massive fraud at his bank, Italy's biggest private bank. A first inquest said he had committed suicide, a second ended with an open verdict. In 1989, a court in Milan ruled that Calvi had been murdered – but that the murderer remained unknown.

In a meeting with five Italian judges in New York in July 1991, the Sicilian supergrass Marino Mannoia alleged that Di Carlo had nine years earlier strangled Calvi with his bare hands before hanging the body from the bridge to make the death look like suicide. Two months after Calvi's death his bank, the Banco Ambrosiano, collapsed with debts of more than a billion dollars in Italy's biggest-ever financial scandal.

Di Carlo, the informer said, had acted on the orders of the Cupola to whom the untrustworthy Calvi owed tens of billions of lire.[33] If true, the account shows how freely the Mafia acts in Britain and may help to solve the mystery which still surrounds the death of Calvi. Mafia rules are universal and apply on British soil as much as in Sicily –

Di Carlo, as a Mafioso expelled from Cosa Nostra, was still beholden to the organisation and had to obey its orders, according to the secret society's code of honour.

Di Carlo's imprisonment did little to defuse Cosa Nostra's interest in the City of London as a centre for recycling its profits or in Britain as a base for drug trafficking. But having already ignored judge Falcone's warning back in 1987 that London was a focal point for drug trafficking, officials there, four years later, refused to believe another warning – this time from their own men in Rome. In October 1991 a diplomat and a Scotland Yard detective on secondment to the British embassy in the Italian capital sent a secret report to London calling for urgent international co-operation to prevent Italian clans from expanding their operations into Britain. The document said the threat of Cosa Nostra to Britain could become very real once the EC abolished its internal border controls in January 1993. But its authors – first secretary John Ashton and detective chief inspector Gus Jones, who had become Britain's first drug liaison officer in Italy in 1990 – were criticised in London for exaggerating the risks.

Far from exaggerating, the report underestimated the speed at which the Mafia was already expanding. As in much of the European Community, Cosa Nostra had not waited for the single market before acting. In 1992, drugs worth more than £500 million were discovered by British customs investigators. Cocaine seizures reached two tonnes (worth £328 million) for the first time, more than double the figure for the previous year. In the twelve months prior to April 1993 almost three tonnes of drugs were seized on flights between Heathrow, Gatwick and Stansted and airports in other EC countries. The street value of the heroin, cocaine, cannabis and amphetamines confiscated was estimated at £70.8 million – a 25 per cent increase on the previous year. Intelligence blamed increases in cocaine trafficking on Colombian cartels busy developing new markets in Europe with the complicity of Cosa Nostra and other organisations. The drugs were shipped to Europe and stockpiled in the Netherlands, Spain and Portugal before being fed in smaller quantities into Britain.

But a sizeable drugs haul in December 1993 – again in Felixstowe where Di Carlo's shipment was discovered some eight years previously – forced the investigators to revise their analysis. For the first time, Cosa Nostra was linked to drug smuggling into Britain, where street prices for hard drugs are the highest in Europe. Until then, police had believed Britain was being used principally as a transit point for drugs on their way to other countries, or to launder profits. The Di Carlo heroin, for instance, had been on its way to Canada. But on this occasion, thirteen people were arrested in Britain, Italy and Colombia after customs officials discovered 263 kilos of cocaine worth £105 million on a Colombian merchant vessel, the *Maipo*. The cocaine was hidden among coffee sacks in lead crates to escape X-ray detection. Another 850 kilos of cocaine were seized in Sicily. The raids broke up a network through which Colombia's Cali cartel sent cocaine to Cosa Nostra.

Britain, together with Germany and France, has also become increasingly attractive to members of Cosa Nostra as a safe haven for fugitives. In early 1993, the National Criminal Intelligence Service (NCIS) estimated there were 'several score Mafiosi and their associates in the United Kingdom'[34] – enough to constitute several clans. Neapolitan families of the Camorra were also in Britain, running protection rackets in London and south-east England which targeted restaurants and other businesses.[35] In 1993, the Italian authorities sought the extradition of alleged Mafiosi including Giovan Battista Maganuco, a thirty-year-old Sicilian living in Rochdale, where he had settled after coming to Britain to work as a chef. The Italian investigators issued a warrant for his arrest on a charge of extortion back in his home town of Gela on Sicily's southern coast.

In January 1994 a confidential NCIS report quoted Italian police as warning their British colleagues that three lieutenants of the Godfather Riina could be hiding in Britain.[36] The three – Bernardo Provenzano, Leoluca Bagarella and Giovanni Brusca – were all wanted for the murder of judge Falcone. But the Palermo anti-Mafia magistrates dismissed the report, saying Cosa Nostra's chiefs of staff never settled outside Sicily – to do so, the magistrates argued, would be to admit defeat on their home territory.

Britain's biggest attraction for Cosa Nostra, however, remains the City of London, which is a natural target for the recycling of illegal profits because it is comparatively stable, has a good reputation and offers established links with the Caribbean, Hong Kong and other offshore islands. A senior British intelligence officer told the author that the Mafiosi have become financial experts, involved in insider dealing, the theft of securities, market manipulation and deals on an illegal commodities market.[37] Ailing British firms are very vulnerable and may unsuspectingly be seduced by Mafia money. The NCIS noted in a January 1993 briefing that Cosa Nostra's methods could be as successful in Britain as they were in Sicily: 'At its most extreme, the money and power [organised crime] generates can subvert legitimate business and corporate activity and there is a real potential to corrupt the administration of justice and even the democratic process itself.'[38]

Beyond the European Community

Over the past few years, Cosa Nostra has not limited itself to the swift building of its own single market. It has also exploited the institutions which have overseen the slower progress to a union of EC states. No other criminal organisation has been as skilled as the Mafia in turning the EC's generous Common Agricultural Policy (CAP) to its own advantage. In 1988, EC aid to Italian farmers – mainly in the oilseed, tobacco and olive oil sectors – totalled 7,520 billion lire against 323 billion lire in 1972. There are no estimates available for how much of this goes to Italian organised crime, but one report put the value of EC frauds in Italy at 150–300 billion lire.[39] Both Sicily and Calabria, homes to Cosa Nostra and the 'Ndrangheta, can boast a huge number of trials for fraud against the EC. The number of frauds perpetrated in the two regions is seven times greater than the European average.

Recent investigations have shown how the Mafiosi make large profits from the bogus destruction of excess crops. According to Falcone: 'Reliable sources confirm that if all the crops which are supposed to have been destroyed had actually been destroyed, a Sicily entirely covered in orange and lemon groves would not suffice to achieve the levels of destruction which have apparently been achieved.'[40]

Equally at ease playing the EC fraud game or colonising its member states, Italian organised crime is looking beyond the external frontiers of 'Fortress Europe' to the eastern half of the continent. On the very night the Berlin Wall collapsed, a member of the Camorra telephoned his brother, who was in the city. The Camorra mobster urged him to cross over to East Germany immediately and buy pizzerias, restaurants and small businesses so that his family could invest its dirty profits.[41] The fall of the Iron Curtain opened up what was potentially one of the world's richest markets. In November 1993, Italian authorities unearthed a 3-trillion-lire (£1.5 billion) plot by the 'Ndrangheta to buy a refinery, steel mill and bank in Russia.

Italy has expressed growing alarm at the eastward spread of Cosa Nostra and its Neapolitan and Calabrian allies since they opened up new smuggling routes for drugs and arms through the former Soviet empire. The war in former Yugoslavia forced heroin-traffickers to seek alternatives to the traditional Balkan route for smugglers on their way from south-east Asia to western Europe. The route has shifted to cross through northern European countries – Hungary and the Czech and Slovak republics have become the main transit countries for drug trafficking, with Poland playing this role for consignments which are bound for northern Europe.

Drugs and arms trafficking are often two sides of the same coin. In October 1992, police in Catania in eastern Sicily discovered an arms cache which included a Soviet-made missile launcher, kalashnikovs, half a tonne of explosives, grenades and a stock of ammunition. A missile fired by the launcher would be powerful enough to pierce an armour-plated car. The discovery was made in the fiefdom of the local boss Nitto Santapaola. Shortly before, the Italian secret services had reported a lively trafficking in weapons, especially in kalashnikovs and Skorpion machine guns, between Cosa Nostra and contacts in what was then Czechoslovakia and Yugoslavia, and in Hungary, in which arms were exchanged for heroin and cocaine. Croat nationals had sold kilos of TNT, the military-type explosive used to murder judges Falcone and Borsellino, to Cosa Nostra. The former East Bloc, where Soviet forces stockpiled huge quantities of arms, has become a new market for Mafia purchases.

'For arms as for drugs, the Mafia has a thousand possibilities,' the supergrass Messina, the first to reveal the syndicate's colonies in Europe, testified to the Rome anti-Mafia commission. 'When the Mafia doesn't have them at its disposal, it steals them or buys them from the North, in Switzerland and in Germany. I acted as an intermediary for purchases worth hundreds of millions [of lire]. No boss will ever admit to being without arms . . . You can get anything you want from NATO bases – weapons, jackets, ammunition. You know how well equipped they are! When I said [the bosses] owned bazookas, people laughed. They have found five of them . . . It's like going to buy sweets.'[42]

The Sicilian men of honour have designs on even more terrible weapons. In early 1993 the Florence public prosecutor Pierluigi Vigna said there was a very immediate and real risk that Italian organised crime, especially Cosa Nostra, was ready to traffic in nuclear, chemical and bacteriological weapons. Vigna was investigating links between a Mafia clan led by Giacomo Riina, an eighty-five-year-old uncle of Salvatore Riina, who had settled in the peaceful hills of Tuscany, and eastern European arms merchants. German federal police had in the previous year alone recorded 120 cases of trafficking, or attempted trafficking, in uranium, caesium and other materials used in nuclear weapons from the former Warsaw Pact countries. A few months after Vigna's warning, the anti-Mafia commission revealed that Italian organised crime had sealed pacts with Russian criminals to carve up the trade in drugs and nuclear materials, and had also established money-laundering channels. Cosa Nostra, the Camorra and the 'Ndrangheta had held summits in Warsaw and Prague to negotiate the deal with their Russian counterparts.[43]

Only a few years after the abolition of EC frontiers, and the opening up of eastern Europe, the tentacles of Cosa Nostra were already reaching further than ever before. The threat of an international Mafia whose advance nations are powerless to stop seems uncomfortably real. Falcone's portrayal of the Sicilian syndicate as a model for other organisations to emulate was beginning to look increasingly prophetic:

> The current situation, in which criminal organisations from a few countries agree limited and local pacts, is one thing: quite another is the eventual evolution of organised crime towards a federation of vast dimensions. The extremely dangerous prospect of a homogenised model of criminal organisation, in which a point is reached where one can no longer distinguish between the methods of the Yakuza, the Chinese triads and Cosa Nostra, would create a kind of global Mafia, and I ask myself how it could possibly be opposed.[44]

8

TAMING THE OCTOPUS

The Fascist Challenge

It should have been a stage-managed visit from start to finish. In May 1924 the Fascist dictator Benito Mussolini toured Palermo and a host of Mafia dominions along the Sicilian coast and in the rugged interior. As if by some invisible hand, the streets where his motorcade was to pass were spruced up overnight and lined by thousands of cheering islanders.

Unfortunately, no allowance had been made for the vanity of the mayor of Piana dei Greci, a small town in the centre of the island. The town, which today has a population of some 6,000 people, is the biggest of the Albanian colonies in Sicily – the locals are faithful custodians of the language and traditions of their ethnic past, and postcards of Piana dei Greci often feature the colourful Albanian costumes worn on feast days. Don Ciccio Cuccia, the mayor charged with showing Mussolini round his 'typical' Sicilian township, was tied to the local Mafia and had several times been accused of murder. Nicknamed '*ù chianalottu*' ('small bottle') because he was short and fat, Don Ciccio prided himself on the supremacy he exercised over his fiefdom. When Mussolini summoned his escort of police motorcycles as they prepared to tour the town in the mayor's car, Don Ciccio took it as a personal insult. Upset by what he saw as defiance of his authority over his kingdom, he cheekily admonished his illustrious guest, using an offensive local word for the police: 'You're coming with me and there's nothing to worry about. Why do you need so many *sbirri*?'[1] The strutting dictator was not amused.

Mussolini's visit to Piana dei Greci epitomised the confrontation between the Fascist regime and the Mafia. At first the Mafia supported Fascism. The Godfather Calo' Vizzini even earned the personal benevolence of 'Il Duce' by raising funds for the latter's March on Rome. But for Mussolini, the Mafia represented not only a state within the State, a violation of order as he understood it, but also a challenge to his totalitarian vision of the Italian State. The dictator could not suffer such a rival. During his five-day visit to Sicily, he thundered: 'We must no longer tolerate that a few hundred blackguards overwhelm, impoverish and harm a magnificent people like yours.'[2]

Fascism's inability to coexist with the Mafia prompted it to throw down the gauntlet and defy organised crime's control of Sicily. Although the government drive had its limits, it was an unprecedented threat to the Mafia and was unrepeated for decades. Of all the Italian leaders, Mussolini came closest to breaking the power of the Mafia. He dubbed his campaign against the bandits and the Mafia 'Fascist surgery', and summed up what he saw as its achievements in a speech to parliament three years after his visit to Piana dei Greci. His host's insult apparently still rankled: 'In Piana dei Greci – and many of you remember that unspeakable mayor who always managed to get himself photographed on all solemn occasions – he is behind bars, and he will stay there for some time'.[3]

The man entrusted with wielding the Fascist scalpel was an authoritarian, inflexible police chief from the northern Piedmont region, Cesare Mori. Mori, schooled in the rigid traditions of ancient Turin bureaucracy, had earned his spurs in the province of Trapani in western Sicily, where he was sent in 1904. Backed by hundreds of policemen and a strong cavalry, he took on the local bandits and shot several dead himself. Named prefect (government representative) in Palermo with extraordinary powers in October 1925 to combat the Mafia and banditry, he soon realised his enemy had long ago expropriated the Italian State. He wrote in his memoirs, an arrogant, rhetorical work littered with tributes to the cult of 'Il Duce': 'The Mafia had created a state within the State, a regime within the Regime: that is, the regime of the Mafia with its own laws and its tributes of money and blood, and its penal sanctions.'[4]

Mori also denounced the Mafia's historical role as mediator between the social classes, chiefly between the rich landowners and the peasantry. He wanted to target 'above all the Mafia's mentality, its prestige, its intimidatory strength . . . to break with a firm resolve the conditions of submission, reciprocity and the compromises which have been created by the violent intervention, be it suffered or requested, of the Mafia in all business transactions and in all private or public activities of whatever kind'.[5] He claimed his method was not just to unleash police forces against the Mafia but also to try to engineer a revolution in the Sicilian mentality, a popular mobilisation – what he called 'an insurrection of consciences'.[6]

But Mori's campaign soon showed that it could be carried out only under a dictatorship. The '*Prefetto di Ferro*' ('Iron Prefect'), as he came to be known, at first sought to cut the ground from under the Mafiosi's feet. He issued a decree in 1925 whose purpose was to attack the Mafia's role as a social go-between, repress cattle-rustling and clandestine butchery. Rigid controls were imposed on the activities of *campieri* and other Mafioso guardians of the rural estates. They had to carry a special licence and swear an oath of submission to the laws of the Italian State in a pompous ceremony that included a mass. With an eye for detail, Mori even banned the planting of canes less than 100 metres from the edges of roads and ordered any beds of giant reeds which broke this rule to be pulled up without delay – passers-by were liable to be ambushed by gunmen hiding behind the canes.

Later, Mori launched huge police raids, each one leading to hundreds of arrests. His first weapon was a new offence, 'criminal association', invented by the judicial authorities to ease his task. His second was an inter-provincial police force, a group answerable only to him and free to roam across provincial borders. He certainly had the resources necessary to support his proud boast: 'If Sicilians are scared of the Mafia, I shall convince them that I am the most powerful Mafioso of the lot.'[7] Mori made 11,000 arrests in the late 1920s, of which 5,000 were in the province of Palermo. He tortured, jailed or sent into exile hundreds of Sicilians, many of whom were innocent. He once arrested an entire town, accusing all its inhabitants of complicity with the Mafia. In parallel to the police round-ups, many trials which had been abandoned for lack of evidence or following pressure from the 'friends of the friends' were reopened. Between 1922 and 1929, fifteen mass trials were held. For the first, a cage 50 yards long had to be built to hold the 154 defendants. Mori also made generous use of the death penalty, but those who were shot were mostly common criminals, rarely Mafiosi.

In one spectacular police operation early in 1926, Mori flushed out bandits who had sought refuge in the rugged Madonie mountains outside Gangi, one of the biggest towns in the area. To humiliate his foes, he ordered his officers into the houses of the fugitives and told them to sleep in their beds. Mori took several locals hostage, mostly women and children. In the end the bandits came down from the mountains and gave themselves up.

Mori did make a courageous attempt to sever the Mafia's ties with Sicilian politicians and aristocrats. This became the Iron Prefect's *bête noire* in the last years of his fight against the brotherhood, because he realised that no State challenge would succeed if it stopped at catching lower-ranking criminals. As he wrote in his memoirs: 'The Mafia is an old whore who likes to rub herself ceremoniously and submissively against the authorities, trying to flatter, deceive and lull them into a false sense of security.'[8] From 1926 onwards, Mori sent several reports to Mussolini denouncing the close links between the Mafiosi and a member of the Rome parliament, Alfredo Cucco, who was head of the Fascists in Palermo. Mori accused Cucco of using the Mafia to gather votes. He also dared to implicate General Antonino di Giorgio, a former Italian Minister of War and the commander of the armed forces in Palermo. In 1929, Mori launched a series of searches at the homes of the Palermo aristocracy.

Such efforts went too far for Mussolini's liking, who recalled his Iron Prefect with a terse telegram in June 1929 and transferred him to the northern province of Venezia Giulia. When once asked how long the war on the Mafia would last, Mussolini had answered in typically bombastic style: 'Until the end and afterwards. It will end when the recollection of its organisation has disappeared completely from the memory of Sicilians.'[9] In fact, the war ended much earlier than this because Mori aimed impossibly high within the Fascist hierarchy.

Did Mussolini manage to break the Mafia's power? Il Duce certainly thought he had. He would boast in parliament of the impressive decline in criminality reflected in the statistics produced by his regime. If these are to be believed, the number of murders in the province of Palermo fell from 223 in 1922 to 25 in 1928. The number of hold-ups was also down, from 246 to 14 over the same period, and extortions of money fell from fifty-three to six. But the press was muzzled by Fascism and these figures may be simply propaganda. As for the men of honour, they were to remember Mussolini's rule as a black period in their history for many years to come. Some six decades later, the supergrass Calderone described how wary he and other Mafiosi were of backing an attempted coup by neo-Fascists, because of the Mori precedent: 'Many Mafia bosses thought: "We'll help them to take power and then they will arrest us all, given that they will have identified us."'[10]

By and large, however, the Fascist repression spared the Mafia bosses and their patrons among the large estate-owners, together with deputies like Cucco. The temptation for Fascism to strengthen its hold on Sicily by co-operating with the Mafia was too great. It proved only too willing to preserve and safeguard the economic and social equilibrium in place, in exchange for the landowners' help in maintaining public order. Only the humbler Mafia of the *campieri* estate guardians, herdsmen, peasants and the poorer bourgeoisie felt the sharp edge of the Fascist scalpel. Neither did Fascism help to overcome the traditional diffidence towards the State, a legacy of the island's history of invasion. Promises made to the peasants by Mussolini in the early days of the Fascist regime were not kept – including claims that he would launch grandiose projects to improve the water supply, reclaim land, throw a patchwork of new roads across Sicily and break up the *latifondi*, resettling the peasants in rural towns or on landed estates.

The Mafia's success in securing acquittals for its senior brethren certainly endured. Genco Russo, who became the Godfather of the Mafia in the 1950s, was still a young man of honour in the years of Fascism. His record is an impressive one. Russo was acquitted first in April 1928 of five murders, then in December 1929 of four more, and again in January 1930 of two killings and three attempted ones. In October 1931 he was acquitted of being part of a criminal association, and finally in November 1932 of three more murders. There was never sufficient evidence to bring a conviction. Russo's predecessor as Godfather, Vizzini, was less fortunate. He was acquitted four times in a row under Mori's rule, but, after an accusation that he belonged to the Mafia, he was deprived of half his assets and spent five years in jail.

A Military Ally

Mussolini's limited success in taming the Mafia evaporated when the Allied troops liberated Sicily in 1943. In order to prepare the ground for the Allied landing, the government of the United States sealed a secret pact with the Mafia.

The US administration exploited the links between the Italian or Italo–American Mafiosi in America and the Mafiosi in Sicily. In return for the bosses' help, the military government appointed Mafiosi as mayors in several dozen Sicilian towns, or to posts within the Allied administration. For the first time in its history, the Mafia was suddenly propelled into the heart of the State apparatus – a status which was furthermore guaranteed by the occupying troops.

The bedrock of this transatlantic collusion was the Italo–American Mafioso Lucky Luciano. A Sicilian who had emigrated from his home town of Lercara Friddi at the age of nine, Luciano became one of the heads of the American Mafia in the 1920s. He was sentenced to thirty years in jail in 1936 for fiscal fraud and sixty-two counts of forcing women to become prostitutes. A drug-dealer as well as the owner of several brothels, he could boast of an efficient network of traffickers spanning Sicily, northern Italy and France.

In the early 1940s the American naval intelligence service was at a loss to explain a series of sabotage attacks in New York harbour on ships about to sail for Britain with weapons, ammunition and food. In the worst of the suspected acts of sabotage, the SS *Normandy*, being refitted as a troopship at the West Side pier, burst into flames in February 1942, and capsized. It was fast enough to outrun any German submarine. The intelligence officers thought these attacks were the work of Fascists operating within New York's Italian community. Hoping the Mafia could root out anybody sympathetic to the Axis powers, they turned to Luciano for information and assistance.

They guaranteed he would be released from prison if he helped them to find the culprits. When Luciano was

told what the American authorities wanted from him by his
associate Meyer Lansky and his lawyer Moses Polakoff, he
exclaimed: 'Look! I'm going to be deported. When I get
out – nobody knows how this war will turn out – whatever
I do, I want it kept quiet, private, so that when I get back
to Italy, I'm not a marked man.'[11] Luciano and his pals
did help the authorities, even protecting the harbour from
espionage and labour unrest.

After the war ended, Luciano's sentence was commuted
in 1946 and he was deported to his native Italy. He settled
happily in Naples, where he organised trafficking in drugs
and cigarettes for more than a decade. Justifying his
decision to free Luciano, Governor Thomas Dewey of the
state of New York sent a message to its legislature: 'Upon
the entry of the United States into the war, Luciano's aid
was sought by the Armed Services in inducing others to
provide information concerning possible enemy attack. It
appears that he co-operated in such efforts, although the
actual value of the information procured is not clear.'[12]

The Governor's explanation was an understatement.
Luciano's contribution to the Allied cause did not stop
at providing information on attacks in New York harbour.
At the authorities' request, he contacted his fellow Mafia
bosses in the United States who themselves mobilised their
cousins in Sicily, thus helping to prepare the ground for
the Allied landings on the island on 10 July 1943.[13] The
Italo–American Mafiosi had singled him out to authorities
as the key intermediary for establishing contact with the
Sicilians, and as the Mafioso with the most extensive ring
of underworld contacts.

According to the Sicilian historian Michele Pantaleone,
the co-operation between the Mafia and the US government
bore fruit four days after the landings on Sicily's southern
coast. Three tanks of the American forces clattered into

the town of Villalba in central Sicily, home of the Godfather
Calogero Vizzini. One of the tanks flew a yellow flag
bearing the initial 'L' for Luciano in black. Only a few
days previously, an American fighter plane had dropped
a message from Luciano and a yellow silk handkerchief
with his initial near the house of Don Calò. A disembodied
voice, buried in one of the tanks, repeated mechanically:
'Fetch Don Calò Vizzini. Fetch Don Calò Vizzini.' The
crews of the American tanks stayed just long enough to
call on him and take him away. The Godfather of the
Mafia joined the American military contingent which
swiftly isolated the southwest of Sicily, where beleaguered
German troops sought refuge before fleeing by sea. [14]

The American Seventh Army, which had the hard task
of cleaning up the mountainous centre and western part of
the island, did so quickly and at little cost. The landing
at Gela, further east along the coast from Agrigento, went
so well that by the afternoon of the first day trucks could
be brought ashore without hindrance. The Americans
encountered little resistance from Italian and German
troops, and took only seven days to reach the northern
coast. The British Eighth Army and a Canadian contingent,
on the other hand, found it much more difficult to liberate
the east of the island. Slowed by heavy fighting which cost
them several thousand casualties, they took five weeks to
reach Messina in the northeast of the island.

The nature of the role played by Don Calò and other
Mafiosi in what General Patton was to call 'the shortest Blitzkrieg in history' is unclear. Pantaleone says
the Mafiosi were recruited to fire at night on German
and Italian positions far ahead of the Allied lines. The
besieged soldiers would withdraw at dawn, convinced
that their American enemies had progressed much faster
than they had originally believed. [15] In the small town

of Mussomeli in central Sicily, the boss Giuseppe Genco
Russo made a public declaration that local people would
not impede the Allies. He captured the commander of
the Italian garrison in the town, disarmed him and had
him locked up in the local social club. The Americans
took over the town without firing a single shot, and they
appointed Genco Russo as mayor. Although the extent
of the Mafia's help is unclear, Luciano was not the only
boss to be deported from the United States just after the
end of the war. The Rome anti-Mafia commission, noting
that sixty-four others enjoyed the same fate, concluded
that this 'could only correspond to a reward for their
contribution to the preparation and the carrying out of
the landing'.[16]

The Allied military government which took over Sicily
after the landing, however, was not slow in showing its
gratitude. Ninety per cent of the 352 new mayors named by
the government's leaders were either Mafiosi or politicians
of the Separatist movement, a force tied inextricably to the
Mafia.[17] The Allies' aim was to set up a governing class
which could stand up to the Fascist government ruling
the mainland, and which might prove able to organise
and lead an eventual resistance movement. They were
fully aware of the links between the Separatists and the
Mafiosi. Two documents from the American consulate
in Palermo, obtained by the anti-Mafia commission and
dated November 1944, were entitled 'Meeting of heads
of the Mafia with General Castellano and the forming of
groups in favor of autonomy' and 'Formation of groups to
favor autonomy under the direction of the Mafia'.[18] The
author of the reports would have been hard pressed to be
more explicit.

The Mafioso's role as a mediator in local conflicts,
and the ultimate arbiter, was institutionalised. Dozens of

leading Mafiosi who had been jailed by the Fascists were appointed mayors of Sicilian towns by the Allied military command, replacing the Fascist town councils. Others were put in charge of stocks of weapons and ammunition as well as provisions or medicine. Don Calò himself was rewarded for his help with an official investiture as mayor of Villalba only a few days after the Americans had occupied the town. An American lieutenant handed him the tricolour sash symbolising the mayor's office, and gave him and his men permission to carry pistols and rifles. 'This is your master,' the officer proclaimed to the assembled townsfolk. One of the new mayor's first acts was to organise a black market in olive oil. His criminal record was to all appearances considered to be defunct – his slate had been wiped clean of charges, which included thirty-nine murders, six attempted ones, thirty-six robberies, thirty-seven thefts and sixty-three extortions.

One of the bosses to be honoured by the Allied government, Vincenzo di Carlo, who came from the town of Raffadali, was appointed head of the office in charge of requisitioning wheat and other cereals. Several other Mafiosi were deemed to have resisted Fascism and therefore had their police records purged of all criminal charges. Michele Navarra of Corleone, one of the first patriarchs to fall victim to Salvatore Riina, was allowed to take over hundreds of military vehicles abandoned by the army. As another favour granted by the Allies, men of honour were spared the onerous task of accounting for their crimes. The Mafioso Vito Genovese, who had returned to Italy to flee incriminations in America, became one of the bosses of the underworld during Fascism and stole supplies from Allied army stores until his arrest in 1944. Genovese was not formally indicted until six months after his arrest, because the officer who arrested him could not find anybody willing to take him before a court.

As Lord Rennel, the head of the Allied military government, reported back to London in August 1943, striking a barely regretful tone: 'I fear that in their enthusiasm to remove the Fascist *podestà* (mayors) and the municipal officials of rural towns, my officers, in some cases out of ignorance of local society, have chosen a number of Mafia bosses or have authorised such persons to propose docile substitutes ready to obey them.'[19] To maintain order, the Allies relied on the large estate-owners, a class which had been unharmed by Fascist rule. The landowners in turn entrusted the protection of their property to local strong-men, almost invariably Mafiosi – as had happened a few decades earlier.

What started out as an attempt by intelligence officers to use Mafia bosses for a purely military objective had lasting political repercussions. The Allied forces' approach paved the way for a relationship of cohabitation which Italy's government, institutions and especially the majority party (the Christian Democrats) established with the Mafia and maintained for decades. The relationship endured with a blossoming Mafia as the chief beneficiary, and a political class that only sporadically sought to counter the Mafia, to little effect.

The Absent State

The long-delayed birth of the Rome parliament's anti-Mafia commission is symptomatic of the Italian State's weak stand against the Sicilian fraternity, which marked almost the entire post-war period. For several years after the Allied forces threw town hall doors open to the men of honour, any denunciation of organised crime's links with politics or requests for a special commission to be set up unfailingly met with a stony response. The Interior Minister Mario Scelba, brushing off just such accusations from a group of opposition politicians in 1948, told his fellow-deputies: 'As the Mafia is an age-old phenomenon, its existence cannot be blamed on a particular line of policy.'[20] For fifteen years from 1948 to 1963, the parties of the ruling centre-right coalition led by the Christian Democrats rejected demands from the left-wing opposition for an anti-Mafia commission.

The Christian Democrats at last agreed to set up a commission in December 1962. At the time, a war between rival clans in Palermo was claiming a victim every seventeen hours. The parliamentary commission, made up of twenty-five deputies and twenty-five senators, was charged with the task of investigating the Mafia and proposing measures to stamp it out. Similar to a Select Committee in the British parliament, it was given powers to question State officials. But it was not until a Mafia car-bomb had killed seven police and army officers in Palermo in 1963, and national and regional elections had been safely conducted, that the commission was able to hold its first meetings. As early as August 1963, only a few months after its birth, the commission put forward a package of measures and recommended their urgent adoption. These proposals included the exile of Mafiosi to central and northern Italy, an end to rivalry between different police forces, closer co-ordination between police and magistrates and reform of public sector contracts. Today, much of the package has still to be implemented. The internal exile of Mafiosi, which was enforced, was

to prove disastrous and contributed to the spread of the
Mafia beyond Sicily. In the 1970s, Tuscany was one of
the regions which received most of these men of honour –
the region became a privileged home for various members
of the Corleonese clan, including Gaspare Mutolo (who
dealt in arms and drugs) and Giacomo Riina, uncle of the
Godfather Salvatore Riina.[21]

The anti-Mafia commission had an uphill task. When
it dared to propose a visit to Sicily in 1964, the right-
wing Cardinal Ernesto Ruffini of Palermo exploded: 'A
relentless propaganda campaign, through the press, radio
and television has persuaded people in Italy and abroad
that the Mafia has contaminated the island and that the
Sicilians in general are all Mafiosi.'[22] When in the same
year the commission launched an inquiry into Mafia
infiltration of the Palermo city council, the national and
regional leadership of the Christian Democrats – the party
in control of Palermo – closed ranks to frustrate the
investigation. The parliamentarian Oscar Luigi Scalfaro,
a Christian Democrat who pressed on with the probe
despite his party's opposition, was forced to resign as
vice-president of the commission. When the commission
did publish a voluminous dossier on the connections
of the Palermo mayor Salvo Lima with the Mafia, it
was quietly shelved. The annual report it published in
1976 under Senator Luigi Carraro, a Christian Democrat,
concluded rather optimistically that Cosa Nostra was on
the point of disappearing and that it was about to be
replaced by a more modest and less alarming form of
urban crime.

For several decades after the war, the authorities and
the media both sought to minimise the importance of Cosa
Nostra. A blatant manifestation of this are the speeches
delivered by successive Palermo chief prosecutors at

ceremonies held to mark the opening of the judicial year. In 1956, one incumbent declared that the Mafioso phenomenon had disappeared. His successor the following year did mention blood feuds, but put this down to rival groups of delinquents. In 1967 another prosecutor said the Mafia was well on its way to inevitable defeat. Judge Giovanni Falcone summed up the Italian State's efforts against the Mafia. It was, he said: 'Emotive, episodic, inconsistent. Motivated only by the impression created by a given crime or by the effect that a particular initiative on the part of the government will have on public opinion.'[23]

While the politicians in Rome slumbered, the Mafia grew so confident that it dared to launch a frontal attack on the institutions of the State in the late 1970s, targeting the few individuals courageous enough to take it on. This was a crossroads for the secret society. For decades it had been guided by the axiom of Palermo's Gaetano Badalamenti, the head of the Cupola until 1976, who dictated: 'We cannot wage war on the State.'[24] Infiltration, threats, corruption were all acceptable but an open clash was out of the question. Violence was used mainly to settle scores within the organisation or to kill dangerous witnesses and political opponents such as trade unionists.

But the Corleonesi clan, which overthrew Badalamenti and the establishment in a purge which lasted from the mid-1970s to the early 1980s, broke the golden rule of chiefly peaceful coexistence. 'Until now they controlled the State. Now they want to become the State,' said the informer Messina.[25] The victims were named the *'cadaveri eccellenti'* ('illustrious corpses') in a phrase coined by the Sicilian novelist Leonardo Sciascia. The Mafia had never, let alone in so brief a period, executed such senior magistrates or politicians. Those who refused to bend to the law of compromise were cut down. Palermo has the sad privilege of being the only city in the western world where, in little less than four years between 1979 and mid-1983, the heads of so many institutions were assassinated by a criminal organisation – they include the prefect and carabiniere General Dalla Chiesa, the head of the Communist opposition Pio la Torre, the Christian Democrat provincial secretary Piersanti Mattarella, the head of the Palermo flying squad Boris Giuliano, the commander of the carabinieri Emanuele Basile, the head of the investigating magistrates' team Rocco Chinnici and the chief public prosecutor Gaetano Costa. In many cases, those who ordered the killings have still not been brought to account. Several of the Mafiosi who carried out these assassinations were arrested but have since been freed.

Few of these victims were as deeply aware of the risks they were running as General Dalla Chiesa. A man hailed as a hero for his success in crushing the terrorist Red Brigades, Dalla Chiesa took a clear stand as soon as he reached Palermo, where he was appointed prefect in charge of combatting the Mafia. He pledged: 'I have come to restore credibility to the State, wherever it has become usual to see preference given to those who are prepared to genuflect and submit to blackmail in order to have something to which they are entitled as a right.'[26] For Dalla Chiesa, a man from northern Italy with a strong faith in the institutions of the State, most of the protection and privileges guaranteed by the Mafia and which Sicilians had to pay so highly for were no more than citizens' elementary rights. He believed it was the State's task therefore to guarantee these rights and turn the servants of the Mafia into its allies.

The General was ready to challenge the apex of the

political establishment if necessary. Dalla Chiesa believed the Sicilian allies of the Christian Democrat statesman Giulio Andreotti were the island's most polluted political family. He once told his son of the Andreotti faction and others of their like: 'They were in it up to their necks.'[27] Here is Dalla Chiesa's own account, which he wrote in his diary on 10 April 1982, of a private meeting with Andreotti before taking up his Palermo appointment: 'I was very clear, and I gave him the certainty that I would have no regard for that part of the electorate from which he draws his party faithful.' In reply, Andreotti told him about the body of a man of honour, Pietro Inzerillo, which was sent home to Sicily from America in a coffin with a 10-dollar bill stuffed into its mouth.[28]

Andreotti, however, who was not a member of the government at the time, has denied having spoken at that meeting of the Mafia's links with the political class, or of his contacts in Sicily. He said he and Dalla Chiesa only discussed drug trafficking. But for the magistrates investigating Andreotti's alleged dealings with Cosa Nostra a decade later, Andreotti was lying and the story of the dead Mafioso amounted to a warning to Dalla Chiesa 'not to push his inquiries into areas where the interests of Cosa Nostra were intertwined with those of degenerate masonic lodges and political sectors involved with the Mafia.'[29]

Dalla Chiesa was never given the opportunity even to begin to tackle the Mafia. According to judge Falcone: 'He did not have the time to make up for the inadequacies of the investigative machinery. All his activities . . . can be understood as a sustained request for better means to fight the Mafia.'[30] The result was that although Dalla Chiesa was potentially dangerous to the Mafia, he was isolated within the Italian State – a fatal combination in Palermo. An entry Dalla Chiesa made in his diary only

a day after his appointment shows how conscious he was
of his isolation:

> I suddenly find myself . . . in somebody else's home
> and in an environment which on the one hand expects
> . . . miracles and on the other curses my nomination
> and my arrival. That is, I find myself at the heart of . . .
> a State which entrusts the tranquillity of its existence not
> to the will to combat and defeat the Mafia and Mafioso
> politics, but to the use and exploitation of my name to
> silence the irritation of the parties . . ., ready to cast
> me aside as soon as certain interests are or have to be
> tackled or encroached upon.[31]

Dalla Chiesa was 'cast aside' on 3 September 1982, only
five months after his nomination. His wife was driving him
in a small car, with a policeman following in an escort car.
Less than a mile away from his office, two cars suddenly
blocked his way. Firing kalashnikovs, the killers sprayed
Dalla Chiesa, his wife and their bodyguard with bullets.
Dalla Chiesa and his wife died instantly, their bodyguard a
few days later. The following day, at the site of the ambush,
someone left a flower with a message: 'Here died the hope
of honest Sicilians.'

The men of honour smugly congratulated themselves.
'After the murder of La Torre and Dalla Chiesa,' said
the supergrass Mutolo, 'we wondered whether the next
man the State would send to Palermo would be just as
dangerous, but our doubts proved unfounded because,
despite all the declarations, we sensed there was less
commitment and we got more contacts and information
[from the institutions].'[32] This was to prove an exces-
sively confident judgement. A few years before Dalla
Chiesa was sent to Sicily, a young, little-known Palermo

investigating magistrate was preparing to revolutionise the State's handling of organised crime. The young magistrate was Giovanni Falcone, and he was to become the symbol of Italy's struggle against the Mafia.

9

JUDGE GIOVANNI
FALCONE

In Enemy Territory

For decades, the rule of thumb for the State had been never
to tackle Cosa Nostra as an organisation. Only individual
crimes were persecuted. But Falcone's novel approach was
to target the Mafia as a structure, rather than focusing on
single offences. It was not until parliament passed the
Rognoni–La Torre law in 1982, however, that Falcone had
the necessary means to implement his strategy to the full.
The brainchild of the Communist politician Pio la Torre –
for years an active member of the anti-Mafia commission –
the bill was submitted to parliament in March 1980. But it
was only after both La Torre and Dalla Chiesa had been
murdered that it was resuscitated and speedily passed into
law – in just ten days, and more than two years after it
had first been published. The law for the first time defined
Mafia association as a crime, and also allowed magistrates

to investigate the bank accounts of individuals suspected of laundering Mafia funds.

Few were better placed than Falcone to exploit this new law to the full. He was born into a bourgeois, conservative family in the heart of Palermo on 18 March 1939. His father was a research chemist and his mother a devout Catholic. He began his career by training as a naval officer before turning to the law, which he studied at Palermo University, graduating with top marks. His first important post was that of assistant public prosecutor at Trapani in western Sicily, where he served for eight years and commanded respect for his integrity and hard work. After serving as a bankruptcy judge, Falcone was sent in 1978 to Palermo, where he was made investigating magistrate at the age of thirty-nine. He found himself working with a judicial team only beginning to emerge from an age-old lethargy as far as Mafia investigations – only a few were under way – were concerned. With the encouragement of the chief magistrate Rocco Chinnici, an obstinate figure little inclined to diplomacy, Falcone was to change all this.

Only two years after arriving in Palermo, Falcone was given what was then the most delicate investigation of those in hand into the brotherhood, and was guaranteed total autonomy in his task. When a senior Palermitan magistrate urged Chinnici to thwart Falcone by saddling him with petty trials so that he would have no time left to deal with Mafia cases, Chinnici brushed the advice inside. The inquiry centred on a drug-trafficker, Rosario Spatola, whose clan had flooded the United States with heroin in alliance with the Palermo Inzerillo family. The case proved an eye-opener for the young magistrate: 'The Mafia, seen through the Spatola trial, appeared to me as a world that was enormous, boundless, and unexplored,' Falcone was to say years later.[1]

Falcone took to his case with enthusiasm. In a radical approach, he bombarded the directors of all the banks in the province of Palermo with letters demanding full details of recent transactions on suspect accounts, including all receipts for foreign exchange operations. His office was soon submerged in rolls of computer print-outs from the banks. He spent entire days painstakingly sorting through these, gradually retracing the route followed by the dollars used to pay for the heroin. Needless to say, such novel methods of investigation were not appreciated by the Mafia. Much later, a scandalised Nino Salvo, a Mafioso with a monopoly over tax-collecting in Sicily, was to protest: 'That magistrate did crazy things. He went and looked in the banks, to see where the money went. Crazy!'[2]

Taking on the Spatola probe changed Falcone's life. It brought him notoriety, something he would shrug off with a quip: 'I'm not a Robin Hood,' he would say. 'I'm not a kamikaze pilot. I'm not a Trappist monk. I'm just working for the State in enemy territory.'[3] For the first time in his career, he was given police protection. All this entailed was an escort car with three bodyguards, a petty precaution compared to the protection he was given later in his career. But it was enough to highlight his isolation – many Palermitans ignored or were hostile to him, including a neighbour who sent a letter to the local newspaper. Describing herself as 'an honest citizen who regularly pays taxes and works eight hours a day', Patrizia Santoro complained about the noise made by the sirens of the police car that escorted Falcone every day, weekends included. 'Now I ask: is one not entitled to rest or at least to be able to follow a television programme in peace? Even with the windows closed, the noise of the sirens is very loud.' She suggested the anti-Mafia magistrates should be lodged in secure villas on the outskirts of Palermo so that citizens would not be hurt in any attacks on them.[4]

Falcone increasingly found himself receiving threats from Mafiosi he questioned. These were often anonymous letters, consisting of a single sheet of paper with a coffin drawn in black ink. One mobster told him with a smile: 'You're working too much. It's bad for your health, you should take a rest.' Another warned him to his face: 'You have a dangerous job. If I were you, I'd take my bodyguards to the bathroom with me.' But the men of honour did not stop at threats. On one occasion, Falcone went into the Ucciardone jail in Palermo to question a businessman about the boss Salvatore Inzerillo. Suddenly an inmate, Salvatore Sanfilippo, kicked the door of the interview room open, brandishing a gun in his hand. Falcone acted fast, slamming the door shut and racing into another room. Taken aback, the gunman pretended to take another magistrate hostage, saying he wanted to be transferred from the Ucciardone.

Five years after Falcone first arrived in Palermo, the Mafia murdered his mentor Rocco Chinnici. A car-bomb exploded as he walked the few steps from his home to his armour-plated car on the morning of 29 July 1983. Two bodyguards and the porter of Chinnici's home were killed. A third bodyguard at the wheel of the judge's waiting car survived, shielded from the blast by the car door.

The killing of Chinnici did nothing to alter Falcone's determination, and shocked the Rome government into appointing a respected Sicilian magistrate, Antonino Caponnetto, to head what became a dedicated pool of investigators who would focus all their efforts on fighting the Mafia. Caponnetto remembers Falcone as a workaholic with a huge memory, but also as a shy man who rarely confided in his colleagues.

Caponnetto also described how Falcone lived with the knowledge that he was in danger: 'Giovanni was not scared of death. He himself wrote that "all Sicily is impregnated with the culture of death." But none the less he was always very careful about security, aware that he was running a serious risk. Except once, when he got married at the city hall, he wanted a ceremony which would lose none of its intimacy . . . That afternoon he arrived without an escort. He was driving the car.'[5]

The Palermo team was to score some of Italy's biggest post-war successes against the secret society. It finally broke with the rule that had prevailed for decades and which decreed that trials should almost invariably end in acquittals for Mafiosi on the grounds of insufficient evidence. For years the men of honour had emerged from these trials with greater prestige and increased power.

The chief weapon in the armoury of Falcone's team was the supergrass Tommaso Buscetta. Until this Palermo boss turned State's evidence, what little information there was about the Mafia had persuaded most people that if a man of honour spoke about its doings he must be mad and therefore not to be believed. The low-ranking Leonardo Vitale, who had revealed much to authorities in the mid-1970s, had been declared insane and his evidence ignored. It was Falcone who took Buscetta's testimony down, by hand, for weeks on end. The judge later described the supergrass as a language teacher, who gave the Palermo team the essential keys enabling them to understand the Mafia. The two found they had much in common. Buscetta said of the man who interrogated him: 'We are both Palermitans. A turn of phrase, a glance, or a reference to a place and an event was enough for us to understand each other.'[6]

Buscetta's evidence, which helped make possible the

Pizza Connection drug-trafficking case in the United States, enabled Falcone to engineer post-war Italy's biggest judicial assault on the Mafia. The so-called 'maxi-trial' of Palermo inflicted nineteen life sentences and a total of more than 3,000 years in jail on no fewer than 338 men of honour in December 1987. It was the first time that such heavy sentences had been handed down to so many Mafiosi. Bosses, including the Godfather Riina and his lieutenant Provenzano, and Palermo's Michele Greco were sentenced to life in jail. Most of the convictions were for criminal association, the crime introduced into the penal code after the murder of General Dalla Chiesa in September 1982. Previously the Mafiosi had been subject at most to minor irritations such as internal exile or the withdrawal of their passports.

But the trial's success was not due to the Italian State – it was the result of the commitment and professionalism of magistrates like Falcone. It dealt a blow to the myth of the Mafia's invulnerability and impunity, but it did not mark a turning-point in the State's efforts against organised crime. In the years that followed, State institutions underscored the extent to which the Palermo magistrates were fighting a lone battle. In 1990, an appeals court reduced the number of life sentences to twelve, and acquitted eighty-six of the convicted Mafiosi. It refused to accept the evidence of supergrasses as valid and rejected the magistrates' explanation of the Mafia as a tight-linked structure. The following year, Italy's Supreme Court, presided over by the 'sentence-killer' judge Corrado Carnevale, also overturned several heavy sentences. It was not until the following year, after the court was overhauled, that the original sentences were confirmed.

In the aftermath of the trial, Falcone and his colleagues were isolated within the State. The prestige he acquired,

at both national and international level because of the
unprecedented results he obtained, prompted the jealousy of his superiors. Infighting ensured that, despite
his achievements, he was not given the job of chief
magistrate when it became vacant in 1988. The new
incumbent, Antonino Meli, set about destroying what
the pool had accomplished. Arguing that Cosa Nostra
was not a unitary structure, Meli assigned Mafia cases
to investigating magistrates outside Falcone's specialised
team, and to other Sicilian tribunals. He tried to force
the anti-Mafia team to investigate a whole range of cases
– from wife-beating to car thefts – prompting Falcone and
seven other colleagues to threaten to resign.

A fellow-magistrate and close friend of Falcone's, judge
Paolo Borsellino, courageously denounced the destruction
of the team in which he and Falcone had played a
predominant role, together with the flagging efforts of the
judiciary and the police:

Until recently all the anti-Mafia investigations, precisely
because of the unitary structure of the Cosa Nostra
organisation, were strongly centralised in the pool of
investigating magistrates . . . Today, on the contrary,
all the trials are dispersed into a thousand little streams.
Everybody must look after everything – that's the official
explanation. The truth is that Giovanni Falcone is
sadly no longer the point of reference . . . I have the
unpleasant feeling that somebody wants to take a step
backwards.[7]

Falcone was condemned by those who obstructed him
– among them senior magistrates and politicians at both
regional and local level – to a dangerous and fatal isolation.
It was a combination very similar to that which condemned

Dalla Chiesa to death. In June 1989, an attempt against Falcone's life was narrowly prevented. Police found a bomb of fifty-eight sticks of dynamite on rocks a few yards away from the seaside villa he rented outside Palermo. 'They'll try again, you'll see. They'll try again; the Mafia doesn't forget and it doesn't forgive,' Falcone said two days after the discovery. 'I was expecting it, it was in the air. I've been on the blacklist for some time – I'm not saying it out of vainglory but I shouldn't think I was at the bottom of the list.'[8] That summer, the jealousy of Falcone's rivals climaxed in a series of anonymous letters sent to leading figures in the State hierarchy accusing him of illicit working methods and negligence in handling supergrasses. The charges were a fabrication, but the long-drawn-out controversy greatly benefited the Mafia because it weakened Falcone's battle against the organisation.

With regret, but convinced he would be able to do little if he stayed in Palermo, Falcone eventually left for Rome and a new job as director of penal affairs at the Justice Ministry. He believed that the post, which he took up in April 1991, would allow him to help reorganise the anti-Mafia legal apparatus. He wanted to devise new laws to co-ordinate the fight, drawing on his experience on the front line. Falcone was to live thirteen months in Rome, and this brief period proved one of the most intense in the history of Italy's long battle against the Mafia. To a great extent because of his sheer determination, a series of laws were passed in quick succession – in June, a decree enabled police to restrict the movements of suspected men of honour; the following month, a law allowed the government to dissolve town councils infiltrated by the Mafia. An Italian version of the FBI was set up in October, followed in November by a special task-force of magistrates to oversee investigations into Cosa Nostra nationwide, and finally in December a law against extortion rackets.

A Death Foretold

In an interview with the author eight months into his Rome post, Falcone showed himself as much as ever a dedicated 'servant of the State'. Forced to live the life of a recluse, he slept in a military barracks near the Justice Ministry in the city centre. Fast armour-plated cars and bodyguards whisked him to and fro between the barracks and the ministry near the river Tiber, where he sealed himself in a fortified office. Outside, an armed officer lounged in an armchair in the corridor. Visitors had to go through two bulletproof doors to reach the room, where Falcone's collection of miniature china and crystal geese sat at odds with the coats of arms and insignia given to him by the police forces of five continents.

Then fifty-two, the stout, moustachioed judge was at pains to stress that he was only doing his job in battling the organisation which had been sending him death threats for the past quarter-century. 'What drives me? Just the knowledge that everyone must do their duty. *Basta* [Enough].'9 He did not hide his irritation at questions about his personal commitment. 'We'll talk only about the Mafia. Not about me. I don't have anything to do with it,' he said in typically sardonic style. 'It seems really odd to me that such questions can be asked of an employee of the State . . . A phenomenon like the Mafia isn't resolved by heroism – only by hard, tiring, humble day-to-day work.' When

I apologised at the end of the interview for pressing him on his personal commitment, he smiled mischievously, and quipped: 'You were only doing your job.'

For the pugnacious Falcone, for so long a man who had been isolated because of his exceptional dedication, this was the key to fighting the secret society. 'What we need is an acceptable standard of commitment against the Mafia – a standard for people to do their duty, and then there won't be the need for so-called "heroes".' But despite all his efforts, there was still a need for 'heroes' like Falcone. His aggressive use of his powers as a magistrate to conduct investigations, to call in witnesses and issue indictments against untouchable business and political potentates, had given him an unrivalled insight into the Mafia. Falcone was well aware of the price he might have to pay for his position as Italy's leading organised-crime-fighter – fatalistically so. 'Those who believe they are doing something useful are more exposed than others, for many reasons – because of the inertia, ignorance and cowardice of others. And they are murdered – inexorably. That's all there is to it.'

Falcone's prophecy was fulfilled only seven months later. In the spring of 1992, men of honour planted a huge bomb in a service tunnel running below the motorway that links the Punta Raisi airport to Palermo. According to informers, it took as many as eighteen Mafiosi to prepare the assassination. To test the remote control that would detonate the bomb, they staged several dry runs with cars speeding along the motorway at 160 kmh (the expected speed of Falcone's convoy), setting off flash-bulbs to get the timing right. Once all was ready, a group of mobsters set up the remote control on a hillside overlooking the motorway. They lay in wait for five days.

On the afternoon of 23 May, a Friday, a lookout posted at

the Palermo garage where Falcone's armour-plated car was parked phoned his accomplices when he saw the car being taken out by the judge's driver. Shortly afterwards, another lookout at the airport saw Falcone's plane, provided by the secret service, land there. The arrival was supposedly known only to the secret service. Two minutes after the plane touched down, the Mafioso used his mobile phone to tip off his acolytes waiting by the motorway a few miles away. The call lasted six minutes – it was interrupted just after the bomb exploded, killing Falcone, his wife and three bodyguards.

The Mafia has no preference for any single technique of assassination, Falcone had written a few months before his death: 'The Mafia always choose the shortest and least dangerous path. That is its only guiding principle . . . Each victim was killed at their most vulnerable moment. Only technical and strategic considerations determine the type of assassination and the weapon to be used. With a man like Rocco Chinnici who travels in an armour-plated car, it is necessary to resort to more spectacular methods.'[10]

Cosa Nostra rejoiced. 'When the news bulletin came, there was an explosion of celebration, people applauded . . . in the cells, we toasted each other and drank,' said the informer Messina, who was behind bars in the Caltanissetta jail at the time of Falcone's death.[11] According to other supergrasses, Riina himself celebrated in style two weeks later, with a champagne toast in a villa on the outskirts of Palermo.[12] He had allegedly ordered the killing as a favour for 'very important people' outside Cosa Nostra who had promised to guarantee judicial leniency towards organised crime.[13]

Fifty-seven days after Falcone was murdered, a car-bomb killed his friend and colleague judge Paolo Borsellino, along with five bodyguards. Fifty kilos of explosives packed into a Fiat 600 exploded as Borsellino, who had vowed to carry on Falcone's mission, rang the doorbell of his mother's flat in Palermo. Borsellino and his bodyguards, among them a twenty-four-year-old woman, took the full force of the blast. Escorts and bulletproof cars did not prevent the Mafia from carrying out a sentence which had been made public previously. The Palermo supergrass Vincenzo Calcara had told Borsellino during questioning in the Ucciardone jail a few weeks earlier: 'I was ordered to kill you. We were to shoot you with a rifle equipped with a telescopic sight – a real professional job. They had chosen me as the killer. They even gave me the weapon. I would only have had to press the trigger . . . If the attempt failed, there were plans for a car-bomb.'[14] Just as had been announced, it was a car-bomb that blew up Borsellino.

The murders of Falcone and Borsellino prompted an unprecedented public protest against Mafia intimidation. More than ever Sicilians gave the lie to Don Fabrizio Salina's fatalistic view of the island in The Leopard: 'Sleep, my dear Chevalley, sleep is what the Sicilians want, and they will always hate those who seek to awake them.'[15] Falcone's funeral in Palermo was followed by thousands of people who lined the streets and packed the cathedral. Although this was a State funeral, the ceremony brought a bitter indictment of the country's leading politicians. Dignitaries were heckled and booed by the crowd, who saw them as representatives of a class which had done nothing to prevent Falcone's fatal isolation, or worse, had actually colluded with the Mafia. Similar scenes accompanied Borsellino's funeral. 'Politicians out,' the crowd chanted. 'Get the Mafia out of the church.'

Buscetta, whose evidence had been recorded by Falcone, highlighted the extent to which both had been isolated in their combat:

> Judge Falcone was for me a beacon in the fight against the Mafia. The Italian State never realised who Falcone and Borsellino were – it didn't value them, it denigrated them, especially Falcone . . . I saw the disappointment in the eyes of Falcone every time I met him, but he was always laughing. They accused him of being a prima donna . . . but he was a prima donna who wanted to fight the Mafia in earnest.[16]

Across the Sicilian capital, people hung sheets from their balconies daubed with defiant anti-Mafia slogans. Palermitans stuck tributes and messages on a magnolia tree outside Falcone's home in the central via Notarbartolo, a street named after the banker killed by the Mafia in the late nineteenth century who had been the first 'cadavere eccellente' ('illustrious corpse'). 'There are a million things to say to you, but the first we can think of is: Thank you,' read one note left by schoolchildren. A schoolboy called Dario wrote: 'Falcone and Borsellino, your deaths were a great blow to our hopes, but they have also awakened our conscience. We shall continue your struggle so that one day the Mafia can be defeated.' A year later, some 150,000 people marched through Palermo in June 1993 to commemorate the deaths of Falcone and Borsellino in what was Italy's largest ever anti-Mafia demonstration. Hundreds of local shopkeepers, infuriated by the extortion rackets, hung posters in their windows reading simply: 'No to the Mafia.' One huge banner bore the names of dozens of victims of the Mafia and the slogan: 'Too many dead – nobody guilty.'

A Lasting Offensive?

The murders of two of Italy's bravest anti-Mafia fighters
proved a crossroads both in the willingness of the State
to fight organised crime and in public attitudes towards
it. For the first time since the war, the State's response
to the murder of its 'servants' was more than just a
brief knee-jerk reaction. Immediately after the killings,
the government sent 7,000 troops to Sicily, not only to
assist the police in their task but also to convince Sicilians
that 'they have not been abandoned', in the words of the
new premier Giuliano Amato.

In August 1992, a few months after the murders, parliament rushed through a package of anti-Mafia measures
– laws which Falcone and Borsellino had persistently
lobbied for but without success. Police were authorised to
conduct house searches without warrants, an action which
had greatly bolstered Italy's fight against the terrorist Red
Brigades. Police were also granted extensive powers to
infiltrate clans in undercover 'sting' operations, and to
bug private phone calls and conversations. Evidence
from an informer given to investigators before a trial
would remain valid even if the supergrass withdrew it
in court. Politicians caught paying for votes supplied by
Mafia bosses faced sentences of up to six years in jail.
Soon after the package was approved, life was breathed
into two institutions which had until then existed only
on paper. First, the DIA (Italy's FBI) was given the
means to co-ordinate anti-Mafia police activity and to
carry out operations nationwide. This reflected the spread
of the secret society throughout the Italian mainland.
Similarly, a national anti-Mafia prosecutor was appointed
– a post which was to have been Falcone's – to oversee

and co-ordinate the work of twenty-six local anti-Mafia prosecutors' offices spread throughout Italy.

Crucially, Mafia turncoats were at last guaranteed a solid, American-style, protection scheme. For decades Italy had had no equivalent to the US federal witness programme which was used to great effect in persuading American Mafiosi and other leading criminals to co-operate. Under a new Italian law, the State agreed to issue supergrasses with false names and false identity papers, even forging school certificates and university diplomas if necessary. Public prosecutors were empowered to order the removal of an informer from the jail where he was being held if he was in danger there. The turncoat's family would be helped to leave their homes and start a new life elsewhere in Italy or abroad, and given the protection of the State. Galvanised by such reforms, the supergrass Calderone urged the anti-Mafia commission: 'Now is the best time to bring the Mafia to its knees. Even more must be done, a superhuman effort must be made because success is possible. Otherwise, they are capable of doing anything. They are like rats on a sinking ship who hang on to anything: they are capable of everything, and they have shown it.'[17]

The government's offensive soon yielded results. The number of informers mushroomed, swelling to seven hundred or so by April 1994.[18] Significantly, the supergrass Buscetta at last agreed to testify about links between the Mafia and politicians. He had refused to be drawn on the sensitive issue for years – save for denouncing a Christian Democrat councillor in Palermo, Giuseppe Trapani, who was safely dead and buried. When pressed by Falcone and other magistrates, Buscetta would justify his refusal to answer questions about politicians by saying that the

Italian State lacked the will to combat the Mafia. On one occasion, he told Falcone and the latter's chief Caponnetto:

> Look, I don't believe in this State. I am collaborating with you because I respect you, but for me you are members of something which is hostile to me . . . Don't ask me about this, because I am convinced that the State would not be able to bear the reactions that would be prompted by my testimony.[19]

Only in September 1992, after the murders of the former Palermo mayor Salvo Lima, and of Falcone and Borsellino, did Buscetta agree to talk, denouncing Lima as a man of honour and a political reference-point for Cosa Nostra.[20] When the anti-Mafia commission asked him whether he believed his choice not to speak out earlier about the Mafia's political links had been a wise one, Buscetta answered:

> You're putting me on the spot. I think that the choice was wise from a material point of view. From a human point of view perhaps I made a mistake . . . If I had spoken about politics at that time, I would have made my testimony useless. I would have become a nothing, because people would have said: 'You believe this rascal who talks of things he doesn't know anything about?'[21]

In 1993, some 240 bosses of Italy's four criminal organisations – Cosa Nostra, the Camorra, the 'Ndrangheta and the Sacra Corona Unita – were arrested. Assets worth 5 trillion lire (£2.5 billion) were seized.[22] Easily top in the hierarchy of those arrested was Salvatore Riina. But prize catches also included Nitto Santapaola, fifty-two, a boss from Catania who had bludgeoned his way into Cosa Nostra's Cupola from humble beginnings as a shoe salesman. After a dozen years on the run, '*il cacciatore*' ('the hunter', as he was known) was arrested at dawn on 18 May 1993, as he slept with his wife in a remote farmhouse outside Catania.

A few months later, in early 1994, the dominant figure among the Camorra bosses, Carmine 'Fatty' Alfieri, a key ally of Cosa Nostra, turned informer after more than a year behind bars. One of Italy's richest gangsters with an empire worth some 1.5 trillion lire (£750 million), and a liking for Dante and Bach, Alfieri had been arrested in September 1992 after ten years on the run. He was suspected of having forged ties with senior members of the Christian Democratic Party, including the Neapolitan former Interior Minister Antonio Gava. 'The State has defeated the Camorra, a historical phase has ended. I say to all the bosses who are still free: "Follow my example, co-operate with the judges, it's over now",' the fifty-one-year-old Alfieri told the magistrates who took down his evidence.[23] In a letter to the Naples judges, Alfieri wrote: 'I understand my mistakes, the damage I have done to society . . . I fear the serious consequences of my mistakes on the lives, the habits and the culture of young people in our region . . . I want to bring myself closer to God. I've always respected the values of religion even if I've lived them in a contradictory and warped way.'[24]

The previously taboo question of the Mafia's ties with politicians was tackled head on for the first time by parliament's anti-Mafia commission — three decades after its creation. The commission dedicated an entire report to such links, tracing their historical development and naming untouchables such as Andreotti and his Sicilian lieutenant Lima — this was several months after the magistrates had launched an investigation into Andreotti's alleged dealings with Mafia bosses. The report was read and discussed at length in schools and universities across Italy.

This offensive against the Mafia was made possible by the body-blow which Italian voters delivered to the parties which had traditionally dominated post-war governments. The rout of established parties like the Christian Democrats and the Socialists in the April 1992 general elections and in polls since then, together with a long-running political corruption scandal based in Milan, prompted an unprecedented purge of the old governing class. The scandal exposed a web of illicit dealings between politicians, businessmen and criminals engaged in the carve-up of business contracts, including those in the construction sector traditionally privileged by the Mafia. Once supported by the United States and the Vatican as a vital bulwark against the spread of Communism in Europe, the Christian Democrats had begun to fall apart after that role was destroyed by the collapse of the Berlin Wall in November 1989 and the opening of eastern Europe. For more than four decades after the war, the Christian Democrats had been able to present themselves as the champions of anti-Communism. Since 1943, the Communist threat had helped foster an alliance between Cosa Nostra and the authorities. That alliance was justified on the grounds of State security – the Mafia became an arm of the fight against Communism in return for tacit tolerance of their activities. But in the early 1990s, discredited and weakened, the parties of the establishment were unable to guarantee that they would be able to look after the Mafia's interests as they had in previous years.

Worse, in the eyes of Cosa Nostra, Sicilians mobilised

behind a new anti-Mafia movement, the 'Rete' ('Network') which swiftly became Italy's fastest-growing political party of the early 1990s. It was founded by Leoluca Orlando, a former Christian Democrat mayor of Palermo. Born the eldest son of a wealthy, aristocratic Palermo family, Orlando studied law and became at the age of twenty-four the youngest university professor in Italy. A devout Catholic, he joined the Christian Democrats – the start of a meteoric political career. Elected mayor of the Sicilian capital in 1985, he challenged Mafia interests and his party in the so-called 'Palermo Spring' of 1985–90.

After he stormed out of his party, his harsh attacks on leading politicians, whom he accused of corruption and collusion with the Mafia, won him a wide audience. Buoyed by popular support, he founded the 'Network', which managed to win twelve seats in the Rome lower house on its first showing in the 1992 elections. A year later, in November 1993, Orlando was re-elected mayor of Palermo with an astonishing 76.4 per cent of the vote in the first round – a decisive blow to the political order (Mafia and Christian Democrats) which had ousted him from the city hall in 1990.

Cosa Nostra's response to the loss of several political allies and to the government offensive was not slow in coming. Its reaction underlined a process already in train – the severe challenge to the traditional co-existence of the Mafia and the State. For almost the entire post-war period right up to the end of the 1970s, Cosa Nostra had in its relationship with State institutions always treated the latter as a distinct sovereignty. Neither had attacked the other as long as each played by the rules.

But in recent years the Mafia seems to have been deliberately seeking a frontal clash with the State. Mafiosi and politicians are on an increasingly unequal footing. It is Cosa

Nostra which calls the shots. The killing of Lima, the European parliamentarian who had been denounced as the Mafia's political guarantor in Palermo, underscores the organisation's desire to dominate the political class. According to Luciano Violante, former president of the anti-Mafia commission: 'Cosa Nostra no longer wants a relationship between equals or one which is based on the exchange of favours, as conceived by [the patriarch Gaetano] Badalamenti, who used to say: "We cannot wage war on the State." I have the impression that Cosa Nostra no longer recognises a political authority. Today it seeks to impose its will on everything, believing itself in some way betrayed by the political world, because it no longer safeguards its interests.'[25]

Cosa Nostra retaliated by unleashing a terrorist-like counter-offensive. In just the first half of 1993, in several Italian cities, eleven people died and dozens were injured in five car-bombings. The investigators attributed them to an alliance of the Mafia and right-wing terrorists, aided and abetted in all probability by secret service agents. In March, a car-bomb exploded in the Parioli district, one of Rome's smartest residential neighbourhoods. Twenty-three people were injured. The bomb went off shortly after the host of a popular television talk-show, Maurizio Costanzo, had driven past. He had often turned his programme into an anti-Mafia platform. Less than two weeks later, a much more powerful bomb went off in the middle of the night near the Uffizi Gallery in Florence, killing six people and heavily damaging the museum. Again, in late July, three car-bombs went off in Milan and in Rome, killing another five people.

'The bombs in Rome and Florence indicate that Cosa Nostra does not intend to remain idle while its bosses and allies are seized one by one,' said Violante that summer. 'They are warnings, not Cosa Nostra's answer. The anti-Mafia has not allowed itself to be intimidated and has persevered . . . Therefore we must now expect the real response: they will try to blow apart strategic linchpins in the struggle against the Mafia.'[26] The Mafia had resorted to terrorist tactics in the past. After Buscetta had shocked Cosa Nostra by revealing its secrets to Falcone in the early 1980s, the Cupola was anxious to distract the attention of the forces of law and order, and of public opinion, away from Sicily. The boss Pippo Calò, a member of the Cupola and the head of the Mafia's colony in Rome, contacted the Camorra and right-wing terrorists and ordered them to plant a bomb on a train. The explosion two days before Christmas in 1984, on a passenger train travelling from Florence to Bologna, killed 16 people and injured 266.

After the general elections of March 1994, the government offensive against Cosa Nostra appeared to be running out of steam. The poll was a stinging defeat for the Network of Palermo mayor Orlando, which had made the battle against organised crime its main electoral platform. Across Sicily, the rightist National Alliance of the media baron Silvio Berlusconi, which included former Christian Democrat politicians allegedly linked to the Mafia, swept aside many leading figures of the Network such as the former judge Caponnetto.

To the dismay of the anti-Mafia investigators, parliamentarians of the victorious right-wing coalition in Rome began casting doubt on the validity of informers' testimony, the keystone of the State's campaign. Members of Berlusconi's government called for new restrictions on informers, including a limit on how long they could testify for and a new credibility test. The criticism echoed the attacks launched by Riina after his arrest – he had accused supergrasses of being manipulated by an unknown entity. Italian law already stipulates that evidence given by Mafia turncoats must be corroborated independently, and the new climate was seen as sign of flagging political will to exploit this tool to the full – in effect, a return to the wasted years before Falcone interrogated the first leading informer, Buscetta.

Riina, quick to sense a change in the political climate, went so far as to make a public attempt to forge a pact with Berlusconi's new government. During a court appearance in May 1994, a year after attacking informers, Riina advised the government to abolish the law providing for supergrasses. In a thinly-veiled death threat, he also advised the government to beware of three men he branded communists and mischief-makers – Palermo chief prosecutor Giancarlo Caselli, the former head of the anti-Mafia commission Luciano Violante, and sociologist Pino Arlacchi. It was the first time that a godfather had dared to issue such a public threat since Riina's mentor, Leggio, in the late 1970s. Caselli confided to a friend: 'I am convinced that I am now in the hands of God. There is no salvation on Earth for me.'[27]

A Lasting Rebellion?

The demonstrations that followed Falcone's murder were not restricted to Palermo. Further inland in Corleone, Riina's fiefdom, several hundred pupils from local schools and their teachers marched through the streets shouting defiance of the men of honour. In July 1992, three hundred people attended a mass in the Corleone parish church to pay tribute to Falcone's colleague Borsellino. After the service, the congregation marched through the narrow, winding streets of the town. The local recoil at the judges' murder led the authorities to rename Corleone's main square after the two victims – a challenge to Mafioso power and culture in the town that had symbolised Cosa Nostra and its most violent expression. The society did not take kindly to this, and dumped a calf's head outside the mayor's home, a typical Mafia death threat.

According to the commander of the local carabinieri, Captain Francesco Iaccono, Riina's arrest in January 1993 brought about a change in people's attitudes: 'People have come up to us to ask for our forgiveness. They feel guilty for not having shown themselves to be our friends in public before. All sorts of people – peasants, bar-owners, professionals – come up to us now and shake our hands on the piazza, quite openly.'[28] Traditionally the carabinieri had been dismissed as '*sbirri*', the pejorative term for the police.

Is Corleone finally rebelling against the Mafia? It is a little-known truth that the history of resistance to the Mafia in the town stretches as far back as the history of the Mafia itself. People invariably think of Corleone as the home of Cosa Nostra's fiercest clan. Yet as far back as 1893, a Socialist mayor, Bernardino Verro, fathered what came to be called the Corleone Pact, the first contract to define the relationship between peasants and landowners. It defied the Mafia because it eliminated the intermediaries between the two classes, a role traditionally played by the Mafiosi. In October 1910, the courageous Verro denounced the Mafia at a public meeting, accusing it of having turned Corleone into the 'unhappiest of Sicilian towns in leaving it only the sad advantage of being the seat

of its supreme tribunal'.[29] Verro was murdered five years
later, in November 1915. Eleven bullets were pumped
into his body. Decades later, after the Second World War,
the local young trade unionist Placido Rizzotto became a
symbol of the peasants' struggle against the Mafia, until he
was murdered by Luciano Leggio.

Today, a former councillor of the ex-Communist Party
can claim to be the descendant of Verro and Rizzotto.
Dino Paternostro edits a local newspaper, *Città Nuove* (*New
Cities*), which he founded with a staff of thirty volunteers in
1990 as a platform to counter Cosa Nostra. In April 1991
someone tried to burn the newspaper office down by pouring
petrol under the door and setting fire to it. In the months
that followed, Paternostro received several threatening
telephone calls. A heavily-built figure, he shrugged off
the threats. 'I don't give these calls much weight, but
I'd be crazy not to be afraid. Maybe I'm foolhardy, but I
always think that things happen to others.'[30]

Despite Paternostro's best efforts, the people of Corleone
have stopped short of challenging outright what is the key
manifestation of Mafia territorial control — its extortion
racket. This reluctance, which is true of most towns across
the island and of Palermo, casts a shadow over recent signs
of an anti-Mafia awakening. The town of Capo d'Orlando,
a prosperous resort below the mountains of the rugged
north-eastern coast of Sicily, is the exception to the rule.
It is one of the first communities to organise a common
front against extortion and to denounce Mafiosi seeking
protection money. In 1991, on evidence from twenty-seven
shopkeepers and businessmen, who braved threats to take
Cosa Nostra to court, a judge was able to jail fourteen men
of honour for a total of 108 years.

Earlier that year, a businessman in Palermo had dared to
declare publicly his refusal to pay protection money ('*pizzo*')

to the Mafia. Libero Grassi, a textile manufacturer, sent an open letter to the *Giornale di Sicilia* headed: 'Dear racketeers, I will not pay you.'[31] His act of rebellion took on a symbolic value because, for the first time, not only was the imposition of the '*pizzo*' rejected but, worse, publicity was given to this refusal. The sixty-seven-year-old Grassi was hailed as an example to follow, but gunmen shot him dead as he walked to work one summer morning, eight months after he took his stand. His embittered relatives denounced Grassi's isolation – no one had followed his example in Palermo: 'Today, even a better State would not save us from the Mafioso mentality of the people of Sicily.'[32]

The State's representatives – the Palermo magistrates who have succeeded Falcone and Borsellino as 'servants of the State in enemy territory' – are wary of making too much of the popular reaction against the Mafia which followed the judges' murders, or of the government offensive. Even the building in which the magistrates work shows their isolation from the rest of the Sicilian capital. The cavernous grey Palace of Justice almost turns its back on the city centre. Built under Mussolini in the Fascist style, it is a massive white marble building with tall square columns. High, narrow windows let little light filter through. There is a huge flight of steps in front of the building, but anti-Mafia magistrates are banned from climbing it for security reasons. Instead, they are driven up a steep ramp which runs along the top of the steps, sirens blaring and blue lights flashing, to be hustled in through the main entrance. Each magistrate has at least three bodyguards, young men in jeans and T-shirts who carry their guns in gaily-coloured pouches slung round their waists.

'The demonstrations show people are more aware of what the Mafia represents,' said the magistrate Alfredo

Morvillo, whose investigations into extortion rackets in Palermo were hampered by the lack of witnesses. 'But concretely there's been little change as far as people assuming their responsibilities is concerned. It's still true that no witnesses come forward after a Mafia crime. People are still scared. There is still the old attitude that it's up to judges and police to deal with the problem. We need a cultural revolution, which is impossible in so short a time.'[33] The end of Cosa Nostra has been proclaimed too many times in the past, as in 1965 when ten bosses were arrested, or in the mid-1980s at the time of the Palermo maxi-trial. The revulsion that followed the murders of Falcone and Borsellino must first spawn a real political alternative, a force capable of engineering a radical renewal of the discredited State.

But, for the time being, old habits die hard, according to the magistrate Roberto Scarpinato, who led the investigations into the ex-premier Giulio Andreotti's and the police officer Bruno Contrada's alleged ties with Cosa Nostra: 'We have the sensation of living in front of a firing-squad. The guns are trained on us but we are the ones who have to pull the trigger. And the message is: your life is in your hands. If the trigger is pulled, that will be because you have made a move. In short, it's as if they were saying: don't go any further, stop right where you are.'[34]

The man leading the team of anti-Mafia magistrates, Giancarlo Caselli, secured his appointment in December 1992 on the strength of ten years' experience fighting terrorism in northern Italy. But the Mafia cannot be beaten as quickly as the Red Brigades which plagued Italy in the 1970s and 1980s. All the political forces had mobilised in that battle. Unlike the Mafia, the Brigades had always refused any link with State institutions, and could not claim to be a force as entrenched. The battle against the Mafia demands far more than new laws. All too often, people have no faith in the State because it is seen as the Mafia's accomplice – the State has shown itself strong with the weak and weak with the strong, and lost its credibility for most citizens.

Shortly after huge crowds marched through the streets of Palermo to mark the deaths of Falcone and Borsellino, Caselli cautioned:

> I remember General Dalla Chiesa saying: what the Mafia gives to citizens as favours, let us give to them as rights, and we shall turn adversaries into allies . . . We are living through a phase of euphoria, but many people warn us to be wary of it. If we do not succeed in satisfying these basic rights . . . the popular tide in favour of the magistrates will ebb away. We shall no longer have 150,000 people demonstrating in the streets of Palermo. And it will be more difficult to fight, and even – who knows when – defeat the Mafia.[35]

10

THE TASK AHEAD

The Head of the Octopus

From its origins as a buffer between the peasants and landowners of nineteenth-century Sicily, and a protector of the latter's property, the Mafia has grown to expropriate the State from much of the island. Outrages including the murders of judges, police officers and politicians have emphasised the true nature of the Honoured Society. But, for its part, the Italian State has failed to launch a lasting attack on the brotherhood. The efforts of the Fascist regime were nullified at the end of World War Two, and the next Mafia 'maxi-trial' only took place four decades later, in the mid-1980s. Like a malevolent giant octopus, the Mafia's tentacles now spread throughout Italy and extend into Europe. The head of the octopus is firmly entrenched in Sicily, and in Palermo in particular. Whether or not European governments finally decide to try and hack off some of the octopus' tentacles, it is in Sicily that the toughest battles will have to be fought.

How can Italy defeat the Mafia? To be effective, any strategy must take it on both as a military corps, with a formalised organisation, and as a network of alliances which have infiltrated State institutions. According to Luciano Violante, the former head of the anti-Mafia commission: 'The key problem is not the Mafia's alliances but the Mafia as an army. We are fighting an army, and it is not enough simply to attack its allies who are supplying it with planes and petrol. We have to wage a war as well.'[1] The State offensive launched after the murders of judges Falcone and Borsellino has yielded some results, but it is by no means sufficient. Much remains to be done:

- *Catching the fugitives.* So far, the best results have been obtained by teams of elite police officers from outside Sicily who are sent in to hunt one Mafia boss in particular. This tactic was used to capture the Godfather Riina and his lieutenant Santapaola, and should be extended to searches for lower-ranking figures. All too often, the local police forces are more concerned with ensuring public order than with combatting the Mafia. According to the anti-Mafia commission: 'Generalisations would be out of place, but there is no doubt that this state of affairs does not facilitate repression. It contributes to the climate of co-existence, and leaves the loyal servants of the State alone and exposed.'[2] The prison authorities should ensure that, once in jail, Mafia bosses are unable to go on managing their clans' affairs and should stop them issuing orders from behind bars like Riina's mentor, Luciano Leggio.

- *Co-ordinating the efforts of different police forces.* Italy has six élite police forces fighting organised crime, but they are doing so in a disorganised way – this includes the carabinieri's ROS corps, the SCO police division and the civilian and military secret services. The new DIA investigative body (billed as Italy's FBI), which gathers members of the carabinieri, the police and the finance police, a military organisation under the aegis of the Finance Ministry, should be given more resources to enable it to co-ordinate the efforts of the various police forces. Italy badly needs a sophisticated and flexible police structure capable of conducting wide-ranging investigations on a par with the Mafia's spread across the country.

• *Breaking the Mafia's hold at local level.* Extortion rackets, levying a 'protection' tax on almost all shopkeepers and small businesses under a clan's jurisdiction, are the clearest manifestation of the Mafia's territorial supremacy. So far, few attempts have been made to break this grip. Shopkeepers in Capo d'Orlando in eastern Sicily set up an association to take the racketeers to court, but this was an exception. The government should encourage similar business associations. But, as Falcone stressed, 'there must be at the heart of any anti-racket drive a co-ordinated and effective intervention by the police and not a mere, useless appeal for "civil resistance" by businessmen with no real backing from the authorities.'[3]

• *Bringing Cosa Nostra to trial.* In Sicily, the State's battle against the Mafia has long been blighted by a shortage of investigating magistrates. In some areas, as many as one-third of vacancies have yet to be filled. In August 1993, just eight months after his appointment, Palermo's Giancarlo Caselli appealed for reinforcements, saying he needed another forty examining magistrates to combat crime – double the number he had at the time. Only ten of those under his responsibility were assigned to Mafia cases, a paltry number compared to the 2,500 people under investigation. Caselli's office had to cope not only with Palermo but also with courts in several other towns, including Agrigento and Trapani. 'These are all towns,' said Caselli, 'where the Mafia is strongly implanted and they discharge on to Palermo an immense, endless workload which needs an equally huge staff to tackle it.'[4] Minor crimes such as offences against the environment, or neglect of safety precautions in the workplace, should be decriminalised to allow magistrates to concentrate on weightier investigations.

- *Gathering intelligence.* The anti-Mafia commission has already produced a wealth of reports based on the interrogations of supergrasses, magistrates and police officers, and on visits by its members to Mafia fiefdoms. But it took the commission more than three decades to publish a report on the sensitive issue of the Mafia's links with politicians. The commission should shed light on other delicate areas of Mafia infiltration – its ties with senior investigating magistrates, the secret services and freemasons. It should also publish detailed reports on a wide variety of other issues such as the Mafia's role in local and general elections, the awarding of public sector contracts, the Roman Catholic Church's attitude to organised crime, and European Union fraud.

Every effort should be made to encourage Mafiosi to turn State's evidence. They can play a vital role in breaking the internal solidarity which is one of the strengths of Cosa Nostra. Jailed Mafiosi who signal their wish to break their oaths of silence should be instantly moved to special isolated cells where they are safe from reprisals by fellow-inmates. They should be found a home and a job in towns far away from where they previously operated.

Cosa Nostra's Allies

- *Purging the ballot-box.* No electoral system can guarantee freedom from Mafia involvement. But more can be done to prevent candidates and bosses from forging pacts during election campaigns. In the autumn of 1992, a parliamentary committee drafted a bill which made it an offence for candidates to seek electoral backing from the Mafia in return for, once elected, granting public-sector contracts to its front companies or in any way boosting the society's illicit profits. But this proved too much for the government, which watered down the bill so much that only seeking Mafia votes in return for a direct payment was decreed punishable. The gratitude of an elected politician rarely stops at this, and the law should be widened to stand as in the original draft.

- *Purging the political parties.* The parties should themselves set the example and purge their ranks of those who have been linked to the Mafia. Parliament's anti-Mafia commission has acknowledged that, in order to restore citizens' faith in State institutions, 'it is indispensable that the political parties, independently of judicial measures, expel those who have been elected – be they leaders or members – who in a direct or indirect way have [been linked to the Mafia] . . . If parties do not do so, this means they believe that such activities are compatible with their political outlook.'[5] The parliamentarians in the commission could have taken their reasoning a step further – the Mafia will not be eradicated until the political class is cleansed of all corrupt elements. In addition, stronger safeguards should be instituted to protect the independence of judges, magistrates and investigators from attack by the political authorities.

- *Prosecuting political allies.* Parliamentary immunity should be lifted automatically to allow investigation into individual politicians' links with Cosa Nostra. This would greatly facilitate the prosecution of incriminated politicians. Stricter rules should be imposed on the allocation of contracts for public works, which corrupt politicians all too often hand out to their Mafiosi friends. In the name of greater transparency, public administrators should be ordered to declare their assets. The assets of businessmen and politicians convicted of dealing with the Mafia should be confiscated – this would signal a strong determination on the part of the government to combat crimes in which the public purse is the chief victim.

- *Beyond the political partners.* Targeting Cosa Nostra's penetration of the political parties and State institutions must be a key part of the assault on its network of allies, but it is by no means enough. As the anti-Mafia commission explained: 'The relationship between Cosa Nostra and parts of the institutions and the liberal professions have a formidable weight in the development of the Mafioso organisation. For this reason, if these relationships remain intact – that is to say its links with professionals, members of the magistrature and of the forces of order, officials of all kinds, and with businessmen – the breaking of those with politicians alone will not be sufficient.'[6]

So far, one of the feeblest parts of the Italian State's anti-Mafia efforts has been its supposed attempt to confront accomplices in the financial sector – the banks which handle and help to launder organised crime's illicit profits. The Rognoni–La Torre law of

1982, which allows the seizure of Mafiosi assets, has had some results. But by the time the law was passed, it was realised that the main problem was not so much seizing the assets as tracking down the enormous sums accumulated by the Mafia and discovering how they were being laundered. What is needed is a stronger version of that law, which would enable magistrates to target the financial strength of the Mafia bosses, together with the politicians, public officials and bankers who are often also involved. To date, the notification of suspect transactions has been left to the banks and other financial institutions. A central databank on cash transactions could prove a key tool against money laundering. But it would have to be complemented by a body of investigators able and equipped to make sense of the huge mass of data.

- *Fostering cultural change in Sicily.* For too long now, Italian politicians have been divided between those who advocate repressive measures against the Mafia and those who urge the improvement of social services in order to restore people's trust in the State. The truth is that legislators must do both at the same time. So far, institutions in Sicily have preferred to yield to the interests of a powerful caste, even though it meant sacrificing the general good. Men of honour need the disintegration of the social framework to be able to impose themselves as mediators in the resolution of disputes within a community. As General Dalla Chiesa stressed before his murder, the State must guarantee the fundamental rights of citizens if it is to end Mafia supremacy — by offering better social services, including education, health and social security. Too many youngsters never finish school and are caught in the unemployment trap.

Following the murders of Falcone and Borsellino, many Sicilians have publicly rebelled against the supremacy of Cosa Nostra. But anti-Mafia demonstrations in the streets of Palermo, and commemorations of the judges' deaths, can be only a beginning. The next step is to engineer a deep change in people's outlook and overturn the Mafioso logic which is based on the law of *omertà*. According to the Sicilian historian and tireless anti-Mafia campaigner Michele Pantaleone: 'We need a culture of the automatic denunciation of any illegality whatsoever, however small it may seem. If we have to denounce a friend, a partner, a fellow-member of a political party or a relative, we mustn't stop or hold back. People must be persuaded that to stay silent is wrong.'[7] Such rebels need the support of State and other institutions – they cannot go it alone. The Roman Catholic Church, many of whose members have offended the morality they preach by the abuse of their power in Sicily, must take an uncompromising stand against the Mafia – starting by rooting out clergy who have been associated with the secret society.

Cosa Nostra on Foreign Territory

European countries have in recent years shown that Cosa Nostra can be tackled on an international scale, as in the case of operation Green Ice which broke an alliance between the Mafia and the Colombian cocaine cartels. But such examples are rare, and they are usually the fruit of co-operation between police forces in different countries, and little more. What policies have been adopted so far by European states have failed to encroach much on the Mafia's spread abroad because investigators lack the valid tools to enable them to work together. They need a unitary strategy, which implies both new solutions and convergent measures.

- *Mafia association as a 'European crime'.* Until 1982, the efforts of Italy's investigating magistrates were often frustrated because their penal code did not reflect the true nature of Cosa Nostra. All they had was an offence similar to Britain's 'conspiracy' charge, which applied to three people or more meeting to commit a crime. Italian lawmakers eventually accepted that this could not be used to any great effect against the Mafia because it was incomplete, and the La Torre law was born. This created a new offence, that of Mafia association, which takes into account the law of *omertà* imposed by the organisation, and the way it controls economic activity. It is a catch-all charge, used to great effect against Mafiosi.

If Italy's efforts, as well as those of its partners, are to make any inroads against the Mafia, European governments should harmonise their penal codes, adopting a similar charge and making it illegal to belong to a criminal or Mafioso organisation. This would be to all intents and purposes a 'European crime', implying that the judicial authorities in different countries would be entitled to co-operate automatically when investigating a suspect. It would help to guarantee stronger relations between investigators and a faster exchange of intelligence. And, not least, the charge would show that European investigators understood the true nature of Cosa Nostra as a tightly-knit organisation. All too often, police outside Italy treat a Mafioso suspect as a run-of-the-mill offender, and fail to give enough importance to his position inside a Mafia clan firmly rooted in the organisation. Their approach is similar to that which prevailed until Falcone spearheaded a new strategy and tackled Cosa Nostra as an association rather than investigating each individual Mafioso on an isolated basis.

- *Drawing on Italian efforts*. Although the Mafia is not as entrenched abroad as it is in Italy, European governments must learn from the latter's experience and adopt several measures which have had some results in Italy. Germany, France and the United Kingdom are the countries where the Mafia has made the biggest inroads. They should set up parliamentary committees modelled on the anti-Mafia commission of the Rome legislature. Because investigators in these countries know little about the nature of the Mafia, these committees could play an important role in gathering and distributing information. Professional organisations anxious about attempts to infiltrate companies or suspicious capital movements could consult the committees, as could local authorities before seeking public tenders. The committees could also meet their Italian counterpart to find ways of harmonising legislation in the European Union.

France in particular should introduce a law which in Italy helped to break some links between elected politicians and the Mafia at local level. This would allow the French Interior Ministry to dissolve town councils plagued by corruption. The Ministry would then appoint a special commissioner to administer the town and erode the power of local criminal interests. In areas at risk, mainly the French Riviera, authorities could demand that companies who compete for public-sector contracts present an anti-Mafia certificate guaranteeing they are free from underworld ties which would be delivered by the local prefects.

On a broader level, members of the European Union should seek to combat the influence of and infiltration by organised crime in public administration with a 'Charter of Transparency'. This would cover tender procedures and public appointments and demarcate political and administrative tasks. Any elected official or politician convicted of links with organised crime should be barred from office.

- *Closer international co-operation.* Both the police forces and the investigating magistrates in European countries must forge closer links if they are to present a united front in tackling Cosa Nostra, which itself loses none of its internal cohesion when it crosses national boundaries. As far as police co-operation is concerned, governments of the European Union have placed much of the emphasis on Europol, the new police body charged with tackling drug trafficking and organised crime. But its beginnings are hardly encouraging. Ambitiously dubbed Europe's future FBI, Europol settled in its new headquarters in The Hague in February 1994 and set itself the objective of becoming a central intelligence database at the heart of the European Union's fight against drugs. But the treaty giving Europol a legal basis and laying down the guidelines for its activities was still in the process of being drafted when it moved into its new offices. Obtaining the backing of all twelve EU members could take up to two years after they agree on the wording of the treaty. Despite its high hopes, Europol had no authority to set up a European databank of people suspected of drug trafficking.

Such databanks already exist. European countries have

several at their disposal, including Interpol, the Trevi group (founded in Rome in 1972, originally to combat terrorism) and the struggling Schengen information service (planned by the twelve EU countries excluding Britain, Denmark and the Irish Republic). Many investigators dismiss Europol as yet another tier of policing in a European Union where police are still unable to conduct cross-border operations. Long before Europol was set up, a report of the European parliament had cautioned: 'The primary function of a police force is to enforce the law of the land by detecting and arresting those who break the law and by gathering evidence for prosecution to be brought before the courts. On this definition the idea of a "Europol" – if it means a European federal police force – is premature because there does not yet exist a corpus of European criminal law in which such a police force could act across national frontiers.'[8]

As it is, Europol is not an adequate basis for a more co-ordinated battle against the Mafia in the European Union. Bilateral accords could be part of the solution, modelled for example on that signed by the Italian and German Interior Ministers in October 1993. The most comprehensive of its kind in Europe, it provides for close co-ordination and rapid exchange of both information and manpower. It also provides for the expansion of police liaison offices, staffed by Germans in Italy and Italians in Germany, and for the investigators of both countries to work together when following the activities of criminals in third countries.

Teams of expert anti-Mafia investigating magistrates should be formed in several countries, modelled on Falcone's pool in Palermo which achieved such significant results. These investigators could form a 'European magistrature' of specialists to tackle the Mafia as an organisation that knows no borders. The magistrates' remit should extend further than that of normal local offices, stretching nationwide if necessary. These task forces could be the basis for the investigation of money laundering by the Mafia. So far, the European Union has plans only for a central bank to govern the financial sector – but an agency to monitor illicit funds is also necessary, backed by a mandatory system for financial institutions to report suspicious operations to the authorities.

There is much European countries – and not only Italy – can and must do to counter the spread of Cosa Nostra. If governments stand idly by and fail to lend their support to Rome, the sacrifice of judges like Giovanni Falcone will have been in vain. For the time being, governments are fighting a losing battle. But the Mafia is not invincible. It is simply that the Italian State as a whole has yet to take on the secret society. Many servants of the State, like Falcone, did not live to see this. But he believed that the Mafia would one day be eradicated: 'The Mafia is a human phenomenon and, like all human phenomena, it has a beginning, it has a peak and it has an end.'[9]

NOTES

1 The First Mafiosi

1 Arnone, *Mafia: Il processo di Agrigento*, p16
2 Interview by Enzo Biagi in *Panorama*, *Mafia: Dentro i misteri di Cosa Nostra*, p35
3 Gaspare Mutolo's testimony to the anti-Mafia commission of the Rome parliament, 9.2.92, p1222
4 Linares, 'Racconti popolari', quoted in Mori, *Con la Mafia ai ferri corti: Le memorie del 'Prefetto di Ferro'*, pp50–1
5 Mori, p51
6 Stajano, *Mafia: L'atto d'accusa dei giudici di Palermo*, p7
7 Hess, *Mafia: Le origini e la struttura*, pp42–3
8 Schneider, *Classi sociali, economia e politica in Sicilia*, p51
9 Lampedusa, *The Leopard*, p123
10 Schneider, p78
11 Ibid., p235
12 Galluzzo et al., *Obiettivo Falcone*, pp24–5
13 Catanzaro, *Il delitto come impresa*, p29
14 Dalla Chiesa, Carlo Alberto, *Michele Navarra e la Mafia del Corleonese*, p23

15 Ibid., p23
16 Hess, pp66–7
17 Novacco, 'Considerazioni sulla fortuna del termine "Mafia"',
    in *Belfagor*, XIV, p207
18 Quoted in Novacco, p4
19 See Hess, p4 and Gambetta, *La Mafia Siciliana*, pp363–5
20 Quoted in Duggan, *Fascism and the Mafia*, pp26–7
21 Falzone, *Storia della Mafia*, p26
22 Catanzaro, p26
23 Ibid., pp127–8
24 Turone, *Politica ladra*, p72
25 *Panorama*, 28.2.93
26 Anti-Mafia commission, Relazione sui rapporti tra Mafia e
    banditismo in Sicilia (1972), in Tranfaglia, *Mafia, politica
    e affari 1943–91*, p16
27 Anti-Mafia commission, Relazione su Mafia e politica
    (1993), p76
28 Catania and Sottile, *Totò Riina*, p72
29 Anti-Mafia commission, p55
30 Gambetta, ibid., p194
31 Lupo, *Storia della Mafia*, p97
32 Arlacchi, *Mafia Business*, p18
33 Tommaso Buscetta's testimony to anti-Mafia commission,
    16.11.92, p363
34 Arlacchi, *Gli uomini del disonore*, p144

2 The Mafia Canon

1 Arlacchi, ibid., p5
2 Biagi, *Il Boss è solo*, p142
3 Pantaleone, *Mafia è antimafia*, p110

4 Hess, *Mafia*, p16
5 *Giornale di Sicilia*, 6.7.66
6 Falcone, *Men of Honour*, p43
7 Gambetta, *La Mafia Siciliana*, pp366–7
8 Leonardo Messina's testimony to anti-Mafia commission, 4.12.92, p611
9 Kermoal and Bartolomei, *La Mafia se met à table*, p9
10 Catania and Sottile, *Toto' Riina: Storie segrete*, p34
11 Lodato, *Dieci anni di Mafia*, p195
12 Mignosi, *Il Signore sia coi boss*, p36
13 Gaspare Mutolo's testimony to anti-Mafia commission, 9.2.92, p1222
14 Ibid., p1238
15 Arlacchi, ibid., p7
16 Antonino Calderone's testimony to anti-Mafia commission, 11.11.92, p281
17 Buscetta's testimony, p351
18 Santino, 'Mafia e maxiprocesso: Dalla supplenza alla crisi della giustizia', in Chinnici, Santino, La Fiura and Adragna, *Gabbie vuote*, p108
19 Falcone, p68
20 Brancati and Muscetta, *La letteratura sulla Mafia*, pp138–9
21 Galluzzo, *Buscetta*, p49
22 Calderone's testimony, p3
23 Lodato, p204
24 Arlacchi, ibid., p24
25 Correnti, *Il miglior perdono è la vendetta*, p163. see also pp144–61 for a glossary of Mafia jargon
26 Quoted in Hess, p79
27 *Panorama*, 21.2.93
28 Arlacchi, ibid., p57
29 Russo, *Antologia della Mafia*, pp22–3
30 Pitrè, *Usi e costumi, credenze e pregiudizi*, p289
31 Falcone, p12
32 Mutolo's testimony, p1239
33 *La Repubblica*, 20.11.93

34 Catania and Sottile, p199
35 Mutolo's testimony, p1238
36 Arlacchi, ibid., p16
37 Calderone, quoted in *Panorama*, 18.7.93
38 Calderone's testimony, pp182–3
39 Caponnetto, *I miei giorni a Palermo*, p137
40 Servizio Centrale Operativo della Polizia di Stato, Informativa 10 September 1992, p2
41 Stajano, *Mafia*, p14
42 Ibid., p14
43 Shawcross and Young, *Mafia Wars*, p62
44 *Panorama*, p22
45 Ibid., p19
46 Catania and Sottile, p39. See also description of meeting in Shawcross and Young, p26
47 Mutolo's testimony, p1224
48 Anti-Mafia commission, p28
49 Biagi, p243
50 Messina's testimony, p525
51 Biagi, pp181–2
52 Arlacchi, ibid., p27
53 Mutolo's testimony, p1275
54 Falcone, pp7–8
55 Pantaleone, *Mafia e droga*, pp8–9
56 Falcone, p8
57 Tribunale di Palermo, Gaspare Mutolo's testimony in trial of Francesco Madonia, 29.1.93, p94
58 Arlacchi, ibid., pp307–8.

3 A State Within a State

1 Gambetta, *La Mafia Siciliana*, p147

2 Tranfaglia, *Mafia, politica e affari: 1943–91*, pp333, 343
3 Mutolo's testimony, p1234
4 Santino, *L'Antimafia difficile*, p105
5 Messina's testimony, p515
6 Servizio Centrale Operativo, p5
7 Interview with Antonio Manganelli, director, Nucleo centrale anticrimine, Servizio Centrale Operativo, Rome, 29.4.93
8 Calderone's testimony, p26
9 Ibid., p125
10 Lewis, *The Honoured Society: The Sicilian Mafia Observed*, p17
11 Montanelli, *Incontri italiani*, pp66–7
12 Duggan, *Fascism and the Mafia*, p66
13 Montanelli, p66
14 Fava, *Mafia: Da Giuliano a Dalla Chiesa*, p34
15 Calderone's testimony, pp150, 151
16 *Il Corriere della Sera*, 27.7.93
17 Interview with Francesco Iaccono, Corleone, 16.6.93
18 Francesco Marino Mannoia's testimony, quoted in anti-Mafia commission, relazione di minoranza, 24.1.90
19 Mutolo's testimony, p1224
20 Calderone's testimony, p292
21 Calderone's testimony to judge Falcone, 19.3.87 to 25.6.88, pp256–9
22 Martorana and Nigrelli, *Così ho tradito Cosa Nostra. Leonardo Messina: la carriera di un Uomo d'Onore*, p104
23 Lodato, *Potenti*, p64
24 Ibid., p63
25 Galluzzo, *Buscetta*, p96
26 Mutolo's testimony, p1303
27 Interview with deputy public prosecutor Alfredo Morvillo, Palermo, 15.6.93
28 Ibid.
29 Grasso, *Contro il racket*, p67
30 Servadio, *Mafioso: A History of the Mafia from its Origins to the Present Day*, p59

31 Mutolo's testimony, p1223
32 Ibid., p1223
33 CENSIS, *Contro e dentro: Criminalità, istituzioni e società*, p83
34 Tribunale di Caltanissetta, Ordinanza di custodia cautelare, Madonia Giuseppe+240 (1992), p36
35 Martorana and Nigrelli, p77
36 Calderone's testimony, p189
37 Mutolo's testimony, p1308
38 Violante, *I Corleonesi*, p65
39 Messina's testimony to anti-Mafia commission, p545
40 Mario Mori, vice-commander of Raggruppamento Operativo Speciale (ROS), testimony to anti-Mafia commission, 20.10.92
41 Calderone's testimony, p141
42 Ibid., p316
43 Galluzzo, Nicastro and Vasile, *Obiettivo Falcone*, p63
44 Calderone's testimony, p121
45 Mutolo's testimony, p1320
46 Interview with deputy public prosecutor Vittorio Teresi, Palermo, 14.6.93

4 The Peasant from Corleone

1 Martorana and Nigrelli, *Totò Riina: Trent'anni di sangue da Corleone ai vertici di Cosa Nostra*, p44
2 Salvatore Contorno's testimony, p242
3 *La Repubblica*, 2.3.93
4 Ibid., 20.1.93
5 *Il Corriere della Sera*, 9.1.93
6 Martorana and Nigrelli, p39

7 Arlacchi, ibid., p29
8 Servizio Centrale Operativo, Scheda su Salvatore Riina (March 1993), p2
9 Dalla Chiesa, Carlo Alberto, *Michele Navarra e la Mafia del Corleonese*, p22
10 Arlacchi, ibid., p91
11 Arlacchi, ibid., p72
12 Buongiorno, *Totò Riina: La sua storia*, pp52–3
13 *Il Giornale*, 16.1.93
14 Catania and Sottile, *Totò Riina*, p75
15 Buongiorno, p53
16 Ibid., p56
17 Tribunale di Palermo, Ordinanza di custodia cautelare in carcere, Agate Mariano+57 (1993), p93
18 Messina's testimony, p518
19 Mutolo's testimony, p1232
20 Bolzoni and D'Avanzo, *Il capo dei capi*, pp91–2
21 Catania and Sottile, p36
22 Ibid., p38
23 Arlacchi, ibid., p6
24 Ibid., p86
25 Buongiorno, pp83, 84
26 Di Forti, *Per una psicoanalisi della Mafia*, p89
27 Mutolo's testimony, p1229
28 Interview with Piero Arru, 13.5.92

5 The Godfather

1 Tribunale di Palermo, Ordinaria sentenza, Greco Michele+18, p1748
2 Arlacchi, ibid., p279
3 Mutolo's testimony, p1232

4   Calderone's testimony, p326
5   Arlacchi, ibid., pp159–160
6   Stajano, *Mafia*, pp17–18
7   Tribunale di Palermo, Ordinanza di custodia cautelare, p139
8   Buongiorno, *Totò Riina*, p125
9   Buscetta, vol 1, p92
10 Tribunale di Palermo, p165
11 Ibid., p141
12 Ibid., p171
13 Greco, vol 3, p16
14 Catania and Sottile, p26
15 Ibid., p188
16 Ibid., p65
17 *Il Corriere della Sera*, 9.1.93
18 Tribunale di Caltanissetta, p37
19 Mutolo's testimony, p1320
20 *Epoca*, 10.2.93
21 *La Stampa*, 16.1.93
22 *La Repubblica*, 17.1.93
23 Interview with Guido lo Forte, Palermo, 14.6.93
24 *La Repubblica*, 2.3.93
25 *Città Nuove*, February 1993
26 Interview with Francesco Iaccono, Corleone, 16.6.93
27 Arlacchi, ibid., pp308–9

6 The Friends of the Friends

1   Mutolo's testimony, quoted in Domanda di autorizzazione a procedere contro il senatore Giulio Andreotti, Tribunale di Palermo, 27.3.93, pp29–30
2   Messina's testimony, p19
3   Marino Mannoia's testimony, quoted in Integrazione, Tribunale di Palermo, 14.4.93, p7

4 Di Maggio's testimony, quoted in Seconda Integrazione, 19.4.93, pp8–9, 14, 15

5 Messina's testimony, p20

6 Ibid.

7 Domanda di autorizzazione, p30

8 Buscetta's testimony to anti-Mafia commission, p422

9 *La Repubblica*, 8.2.94

10 News conference by Andreotti, Foreign Press Club, Rome, 5.5.93

11 Domanda di autorizzazione, p9

12 Suddovest documenti, ed., *Delitto Lima*, p25

13 Marino Mannoia's testimony to judge Falcone, 8.10.89 to 19.6.80, p55

14 Calderone's testimony to anti-Mafia commission, p309

15 Buscetta's testimony, p389

16 Anti-Mafia commission, Relazione su Mafia e politica, pp131–2

17 Lampedusa, *The Leopard*, p76

18 *Il Mondo*, 9.3.92

19 Arlacchi, ibid., p212

20 Martorana and Nigrelli, ibid., p87

21 Vincenzo Sinagra's testimony to judge Vittorio Aliquò, 30.11.83 to 30.4.85, p30

22 *Panorama*, 7.7.91

23 Servadio, *Mafioso*, p165

24 Anti-Mafia commission, p88

25 Arlacchi, ibid., pp208–9

26 Interview with Giovanni Falcone, Rome, 11.11.91

27 Messina's testimony to anti-Mafia commission, pp553–4

28 Arlacchi, ibid., p27

29 *La Repubblica*, 21.5.93

30 Mutolo's testimony to anti-Mafia commission, p1247

31 Ibid., p1298

32 Mannoia's testimony, quoted in Integrazione, ibid., p8

33 Buscetta's testimony, p426

34 Arlacchi, ibid., pp40–41

35 Messina's testimony, p571
36 Calderone's testimony to judge Falcone, p88
37 Calderone's testimony to anti-Mafia commission, p300
38 L'Unità, ed., *Mafia e potere*, p5
39 Messina's testimony, p523
40 Calderone's testimony, p294
41 Messina's testimony, p557
42 Interview with Francesco Morvillo, Palermo, 15.6.93
43 *La Repubblica*, 30.3.93
44 *Le Monde*, 16.10.93
45 Galluzzo, Nicastro and Vasile, *Obiettivo Falcone*, p58
46 For a detailed account, see Fava, *Mafia*, p42
47 Mignosi, *Il Signore sia coi boss*, p20
48 Messina's testimony, p602
49 Galluzzo, Nicastro and Vasile, ibid., p184
50 *Il Corriere della Sera*, 22.6.93
51 Ibid., 27.12.93
52 Ibid., 6.5.93
53 *La Repubblica*, 7.5.93
54 *La Corriere della Sera*, 9.5.93

7 Tentacles Spread into Europe

1 *Il Messaggero*, 29.2.92
2 *The Times*, 30.9.92
3 Anti-Mafia commission, relazione su mafia e politica, p48
4 FBI report on Italian organised crime, 1992, quoted in *The Times*, 24.11.92
5 *Narcomafie*, February 1993
6 Messina's testimony to anti-Mafia commission, pp523, 528
7 Relazione su iniziative in ambito comunitario e internazionale per la lotta al narcotraffico ed al riciclaggio del danaro di illecita provenienza, anti-Mafia commission, p8

8   Report by OIPC/Interpol, quoted in Labrousse and Wallon, *La Planète des drogues*, p128

9   Interview with Antonino Caponnetto, Florence, 19.2.93

10 Report drawn up by Committee of Enquiry into spread of organised crime linked to drugs trafficking in Member States of the European Community, 23.4.92, p4

11 *Le Monde*, 26.1.93

12 Ibid., 30.1.93

13 Calderone's testimony to anti-Mafia commission, p337

14 Servizio Centrale Operativo, Informativa, p11

15 Alto Commissario per la lotta contro la Mafia; Rapporto sulle condizioni socio-economiche e sulla situazione dell'ordine e della sicurezza pubblica di Palma di Montechiaro, 13.12.89

16 *Panorama*, 26.9.93

17 Interview with Max-Peter Ratzel, deputy chief, organised crime unit, BKA, Bramshill, 25.5.93

18 BKA report quoted in *Der Spiegel*, 4.8.92

19 *La Repubblica*, 7.9.93

20 Ibid., 30.7.92

21 Speech by Ratzel to conference on organised crime, Bramshill, 25.5.93

22 Raufer, *Les superpuissances du crime*, p118

23 Quoted in *La Repubblica*, 26.10.93

24 Arlacchi, ibid., pp289–90

25 Rapport de la commission d'enquête sur les moyens de lutter contre les tentatives de pénétration de la Mafia en France, 27.1.93, p12

26 *Le Monde*, 23.2.93

27 Interview with Antonio Manganelli, Rome, 29.4.93

28 *Le Figaro*, 21.5.93

29 Testimony of police chief Vincenzo Parisi before anti-Mafia commission, 2.2.93

30 Arlacchi, ibid., p188

31 *Il Corriere della Sera*, 13.1.94

32 Interview with Bob Elliot, organised crime unit, NCIS, London, 18.3.93

33 Calabro, *Le mani della Mafia*, pp98–100
34 Interview with Detective Inspector Graham Saltmarsh, deputy chief, organised crime branch, NCIS, London, 30.3.93
35 Interview with Elliot, 18.3.93
36 *Sunday Times*, 2.1.94
37 Interview with Saltmarsh, 30.3.93
38 National Criminal Intelligence Service, Background Briefing on Organised Crime, London, 1993
39 CENSIS, *Contro e dentro*, p96
40 Falcone, *Men of Honour*, p136
41 Interview with Alessandro Pansa, Rome, 29.4.93
42 Messina's testimony to anti-Mafia commission, p533
43 *The Times*, 11.10.93
44 Falcone, pp100–1

8 Taming the Octopus

1 Servadio, *Mafioso*, p74
2 Lupo, *Storia della Mafia*, p123
3 Servadio, p76
4 Mori, *Con la Mafia ai ferri corti*, p147
5 Ibid., p155
6 Ibid., p153
7 Arlacchi, *Mafia Business*, p16
8 Mori, p158
9 Mori, p162
10 Arlacchi, *Gli uomini del disonore*, p96
11 Campbell, *The Luciano Project*, p98
12 Ibid., p2
13 Report by anti-Mafia commission, quoted in Galluzzo, Nicastro and Vasile, *Obiettivo Falcone*, p41
14 Pantaleone, *Omertà di Stato*, pp114–15

15 Interview with Michele Pantaleone, Palermo, 13.6.93
16 Anti-Mafia commission, *Mafia e politica*, p72
17 Tranfaglia, *Mafia, politica e affari*, p4
18 Anti-Mafia commission, ibid., pp72–3
19 Ibid., p74
20 Pantaleone, *Mafia e antimafia*, p18
21 Testimony of Pierluigi Vigna, Florence public prosecutor, to anti-Mafia commission, 22.1.93
22 Minna, *Breve storia della Mafia*, p124
23 Falcone, *Men of Honour*, pp139–40
24 Quoted in anti-Mafia commission report, 23.2.93
25 Messina's testimony to anti-Mafia commission, p600
26 Dalla Chiesa, Carlo Alberto, *Michele Navarra e la Mafia del Corleonese*, p16
27 Stajano, *Mafia*, p233
28 Dalla Chiesa, Nando, *Storie di boss ministri tribunali giornali intellettuali cittadini*, p101
29 Domanda di autorizzazione a procedere contro il senatore Giulio Andreotti, Tribunale di Palermo, 27.3.93, p103
30 Falcone, pp150–1
31 Stajano, p230
32 Pantaleone, *Omertà di Stato*, pp165–6

9 Judge Giovanni Falcone

1 Lodato, *Dieci anni di Mafia*, p56
2 Chinnici *et al.*, *Gabbie vuote*, p50
3 Falcone, *Men of Honour*, pxi
4 *Il Giornale di Sicilia*, 14.4.85
5 Caponnetto, *I miei giorni a Palermo*, p38
6 Biagi, *Il Boss è solo*, p256
7 *Panorama*, Trent'anni di Mafia, p24
8 Galluzzo, *Obiettivo Falcone*, p1

9 Interview with Giovanni Falcone, Rome, 11.11.92

10 Falcone, pp7, 18

11 Messina's testimony to anti-Mafia commission, p529

12 *La Repubblica*, 13.11.93

13 Ibid., 14.11.93

14 Reuters, 20.7.92

15 Lampedusa, *The Leopard*, pp122–3

16 Buscetta's testimony to anti-Mafia commission, p353

17 Calderone's testimony to anti-Mafia commission, p338

18 *La Repubblica*, 5.4.94

19 Caponnetto, ibid., p56

20 Suddovest documenti, ed., *Delitto Lima*, p79

21 Buscetta's testimony, p426

22 Violante, *I Corleonesi*, p67

23 *La Repubblica*, 1.3.94

24 Ibid., 19.3.94

25 Violante, ibid., p34

26 *Città Nuove*, July/August 1993

27 Disclosed by Bishop Antonio Riboldi at a seminar on the Mafia, Florence 27.5.94

28 Interview with Iaccono, 16.6.93

29 Giraud, *Terres de mafia*, p73

30 Interview with Dino Paternostro, Corleone, 16.6.93

31 *Il Giornale di Sicilia*, 10.1.91

32 Grasso, *Contro il racket*, p19

33 Interview with Alfredo Morvillo, investigating magistrate, Palermo, 15.6.93

34 *Il Corriere della Sera*, 15.7.93

35 *La Republica*, 13.6.93

10 The Task Ahead

1 Interview with Violante, Rome, 22.4.93

2 Anti-Mafia commission, Mafia e politica, p53

3 Cecchini, Vasconti and Vettraino, *Estorti e riciclati*, p14
4 *La Repubblica*, 18.8.93
5 Anti-Mafia commission, pp134–5
6 Ibid., p17
7 Pantaleone, *Omertà di Stato*, p210
8 Report drawn up by Committee of Enquiry, European Parliament, p67
9 Interview with Falcone, 11.11.92

BIBLIOGRAPHY

Italian Official Documents

Testimony of Leonardo Vitale to Palermo magistrates, police and
carabinieri, 30 March 1973.
Testimony of Vincenzo Sinagra to Palermo magistrate Vittorio
Aliquò and others, 30 November 1983 to 30 April 1985, 2
vols.
Testimony of Stefano Calzetta to Palermo magistrate Rocco
Chinnici and others, 12 March, 1983 to 28 February, 1985,
5 vols.
Testimony of Tommaso Buscetta to judge Giovani Falcone and
others, July–August 1984, 3 vols.
Testimony of Salvatore Contorno to judge Giovanni Falcone and
others, October 1984–June 1985.
Testimony of Antonino Calderone to Marseille investigating
magistrate Michel Debacq, judge Giovanni Falcone and
others, 19 March 1987 to 25 June 1988, 4 vols.
Testimony of Francesco Marino Mannoia to judge Falcone and
others, 8 October, 1989 to 19 June, 1990.
(*Copies of the above available at Cambridge University Library*)

Alto Commissario per il coordinamento della lotta contro
la delinquenza mafiosa, Rapporto sulle condizioni socio-
economiche e sulla situazione dell'ordine e della sicurezza
pubblica di Palma di Montechiaro. Rome, sent to anti-Mafia
commission 13 December, 1989. Document no. 1244.

Commissione parlamentare di inchiesta sul fenomeno della
Mafia e sulle associazioni criminali similari, Relazione di
minoranza, 24 January, 1990.

——, Relazione su iniziative in ambito comunitario e internazionale per la lotta al narcotraffico ed al riciclaggio del
danaro di illecita provenienza, approved 13 March, 1990.
Doc. XXIII, no. 16.

——, Relazione sulle risultanze dell'attività del gruppo di lavoro
della Commissione incaricato di indagare sulla recrudescenza
di episodi criminali durante il periodo elettorale, approved 25
July, 1990. Doc. XXIII, no. 20.

——, Relazione sulle risultanze dell'indagine del gruppo di
lavoro della Commissione incaricato di svolgere accertamenti
circa lo stato della lotta alla Mafia ad Agrigento ed a Palma di
Montechiaro, approved 31 July, 1990. Doc. XXIII, no. 21.

——, Relazione sulle risultanze dell'attività del gruppo di lavoro
incaricato di svolgere accertamenti sullo stato della lotta alla
criminalità organizzata nella provincia di Messina, approved
15 January, 1992, Doc. XXIII, no. 45.

——, Audizione di Giovanni Tinebra, procuratore della
repubblica di Caltanissetta, 17 November, 1992.

——, Audizione dei capi del Gruppo Investigativo Criminalità
Organizzata della Guardia di Finanza e del Ragruppamento
Operativo Speciale dell'Arma dei Carabinieri, 20 October,
1992.

——, Audizione del collaboratore di giustizia Antonino Calderone,
11 November 1992.

——, Audizione del collaboratore di giustizia Tommaso Buscetta,
19 November 1992.

——, Audizione del collaboratore di giustizia Leonardo Messina,

4 December 1992.

——, Audizione del collaboratore di giustizia Gaspare Mutolo, 9 February 1993.

——, Audizione del dirigenti e dei funzionari del Servizio Centrale Operativo della polizia di Stato, 3 November 1992.

——, Audizione di Pierluigi Vigna, procuratore della repubblica di Firenze, 22 January 1993.

——, Audizione del prefetto Vincenzo Parisi, capo della polizia, 26 January 1993.

Servizio Centrale Operativo. Scheda su Salvatore Riina, March 1993.

——, Informativa in esito all'attività investigativa svolta sull'organizzazione mafiosa denominata 'Cosa Nostra' a seguito delle dichiarazioni rese da Leonardo Messina. Rome, 10 September 1992.

——, L'Operazione 'Green Ice' in Italia, Rome, March 1993.

SISMI (Italian military secret services), Penetrazione nei paesi dell'est Europeo della criminalità organizzata Italiana. Rome, sent to anti-Mafia commission 22 February 1993. Doc. no. 566.

Procura di Caltanissetta, Struttura e dinamiche attuali delle organizzazioni di carattere mafioso: La situazione nel Nisseno, Caltanissetta, sent to anti-Mafia commission 5 February 1992. Document no. 443.

Tribunale di Caltanissetta, Ordinanza di custodia cautelare in carcere contro Madonia, Giuseppe + 240. Caltanissetta, 1992.

Tribunale di Palermo, Ordinanza-sentenza contro Greco Michele +18 per gli omicidi Reina, Mattarella, La Torre, Di Salvo. Palermo, sent to anti-Mafia commission in 1989. Doc. no. 1843

——, Ordinanza di custodia cautelare in carcere contro Agate, Mariano + 57. Palermo, 1993.

——, Domanda di autorizzazione a procedere contro il senatore Giulio Andreotti. Palermo, 27 March 1993. Addenda of 14 and 20 April, 1993.

——, Testimony of Gaspare Mutolo at trial of Madonia,

Francesco. Session of 29 January 1993.

Tribunale di Roma, Ordinanza di custodia cautelare in carcere contro Porcacchia, Antonella + 43. Rome, 26 October 1992. Arrest warrants for defendants involved in 'Green Ice' investigation.

Foreign Official Documents

French Senate, Rapport d'information au nom de la mission commune d'information chargée d'examiner la mise en place et le fonctionnement de la convention d'application de l'accord de Schengen du 14 juin 1985 sur le trafic de la drogue dans l'espace Schengen. Paris, December 1992. No. 72.

French National Assembly, Rapport de la commission d'enquête sur les moyens de lutter contre les tentatives de pénétration de la Mafia en France. Paris, 28 January 1993. No. 3251.

European Parliament, Report drawn up by the committee of enquiry into spread of organised crime linked to drugs trafficking in the member states of the European Community. Strasbourg, 23 April 1992. No. A3-0358/91.

International Narcotics Control Board, Report for 1992, Vienna.

——, Report for 1993, Vienna.

Books

Andreotti, Giulio, *Il potere logora . . . ma è meglio non perderlo*. Milan: Rizzoli, November 1990.

Arlacchi, Pino, *Gli uomini del disonore: La Mafia Siciliana nella vita del grande pentito Antonino Calderone*. Milan: Arnoldo Mondadori, October 1992.

———, *Mafia Business: The Mafia ethic and the spirit of capitalism*. Oxford University Press, 1988.

Arlacchi, Pino, and Nando dalla Chiesa, *La palude e la città*. Milan: Arnoldo Mondadori, 1987.

Arnone, Giuseppe, ed., *Mafia: Il processo di Agrigento*. Palermo: La Zisa, 1988.

Barrese, Orazio, *I complici: Gli anni dell'antimafia*. Milan: Feltrinelli, 1973.

Barzini, Luigi, *The Italians*. London: Penguin, 1968.

Biagi, Enzo, *Il Boss è solo: Buscetta, la vera storia di un vero padrino*. Milan: Arnoldo Mondadori, November 1986.

Blok, Anton, *The Mafia of a Sicilian Village, 1860–1960: A Study of Violent Peasant Entrepreneurs*. London: Harper & Row, 1975.

Bolzoni, Attilio, and Giuseppe d'Avanzo, *Il capo dei capi: Vita e carriera criminale di Totò Riina*. Milan: Arnoldo Mondadori, September 1993.

Brancati, Elena, and Carlo Muscetta, *La letteratura sulla Mafia*. Rome: Bonacci, 1988.

Bufalino, Gesualdo, and Nunzio Zago, eds, *Cento Sicilie: Testimonianze per un ritratto*. Scandicci: La Nuova Italia, 1993.

Buongiorno, Pino, *Totò Riina: La sua storia*. Milan: Rizzoli, September 1993.

Calabro, Maria Antonietta, *Le mani della Mafia: Vent'anni di finanza e politica attraverso la storia del Banco Ambrosiano*. Rome: Edizioni Associate, October 1991.

Calvi, Fabrizio, *La vie quotidienne de la Mafia de 1950 à nos jours*. Paris: Hachette, 1986.

———, *L'Europe des parrains: La Mafia à l'assaut de l'Europe*. Paris: Grasset, 1993.

Calvi, Maurizio, *Figure di una battaglia: Documenti e riflessioni sulla Mafia dopo l'assassinio di G. Falcone e P. Borsellino*. Bari: Dedalo, September 1992.

Campbell, Rodney, *The Luciano Project: The Secret Wartime Collaboration of the Mafia and the U.S. Navy*. London: McGraw-Hill, 1977.

Caponnetto, Antonino, *I miei giorni a Palermo: Storie di Mafia e di giustizia raccontate a Saverio Lodato*. Milan: Garzanti, November 1992.

Catania, Enzo, and Salvo Sottile, *Totò Riina: Storie segrete, odii e amori del dittatore di Cosa Nostra*. Milan: Liber, June 1993.

Catanzaro, Raimondo, *Il delitto come impresa: Storia sociale della Mafia*. Padua: Liviana, March 1989.

Cecchini, Massimo, Patricia Vasconi and Simona Vettraino, *Estorti e riciclati*. Milan: Franco Angeli, 1992.

CENSIS (Centro Studi Investimenti Sociali), *Contro e dentro: Criminalità, istituzioni, società*. Milan: Franco Angeli, 1992.

Confesercenti, *L'impresa Mafiosa entra nel mercato: L'evoluzione della criminalità organizzata e i suoi rapporti con il potere economico*. Milan: Franco Angeli, 1985.

Chillura, Angelo, *Coscienza di Chiesa e fenomeno Mafia*. Palermo: Augustinus, 1990.

Chinnici, Giorgio, Umberto Santino, Giovanni la Fiura, and Ugo Adragna, *Gabbie vuote: Processi per omicidio a Palermo dal 1983 al maxiprocesso*. Milan: Franco Angeli, 1992.

Ciconte, Enzo, *'Ndrangheta dall'unità a oggi*. Bari: Laterza, May 1992.

Ciuni, Roberto, *Mafiosi: Appunti di un cronista*. Milan: Tranchida, May 1989.

Comarin, Elio, *Rupture à l'italienne: Eglise, Mafia, communisme*. Paris: Hachette, 1994.

Commissione parlamentare antimafia, *Mafia e politica: Relazione del 6 aprile 1993*. Bari: Laterza, May 1993.

Correnti, Santi, *Il miglior perdono è la vendetta: Storia e dizionario del linguaggio Mafioso*. Milan: Arnoldo Mondadori, August 1987.

Dalla Chiesa, Carlo Alberto, *Michele Navarra e la Mafia del Corleonese*. Palermo: La Zisa, February 1990.

Dalla Chiesa, Nando, *Delitto imperfetto*. Milan: Arnoldo Mondadori, 1984.

——, *Il giudice ragazzino: Storia di Rosario Livatino assassinato dalla Mafia sotto il regime della corruzione*. Turin: Einaudi, 1992.

——, *Milano–Palermo: La nuova resistenza*. Milan: Baldini e Castoldi, January 1993.

——, *Storie di boss ministri tribunali giornali intellettuali cittadini*. Milan: Einaudi, 1990.

Di Forti, Filippo, *Per una psicoanalisi della Mafia: Radici, fantasmi, territorio e politica*. Rome: Bertani, 1982.

Duggan, Christopher, *Fascism and the Mafia*. London: Yale University Press, 1989.

Falcone, Giovanni, *Men of Honour: The truth about the Mafia*. London: Warner, 1993.

Falzone, Michele, *La Mafia: Dal feudo all'eccidio di Via Carini*. Palermo: S.F. Flaccovio, 1984.

Fava, Giuseppe, *Mafia: Da Giuliano a Dalla Chiesa*. Rome: Editori Riuniti, 1986.

Finley, Moses, Denis Mack Smith and Christopher Duggan, *A History of Sicily*. London: Chatto & Windus, 1986.

Forbice, Aldo, ed., *Mafia vecchia, Mafia nuova*. Milan: Franco Angeli, 1985.

Franchetti, Leopoldo, *Condizioni politiche e amministrative della Sicilia*. Florence: Vallecchi, 1974.

Frasca Polara, Giorgio, *La terrible istoria dei frati di Mazzarino*. Palermo: Sellerio, 1989.

Gaja, Filippo, *L'esercito della lupara*. Milan: Maquis, April 1990.

Galasso, Alfredo, *La Mafia non esiste*. Naples: Tullio Pironti, 1988.

——, *La Mafia politica*. Milan: Baldini e Castoldi, January 1993.

Galluzzo, Lucio, *Tommaso Buscetta: L'uomo che tradì se stesso*. Aosta: Musumeci, 1984.

Galluzzo, Lucio, Francesco la Licata, and Saverio Lodato,

eds, *Rapporto sulla Mafia degli anni '80*. Palermo: S.F. Flaccovio, 1986.

Galluzzo, Lucio, Franco Nicastro and Vincenzo Vasile, *Obiettivo Falcone*. Naples: Tullio Pironti, May 1992.

Gambetta, Diego, *La Mafia siciliana: Un'industria della protezione privata*. Turin: Einaudi, September 1992.

Ganazzoli, Angelo, *Antimafia post-scriptum*. Palermo: Ila Palma, 1987.

Ginsborg, Paul, *A History of Contemporary Italy: Society and Politics 1943–1988*. London: Penguin, 1990.

Giraud, Henri-Christian, *Terres de Mafia*. Paris: JC. Lattès, April 1993.

Grasso, Tano, *Contro il racket: Come opporsi al ricatto Mafioso*. Bari: Laterza, 1992.

Haycraft, John, *Italian Labyrinth*. London: Penguin, 1987.

Hersant, Yves, *Italies: Anthologie des voyageurs français aux XVIIIe et XIXe siècles*. Paris: Robert Laffont, 1988.

Hess, Henner, *Mafia: Le origini e la struttura*. Bari: Laterza, April 1993.

Januzzi, Lino, *Cosi parlò Buscetta*. Milan: Sugarco Edizioni, 1986.

Kermoal, Jacques, and Martine Bartolomei, *La Mafia se met à table: Histoires et recettes de l'honorable société*. Paris: Actes Sud, 1986.

La Licata, Francesco, *Storia di Giovanni Falcone*. Milan: Rizzoli, May 1993.

Labrousse, Alain, and Alain Wallon, *La planète des drogues: Organisations criminelles, guerres et blanchissement*. Paris: Seuil, November 1993.

Lampedusa, Giuseppe Tomasi di, *The Leopard*. London: Harvill, 1992.

Lewis, Norman, *The Honoured Society: The Sicilian Mafia Observed*. London: Eland, 1984.

Lodato, Saverio, *Dieci anni di Mafia: La guerra che lo Stato non ha saputo vincere*, Milan: Biblioteca Universale Rizzoli, November 1992.

——, *Potenti: Sicilia, anni novanta*. Milan: Garzanti, April 1992.

L'Unità, ed., *Mafia e potere: Cosa Nostra raccontata da Tommaso Buscetta, Leonardo Messina e Gaspare Mutolo davanti alla commissione parlamentare antimafia*. Rome: Editrice L'Unità, April 1993.

Lupo, Salvatore, *Storia della Mafia*. Rome: Donzelli, 1993.

Masini, Vincenzo, *Sociologia di Sagunto*. Milan: Franco Angeli, 1984.

Martorana, Giuseppe, and Sergio Nigrelli, *Così ho tradito Cosa Nostra. Leonardo Messina: La carriera di un uomo d'onore*. Aosta: Musumeci, January 1993.

—— *Totò Riina: Trent'anni di sangue da Corleone ai vertici di Cosa Nostra*. Aosta: Musumeci, March 1993.

Mignosi, Enzo, *Il Signore sia coi boss: Storie di preti fedeli alla Mafia e di padrini timorosi di Dio*. Palermo: Arbor, October 1993.

Minna, Rosario, *Breve storia della Mafia*. Milan: Editori Riuniti, 1986.

Montanelli, Indro, *Incontri italiani*. Milan: Rizzoli, 1982.

Mori, Cesare, *Con la Mafia ai ferri corti: Le memorie del'Prefetto di Ferro*. Naples: Flavio Pagano, February 1993.

——, *Tra le zagare oltre la foschia*. Monreale: La Zisa, August 1988.

Nese, Marco, *Nel segno della Mafia: Storia di Luciano Leggio*. Milan: Rizzoli, 1975.

Padovani, Marcelle, *Les dernières années de la Mafia*. Paris: Gallimard, 1987.

Panorama, ed., *Mafia: Dentro i misteri di Cosa Nostra dal dopoguerra a Falcone e Borsellino*. Milan: Arnoldo Mondadori (series libri inchiesta), 1992.

Pantaleone, Michele, *Anti-Mafia occasione mancata*. Turin: Einaudi, 1969.

——, *L'industria del potere*. Bologna: Cappelli, 1984

——, *Mafia e antimafia*. Naples: Tullio Pironti, May 1992.

——, *Mafia e droga*. Turin: Einaudi, 1966.

——, *Mafia e politica*. Turin: Einaudi, 1962.

——, *Omertà di Stato: Da Salvatore Giuliano a Totò Riina*. Naples: Tullio Pironti, May 1993.

Petacco, Arrigo, *Il prefetto di ferro*. Milan: Arnoldo Mondadori, 1975.

Pitrè, Giuseppe, *Usi, costumi, credenze e pregiudizi del popolo siciliano*. Florence: Barbera, 1939.

Porto, Salvo, *Mafia e fascismo: L'azione del prefetto Mori in Sicilia 1925–29*. Palermo: S.F. Flaccovio, 1977.

Procacci, Giuliano, *Storia degli Italiani*. Rome/Bari: L'Unità/Laterza, February 1991.

Puzo, Mario, *The Godfather*. New York: Signet, November 1978.

Raufer, Xavier, *Les superpuissances du crime: Enquête sur le narco-terrorisme*. Paris: Plon, October 1993.

Raw, Charles, *The Moneychangers: How the Vatican Bank enabled Roberto Calvi to steal $250 million for the heads of the P2 Masonic Lodge*. London: Harvill, 1992.

Rossi, Luca, *I disarmati: Falcone, Cassarà e gli altri*. Milan: Arnoldo Mondadori, October 1992.

Russo, N. ed., *Antologia della Mafia*. Palermo: Il Punto, 1964.

Santino, Umberto, *L'antimafia difficile*. Palermo: Centro Siciliano di documentazione, 1989.

Schneider, Jane and Peter, *Classi sociali, economia e politica in Sicilia*. Soveria Mannelli: Rubbettino, January 1989.

Sciascia, Leonardo, *A ciascuno il suo*. Turin: Einaudi, 1988.

——, *Candido: ovvero Un sogno fatto in Sicilia*. Turin: Einaudi, 1977.

——, *Il giorno della civetta*. Turin: Einaudi, 1972.

Servadio, Gaia, *Mafioso: A History of the Mafia from its Origins to the Present Day*. London: Secker & Warburg, 1976.

Shawcross, Tim, and Martin Young, *Mafia Wars: The Confessions of Tommaso Buscetta*. London: Fontana, 1988.

Short, Martin, *Crime Inc.* London: Thames Methuen, 1984.

Spotts, Frederic, and Theodor Wieser, *Italy: A Difficult Democ-*

racy. Cambridge University Press, 1986.

Stajano, Corrado, ed., *Mafia: L'atto d'accusa dei giudici di Palermo*. Rome: Editori Riuniti, September 1992.

Sterling, Claire, *Pax mafiosa*. Paris: Robert Laffont, March 1994.

———, *The Mafia: The Long Reach of the International Sicilian Mafia*. London: Grafton, 1991.

Suddovest documenti, ed., *Delitto Lima: L'atto di accusa dei giudici di Palermo*. Agrigento: Suddovest, October 1992.

Tranfaglia, Nicola, *Mafia, politica e affari: 1943–91*. Bari, Laterza, March 1992.

Turone, Sergio, *Politica ladra: Storia della corruzione in Italia: 1861–1992*. Bari: Laterza, October 1992.

Uccello, Antonino, *Carcere e Mafia nei canti popolari siciliani*. Rome: De Donato, 1974.

Vannoni, Gianni, *Le società segrete dal Seicento al Novecento*. Florence: Sansoni, February 1985.

Violante, Luciano, *I Corleonesi: Mafia e sistema eversivo*. Rome: L'Unità, August 1993.

———, *La Mafia dell'eroina*. Rome: Editori Riuniti, April 1987.

Vittorini, Elio, *Conversazione in Sicilia*. Milan: Biblioteca Universale Rizzoli, October 1990.

Wallon, Alain, ed., *La drogue, nouveau désordre mondial: Rapport 1982–93*. Paris: Hachette, 1993.

INDEX